PENGUIN BOOKS

A Short History of Slavery

James Walvin taught for many years at the University of York, where he is now Professor of History Emeritus. He also held visiting positions in the Caribbean, the USA and Australia. He won the Martin Luther King Memorial Prize for his book *Black and White*, and has published widely on the history of slavery and the slave trade, including more recently *Black Ivory: A History of British Slavery*. His book *The People's Game* was a pioneering study of the history of football and remains in print thirty years after its first publication. *The Quakers: Money and Morals* was chosen by *The New York Times* as one of their Notable Books of the Year.

A Short History of Slavery

JAMES WALVIN

PENGUIN BOOKS

PENGUIN BOOKS

Published by the Penguin Group
Penguin Books Ltd, 80 Strand, London WC2R ORL, England
Penguin Group (USA) Inc., 375 Hudson Street, New York, New York 10014, USA
Penguin Group (Canada), 90 Eglinton Avenue East, Suite 700, Toronto, Ontario, Canada M4P 2Y3
(a division of Pearson Penguin Canada Inc.)
Penguin Ireland, 25 St Stephen's Green, Dublin 2, Ireland (a division of Penguin Books Ltd)
Penguin Group (Australia), 250 Camberwell Road, Camberwell, Victoria 3124, Australia
(a division of Pearson Australia Group Pty Ltd)
Penguin Books India Pvt Ltd, 11 Community Centre, Panchsheel Park,
New Delhi – 110 017, India
Penguin Group (NZ), 67 Apollo Drive, Rosedale, North Shore 0632, New Zealand
(a division of Pearson New Zealand Ltd)
Penguin Books (South Africa) (Pty) Ltd, 24 Sturdee Avenue,
Rosebank, Johannesburg 2196, South Africa

Penguin Books Ltd, Registered Offices: 80 Strand, London WC2R ORL, England

www.penguin.com

First published 2007
1

Copyright © James Walvin, 2007

The moral right of the author has been asserted

Set in 11/13pt Monotype Bembo
Typeset by Palimpsest Book Production Limited, Grangemouth, Stirlingshire
Printed in England by Clays Ltd, St Ives plc

ISBN: 978-0-141-02798-2

Contents

Introduction
Slavery and Abolition

Britain and the United States of America banned their Atlantic trade in African slaves in 1807 and 1808. In fact the trade survived (mainly to Brazil and Cuba) until it died away in the 1860s. Over the preceding three and a half centuries, some twelve million Africans had been loaded on to the Atlantic slave ships. About ten and a half million of them survived to landfall in the Americas. Most of the major maritime nations of western Europe and the Americas involved themselves to some degree in this Atlantic slave system. But by the mid-eighteenth century, the British had emerged as the commercial and maritime masters of the bleak skills of moving large numbers of Africans speedily and profitably towards the American plantations.

The abolition of the slave trade was followed, in the nineteenth century, by the piecemeal, haphazard dismantling of black slavery across the Americas, beginning with the slave upheaval in St Domingue (Haiti) in the 1790s and ending with the emancipation of the few remaining slaves in Brazil in 1888. Britain ended slavery in its colonies by Act of Parliament (and by paying a staggering amount of compensation to the slave owners) in 1833–8, but slavery in the US ended in the bloodshed of the Civil War (1860–65).

From first to last, slavery was a system characterized by brutality. Moreover, it was a system that had far-reaching ramifications for three continents: for the Americas, whose economic potential was tapped by generations of imported Africans, for Europe, which orchestrated (and benefited from) the whole system, and of course for Africa, for which massive loss of population, with attendant violence and upheaval, caused incalculable and long-term damage. But Atlantic slavery had even more profound consequences than this brief assertion might suggest, for it was a major ingredient in the transformation of the West. Slavery was the means by which the West emerged to a position of unrivalled economic and political dominance. Stated simply, African slave labour, transplanted into the Americas, was critical to the creation of Western wealth and the consequent relegation of other regions and peoples to the overarching power of the West.

Here, then, is a historical episode which is important not simply for its own sake but also for the influence it cast over a much wider historical canvas – much wider indeed than is often recognized. But the history of Atlantic slavery is also interesting for a host of other, sometimes puzzling reasons. Modern readers and students often find it difficult to grasp that the suffering which was the essence of Atlantic slavery could be visited on so many people, on so vast a scale, with so little hesitation, and with no real scruple. It was as if Atlantic slavery was morally neutral for those most actively involved (counted in their tens of thousands), from the humblest of sailors to the grandest of planters and slave merchants. The annals of slavery are brimming with accounts of Western people (mainly white) dealing with black humanity in the most grotesque of fashions – and yet not even noticing what they were doing. Slave captains, planters and colonial officials (often God-fearing men to their fingertips) filled their logs, ledgers and diaries with the most violent and degrading accounts of their dealings with slaves, all without registering the least doubt or hesitation about their actions. Moral self-doubt and religious hesitation rarely intruded into the way they described their working lives, which were dominated by daily face-to-face dealings with Africans and their enslaved descendants.

There is, it is true, another side to this story. There were, from first to last, people of conscience who felt uneasy about African slavery, and who recognized the moral and theological difficulties posed by slavery. But they tended to be outside the slave systems. By and large, their voices were marginalized or silenced by the contrary force of commerce, and by the seductive sound of profitable trade on the backs of African slaves. The material well-being disgorged by slavery was so abundant, so universal (except to the slaves, of course), that moral objections seemed out of place. Why worry about the Africans when their efforts yielded such bounty for so many people on either side of the Atlantic?

To modern eyes, it all seems so odd, so out of kilter with present-day sensibilities and values. Similarly, in the broader story of Atlantic slavery, there is another curious challenge for modern readers. Though it scarcely raised a moral whimper for centuries in the West, slavery ended in a crescendo of outrage and ethical disgust. The institution which had survived for centuries without attracting very much opposition ended its days denounced as an offence to Christian values and a blot on the Western conscience. Clearly, something had changed. What had happened to transform slavery (and the slave trade) into such a moral and irreligious monster? If the slave trade and slavery were so deeply immoral and unchristian in, say, 1830, why had that not been the case in 1730 or 1630? Had slavery changed? Had the West changed? Or had slavery come to occupy an utterly different position in the Western world?

What follows is an effort to come to grips with some of those issues by describing in broad outline both the story of Atlantic slavery and its decline and fall. This book is a study of slavery as it emerged in the Atlantic world, post-Columbus. It concentrates on the British, the people who became the major shippers of Africans at that infamous trade's apogee in the mid-eighteenth century. I have also tried to locate the story of Atlantic slavery in its wider historical setting by looking at some of its major precursors. The book ends with a reminder that slavery did not end with the eradication of black slavery in the Americas.

PART I
Slavery before Modernity

1. Slavery in the Classical World

Slavery was ubiquitous in various ancient and traditional societies. It thrived in Ancient Egypt, where Africans were enslaved to the south, and it was a basic institution in the classical civilizations of Greece and Rome, and in their wider empires and colonies. Later, slavery spread in the wake of an expansionist Islam. In all these societies, slave numbers grew by natural increase: by slaves born to enslaved mothers. But they also recruited slaves from outside their own boundaries. As a result, slave trading routes evolved, along which slaves (like other commodities) passed from distant regions to slave markets and into the cultural and political heartlands of Egypt, Greece, Rome and Islam. The most common form of initial enslavement was via acts of violence. Thus Ancient Egypt absorbed armies of Nubian and Somali slaves, who as well as being enslaved to the south, moved north to work in a range of heavy physical tasks and in the military, though women tended to be enslaved for domestic work and concubinage. Slaves were similarly common in all the Greek city states (again, the sexes tended to divide along the heavy duties/domestic line). Here was the slave labour that enabled Greeks to be free from everyday chores and duties, and to play their role in various civic duties. Thus, at critical points, slavery was – ironically – basic to the conduct of Greek democratic life.

Roman slavery is perhaps more familiar, if only because it is more recent and better documented. The remarkable successes of the Roman legions across the empire, from the Near East to North Africa and northern Europe, provided armies of slaves for the imperial heartlands: for the towns of imperial Rome and for its industrial and agricultural activities. Roman slaves

were ubiquitous. It has been calculated that at the height of
the empire, Roman military successes were able to provide
upwards of half a million slaves every year for Rome. The pattern
we are most familiar with in Atlantic slavery, of captives being
enslaved initially through violence and then transported great
distances, was also common to the slave systems of classical
Antiquity. Between 15 and 35 per cent of the population of
Athens, and perhaps one-third of the population of Rome, were
enslaved. It was clearly economically worthwhile to move slaves,
on foot or by water, huge distances – from Nubia to Egypt,
from England to Rome, from the Black Sea to Greece – just
as, later, it was worthwhile shipping slaves from Africa to the
Americas.

Slaves found their way into all corners of the economies and
societies in the classical world. Much of the heavy labouring
tasks, in agriculture, mining, construction, fell to the slaves. Slaves
dominated domestic work and even many skilled occupations.
Some were highly trusted, skilled and literate; others were mere
brutes of labour or warfare: manning the galleys, or acting as
gladiators entertaining the crowds in the amphitheatres.

These ancient slave systems varied greatly one from another.
But whatever differences set them apart, it was the slave as a
commodity, an item of trade with a value on his or her head,
which characterized many of the major slave societies. Slaves
had a monetary value or equivalence in other material objects
– and thus were accounted, tabulated and calculated as things.
Of course it was rarely that simple, and slave societies often
wrestled in law, philosophy and theology with the inevitable
ambiguities of slavery: of the obvious humanity of slaves set
against their inanimate value, of their moral being as opposed
to their status as a thing, of the presence (rather than the absence)
of the slaves' legal or moral status.

Slavery was a cause and occasion of prolonged philosophi-
cal and moral debate in both Greece and Rome, and was of
interest to writers and playwrights in both civilizations.

Criticism of slavery tended to be largely about the abuses of slavery: the institution of slavery itself remained largely unchallenged. Even the emergence of early Christianity failed to challenge slavery itself, concentrating instead on moderating the worst abuses of Roman slavery. Throughout the classical world, in both Greece and later in the Roman Empire, slavery was too widespread, too important, too valuable, to have its existence threatened.

Since slavery was an inescapable aspect of both urban and rural society in the classical world, inevitably, and despite the limited and fragmentary nature of surviving materials, the person of the slave and the issue of slavery figure prominently in contemporary records. In the words of Thomas Wiedemann, in both Greece and Rome great emphasis 'is placed on slavery as the key principle of social organisation'.[1] Philosophers and playwrights, legal commentators and transactions, simple domestic accounts and more offer tantalizing but revealing insights into the world of contemporary slavery.

Different Greek states had their own particular slave systems, and their own means of dealing with slaves. Plato, in the Laws, explained that, notwithstanding those differences, the condition of slavery always posed basic, inherent difficulties, for all slave-holding societies.

The question of slaves is a difficult one in every respect . . . Of all Greek institutions it is perhaps the Spartan system of Helots which gives rise to the greatest doubts and disagreements, with some people considering it a good thing and others not. The slave system of the Herakleots, who have enslaved the Mariandynians, is less controversial, as is the Thessalian class of Penestai. When we have studied these and all other types, what should we decide to do about the acquisition of house-boys? . . . For there is no element in the soul of a slave that is healthy. A sensible man should not entrust anything to their care. As the wisest poet [Homer, *Odyssey*, 17, 322] puts it:

> When the day of slavery catches up with a man,
> Wide-seeing Zeus takes away half of his mind[2]

The debate about slavery is often captured indirectly, as in this extract (in the form of a Socratic dialogue) from Xenophon's The Householder, *in which the author discusses how best to treat slaves.*

(9) It is possible to make human beings more ready to obey you simply by explaining to them the advantages of being obedient; but with slaves, the training considered to be appropriate to wild beasts is a particularly useful way of instilling obedience. You will achieve the greatest success with them by allowing them as much food as they want. Those who are ambitious by nature will also be motivated by praise (for there are some people who are as naturally keen for praise as others are for food and drink). (10) These are the things I teach those whom I wish to appoint as managers, since I believe that by doing so I can make them more honest persons, and I give them the following advantages: I don't make the cloaks and shoes which I have to provide for my workers all alike, but some worse and others of better quality, so that I can reward the better worker with better clothing and shoes, and give the worse to the man who is worse. (11) I think it is very demoralising for good slaves, Socrates, if they see that all the work is being done by them, while those who don't want to do any work or take any necessary risks get just as much as they do. (12) I myself think that better slaves should not be treated in the same way as worse ones, and I praise my managers when I see that they have given the best things to those who deserve them most, and if I see that someone has been treated too favourably as a result of flattery or some other unproductive favour, I don't let that pass, Socrates, but punish the man, and try to show him that this sort of thing isn't to his advantage [as a manager] either.[3]

There was rarely unanimous opinion on the question of how best to manage slaves. Control remained a perennial problem for Greek slave owners. The debate surfaced in, for example, Greek drama, in theatrical representations of slave owners' uncertainties about how best to keep their slaves in line. Xenophon, again, in his Memorabilia *(in what was in effect a defence of the disgraced Socrates) confronts the difficult issue of how to control and discipline wayward slaves.*

'But let us consider how masters treat slaves of that type. Surely they bring their lustfulness under control through starvation; they prevent them from stealing by locking up the places from which they could take anything; they stop them running away by chaining them; they drive out their laziness by blows. Or what do you do, when you discover that one of your slaves is like that?'

'I punish them with every sort of hardship until I compel them to behave as slaves.'[4]

Stern, unbending management was clearly one way of handling slaves. Punishment and the threat of reprisal obviously played a major role in keeping slaves in awe and submission. But some felt that offering incentives and rewards for good behaviour might be the best way. Slave owners recognized that inducements were also important – including the prospect of freedom. In his Politics, *Aristotle felt that getting the right mix of slaves was important, too.*

If I am to state my own preference, the people who cultivate the land should be slaves; they should not all come from the same tribe or nation, and they should not be too courageous. This will make them useful workers and safe from the danger of revolt. As a second best, they should be non-Greek-speaking serfs (*barbarous perioikous*) with natural characters as similar as possible to those I have indicated. Those of them who are used on private estates must be private property, and those used on community land public property. I will discuss on a separate occasion how slaves ought to be treated, and why it is better if freedom is held out as a prize to all slaves.[5]

Here Euripides comments on the shame of being a slave.

> One thing alone brings shame to the slaves,
> the name; apart from all of that, a slave is no worse
> than free men in anything, if he is good.[6]

> For many slaves the name is shameful, but
>   their minds have
> more freedom than the minds of those
>   who are not slaves.[7]

Roman society being, like Greek civilization before it, rooted in slavery, the problems posed by slaves – how they were acquired, treated, punished, rewarded and freed – and how the issue of slavery was related to, and different from, the freedoms of Roman citizens were all questions which taxed Roman slave holders. In his Life of Cato the Elder, *written in the first century, Plutarch offers a particularly graphic account of domestic Roman slavery.*

Cato possessed a large number of slaves, whom he usually bought from among the prisoners captured in war, but it was his practice to choose those who, like puppies or colts, were young enough to be trained and taught their duties. None of them ever entered any house but his own, unless they were sent on an errand by Cato or his wife, and if they were asked what Cato was doing, the reply was always that they did not know. It was a rule of his establishment that a slave must either be doing something about the house, or else be asleep. He much preferred the slaves who slept well, because he believed that they were more even-tempered than the wakeful ones, and that those who had had enough sleep produced better results at any

task than those who were short of it. And as he was convinced
that slaves were led into mischief more often on account of
love affairs than for any other reason, he made it a rule that
the men could sleep with the women slaves of the establishment, for a fixed price, but must have nothing to do with any
others.

At the beginning of his career, when he was a poor man
and was frequently on active service, he never complained of
anything that he ate, and he used to say that it was ignoble to
find fault with a servant for the food that he prepared. But in
later life, when he had become more prosperous, he used to
invite his friends and colleagues to dinner, and immediately
after the meal he would beat with a leather thong any of the
slaves who had been careless in preparing or serving it. He
constantly contrived to provoke quarrels and dissensions among
his slaves, and if they ever arrived at an understanding with one
another he became alarmed and suspicious. If ever any of his
slaves was suspected of committing a capital offense, he gave
the culprit a formal trial in the presence of the rest, and if he
was found guilty, he had him put to death.[8]

*Slaves could be found in a huge range of occupations in the Roman
Empire. Even in a single household – in the homes of Rome's elite,
for example – we find large numbers of slaves working in a remarkable range of jobs. The household accounts of Livia, wife of the Emperor
Augustus, listed fifty slaves, each allotted a specific role. Some were
highly skilled, literate workers (treasurer, for example), others simple
labourers around the house (water carrier). In such prosperous homes,
domestic slaves were simply inescapable.*

1	aquarius	water-carrier
2	arcarius	treasurer
3	argentarius	silversmith
4	ab argento	servant in charge of the silver
5	atriensis	majordomo

6 aurifex	goldsmith
7 calciator	shoe-maker
8 capsarius	clothes folder
9 colorator	furniture polisher
10 cubicularius	chamberlain
11 supra cubicularios	supervisor of the chamberlains
12 delicium	pet child
13 dispensator	steward
14 faber	craftsman
15 insularius	keeper of apartment block
16 lanipendus	wool-weigher
17 lector	reader
18 libraria	clerk
19 a manu	secretary
20 margaritarius	pearl setter
21 medicus	doctor
22 supra medicos	supervisor of the doctors
23 mensor	surveyor
24 nutrix	wetnurse
25 opsonator	caterer
26 obstetrix	midwife
27 ab ornamentis	servant in charge of ceremonial dress
28 ornatrix	dresser
29 ostiarius	doorkeeper
30 paedagogus	pedagogue
31 a pedibus	supervisor of footmen
32 pedisequus	footman
33 pedisequa	female attendant
34 pictor	painter
35 pistor	baker
36 ad possessiones	financial administrator
37 a purpuris	servant in charge of purple garments
38 rogator	issuer of invitations?
39 a sacrario	servant in charge of shrine
40 sarcinatrix	clothes mender

41 a sede	chair attendant?
42 strator	saddler
43 structor	builder
44 ab suppelectile	servant in charge of furniture
45 tabularius	record keeper
46 a tabulis	servant in charge of pictures
47 unctrix	masseuse
48 ad unguenta	servant in charge of perfumed oils
49 ad valetudinarium	sickbay orderly
50 a veste	servant in charge of clothes[9]

Like the Greeks before them, Romans were rarely totally confident about their slaves. They feared them; they worried that they stole, lied and generally deceived their owners. Slave owners took elaborate precautions to ensure that their domestic life and their material possessions were secure from the slaves, as described here by Pliny the Elder.

Nowadays even food and wine has to be sealed up in order to be protected from theft. This is due to the legions of slaves, the crowd of outsiders in our homes, and the fact that we need someone just to remind us of the names of our slaves [the *nomenclator*]. In the days of old there were just single slaves belonging to Marcus and Lucius (*Marcipores Luciporesve*), part of their masters' kin-groups who took all their meals in common with them; there was no need to lock up anything in the house to keep it from the household slaves.[10]

Another persistent concern was the slaves' instinct to escape – to run away. Time and again Romans advertised for the return of runaway slaves. The case of two Egyptian runaways in a document from 146 BC provides an example.

A boy called Hermon has run away at Alexandria, age about 15, wearing a cloak and a belt. Anyone who brings him back will receive 2 [corrected to:] 3 talents; anyone who gives

information that he is at a shrine, 1 [corrected to:] 2 talents;
if he is with a man who can be trusted to accept a court
ruling, 3 [corrected to:] 5 talents. Whoever wishes is to inform
the governor's officials.

There is also another slave who has run away with him,
Bion.

Whoever brings him back will receive the same as for the
one specified above.

Inform the governor's officials about him as well.[11]

*The greatest fear of all was, of course, violent slave resistance. Slaves
everywhere developed various ways of coping with and resisting the
worst features of their bondage, and turning to violence was normally
the last resort: they all knew that they could expect no mercy if they
failed or, after escaping, they were caught. Nevertheless, in his* Letters
*Pliny describes the fate of one particularly brutal master, Larcius
Macedo.*

(1) The horrible fate which the ex-Praetor Larcius Macedo
suffered at the hands of his slaves deserves to be mentioned in
something more than just a letter. He was an insolent and brutal
master who didn't care to remember that his father had himself
been a slave – or perhaps he remembered it all too well.

(2) He was having a bath in his villa at Formiae. Suddenly
some of his slaves surrounded him; one of them grasped him
by the throat, another hit him in the face, another in the chest
and stomach, another (what an unpleasant thing to mention!)
in the groin. When they saw that he had lost consciousness,
they threw him onto the boiling hot bath-floor to see if he
was still alive. He lay there without moving – either he felt
nothing or he pretended to feel nothing: so that he made them
believe that he was in fact dead. (3) At this point they carried
him out as though he had fainted as a result of the heat; some
of his more faithful slaves took over, and his concubines
appeared, with a lot of noise and wailing. The effect was that

he was aroused by their shouting and recovered because of the fresh air, and showed that he was still alive by opening his eyes and moving some part of his body; it was now safe for him to do this. (4) The slaves all fled; most of them have been arrested and the rest are being sought. He himself was kept alive with great difficulty for a few days and then died; he had the consolation that while still alive he was avenged in the way victims of murder usually are.

(5) So you see how exposed we are to all sorts of danger, insult and humiliation. And it is not the case that anyone can feel himself secure because he is indulgent and mild – masters aren't killed with a just cause (*iudicio*), but as the result of sheer criminality.[12]

The most dramatic of all acts of slave violence – and the ultimate fear of all slave-holding societies – was, of course, the slave revolt. Few were as spectacular or well remembered as the revolt of the Roman slaves led by Spartacus in 74 BC, described in the following two extracts by Appian.

At this time there were in Italy some gladiators who were being trained to appear in spectacles at Capua. A Thracian called Spartacus, who had fought in the Roman army but was among the gladiators as the result of capture in war and sale, had persuaded about seventy of them to gamble for their freedom rather than be put on show at a public spectacle. Together with them he overcame the guards and escaped. He armed them with wooden stakes and swords which belonged to some people they met on the road, and fled to Mount Vesuvius. There he received lots of runaway slaves as well as some free persons from the countryside, and plundered the area round about. He chose the gladiators Oenomaus and Crixus to be his lieutenants. He soon collected lots of supporters, since he divided up the booty absolutely equally.

The first person to be sent out against him was Varinius Glabrus, and after him Publius Valerius: they didn't command regular armies, but all the men they could levy immediately along their route of march – for the Romans didn't yet look upon this operation as a war, but rather as a police action against bandits – and when they engaged Spartacus, they were beaten. Spartacus himself even made off with Varinius' horse – so close was the Roman general himself to being captured by a gladiator.

After this even more people were keen to join Spartacus, and his army already totalled 70,000; he had weapons made and collected supplies.[13]

The revolt ended in the crucifixion of 6,000 slaves – a reminder to all slaves (if one were needed) of the price of failure.

Crassus was keen to get to grips with Spartacus any way he could, so that the glory for the war wouldn't go to Pompey: Spartacus himself wanted to resolve things before Pompey's arrival, and he suggested that Crassus might come to an agreement with him. When this idea was rejected, he decided to risk battle, and since his cavalry had now appeared, he broke through the circumvallation with the whole of his army and fled towards Brundisium, with Crassus in pursuit. When Spartacus learned that Lucullus too had arrived at Brundisium, fresh from a victory over Mithridates, he realised that the whole thing was hopeless and engaged Crassus with his entire army, which was considerable even at this stage. With so many tens of thousands of desperate men, there was a long and hard-fought battle; Spartacus was wounded in the thigh by a spear and fell on to his knees; he held his shield out in front of him and resisted those who attacked him until he was surrounded himself and fell together with a great crowd of people around him. The rest of his army broke ranks, and there was much slaughter; so many were killed that it was impossible to count them. About one thousand Romans died; Spartacus' corpse could not be found. A lot of people fled from the battle up into the mountains, and Crassus went after them. They divided themselves into four sections and continued to resist until all of them had been destroyed, except for six thousand who were captured and crucified along the length of the road from Capua to Rome.[14]

2. Slavery and Medieval Europe

In the thousand years between the fall of Rome and the decline of feudalism, slavery (and other forms of bondage) existed in many parts of Europe. In the Byzantine Empire in the East, and across western Europe, slavery was essential to the way a host of societies functioned. It existed at the heart of Christian Europe, and was to be found from Iceland to Spain, from Ireland to Byzantium; and, of course, it was, as we shall see, widespread in the Islamic world, including Islamic Spain.

There was, however, no single form of slavery. Instead there were a variety of slave systems, ranging from piratical Viking slavery in northern Europe through to the well-established and complex ancient slave trading routes of Central Asia. In effect there was a remarkable mosaic of systems, held together by trade and by slave-trading links. Slaves were forcibly shifted huge distances, along well-established sea-borne, riverine and over-land slave routes, destined for the slave markets of distant societies.

Although there was no single overall slave system across Europe, slaves everywhere shared a common fate. They mostly undertook the tedious, back-breaking chores of life, many in rural work, and often as domestic workers. Yet we also know of medieval slaves (as in the classical and Islamic worlds) who managed to rise to more elevated positions and who were responsible for money, accountancy and administration. The most striking slaves in these years (because they were the most visible) were domestics, employed individually or in groups, living and working close to their masters and mistresses, with all the consequent personal tensions such proximity generated, but medieval urban life was also dotted with skilled and semi-skilled slaves.

Slavery in western Europe was eventually eroded by the rise of feudalism, which involved the merging of slaves and free into a class of serfs. They came to form a dependent peasantry which, though the peasants were tied to the land, was quite distinct from the old forms of slavery. Even so, slavery managed to persist, especially in those European regions which were either physically close to Islam – Spain, for example – or which had important trading links to distant slave communities, notably Italy. But even where slavery in medieval Europe remained important and visible, it was never on the scale of slavery in the classical world or in Islam; nor did it attain the significance it had previously held.

At first glance, it might be thought that slavery in Europe would have faced objections from the Christian church. In fact, from the earliest days of Christianity (in the last years of the Roman Empire) Christians tended to accept slavery as part of the natural order of life. After all, slavery had existed in both the world of the Old and the New Testaments, and biblical texts (including the Koran) are littered with references to slavery and slaves. Indeed, some examples of slavery remain among the Bible's best-remembered stories, the most obvious and famous perhaps being Israel's slavery in Egypt.

Some of the earliest Christians were themselves converted slaves, while others owned 'pagan' slaves. Furthermore, as institutional churches spread across Europe, possessing their own lands, they simply accepted that slaves would toil on church lands, much as they did on the lands of other contemporary landowners. In England, for example, churches were among the last to hold slaves on their lands: Peterborough Abbey used slaves on its properties as late as the 1120s.

Throughout early medieval Europe, warfare seems to have been a major (though not the only) source of slaves. Prisoners of war formed ready-made supplies of slaves for local or long-distance use. In Anglo-Saxon England, most slaves appear to have been used as rural workers, and were characterized by the ploughman.

When the shift from slavery to serfdom took place, serfdom flourished in the growth of large estates, and in their need for a form of labour that was different from slavery. The rise of powerful local lords across western Europe was paralleled by their ability to force through important social changes, most notably in the use of labour. In England, this process was hastened by the Norman Conquest, and by the imposition of a foreign landlord class.

What lay at the heart of this transformation – the ending of slavery – was to be found in other parts of Europe, though the exact timing differed from place to place. In Scandinavia, for example, slavery ended under pressure from many of the economic changes seen at work earlier in England. In Iceland, Norway and Denmark, slavery appears to have died out by the mid-thirteenth century; and in Sweden perhaps a century later. In Scandinavia, as elsewhere, the role of the early Christian church was sometimes ambiguous. The medieval Scandinavian church (as in England) held slaves on church lands, and most churchmen seem to have regarded slavery as a natural feature of the existing social order, though they cautioned that slaves should be treated as humans and as fellow Christians.

Further east, in Russia, the story of slavery was quite different. The expansion of the initially small Muscovite state into the vast, sprawling precursor of modern Russia took place along-side, and related to, the expansion of Russian slavery, though this all came at a much later date.

What happened in southern Europe was quite different again. It was understandable that slavery was more common across swathes of southern Europe. For a start, Islam had conquered much of Spain by 720, and was only stopped from sweeping through northern Europe by military defeat at Poitiers in 732. Islam remained in control of much of Spain until the late thirteenth century, and was only finally expelled with the fall of Grenada in 1492. The Islamic tradition of enslavement, and contacts with other Islamic societies in Africa and the eastern

Mediterranean, meant that, in the very years when slavery was in sharp decline elsewhere in Europe, slavery was confirmed as an unquestioned feature of Iberian life. Muslims used Christian slaves, and Christian areas of northern Spain tended to use Muslim slaves. Muslim prisoners of war were employed as slaves for the building of the cathedral of Santiago de Compostela in the twelfth century; when the Aragonese took Minorca in 1287, they enslaved everyone except the rich, who were able to buy their freedom and flee to North Africa.

Both Christians and Muslims in the Iberian peninsula raided each other's communities for slaves. But the most plentiful source of slaves was Africa. By the 1240s Catalan merchants were buying slaves in North Africa, and Barcelona rivalled Majorca as a major slave market. Spain's major Mediterranean ports teemed with ships loaded with goods (including slaves) from all corners of the Mediterranean. Slaves inevitably found their way throughout Iberian society into domestic work, urban employment and rural labouring. The ownership of slaves was widespread: artisans, monarchs and princes of the church all owned slaves. We know of slaves in 1431 in Catalonia who were owned by carpenters, laundrymen, blacksmiths, weavers, seamen, tailors, notaries, butchers and doctors. Slaves were rowers on the royal galleys in the late fourteenth century, while in the Balearic Islands slaves were essential as agricultural workers.

In the two centuries to 1500 the Mediterranean slave trade thrived, with slaves (Muslim and 'pagan') arriving in Spain from around the Mediterranean and the Black Sea. Spanish slave traders did not, however, buy direct from Black Sea ports, instead securing slaves via merchants in Marseilles, Genoa, Naples, Palermo and around the Adriatic. Thus the ranks of Spanish slaves were filled by Africans from North Africa, Tartars and Turks, Caucasians and Russians, and others from the Balkans and Greece. It is impossible to be precise about the numbers of slaves in Spain; though they seem to have increased between 1300 and 1450, their numbers declined thereafter. Even so, it has been calculated that as late as 1428 one-tenth of the population of Majorca (where slaves were especially numerous) was enslaved.

Perhaps the most important aspect of slavery in Spain was the role of the law. Thanks to the enlightened rule of Alfonso X of Castile, Roman law had been incorporated into local law – the Siete Partidas. One of the many consequences of this change was that slavery was given a legal structure: it was no longer merely a haphazard economic phenomenon. Though the implementation of the Siete Partidas varied greatly, it had important long-term consequences. It ensured that a legal code existed for the treatment of slaves, and it was this code that guided and shaped the early Spanish involvement with slave colonies in the Americas. Thus the Spaniards not only maintained an active involvement with slavery long after it had been effectively abandoned in other parts of Europe but with their legal system they facilitated the transfer of slavery to the Americas.

As in the Iberian peninsula, Italy was familiar with slavery in the centuries when slavery was in sharp decline elsewhere in Europe. In the eleventh and twelfth centuries, Spain had been the major slave market of western Europe, but the Black Death, and the subsequent shortage of labour, saw the trade shift to Italy. Italy, of course, lay at the crossroads of the movement of commodities and peoples to all corners of the Mediterranean and beyond. The merchants of dominant Italian city states traded at all major Mediterranean ports, and their goods were also trans-shipped to the even more distant locations of sub-Saharan Africa, the Black Sea and the East. Among those goods were slaves. Most were young – often children – sold by parents or enslaved by raids, and then sold on to Italian merchants at the slave markets of Tana, Caffa, Constantinople, Cyprus and Crete. The Genoese and Venetians established themselves as the most prominent and enterprising of Europe's long-distance traders, supplying distant ports with slaves – shipping them from the Black Sea to Egypt, for example. The Genoese enjoyed a favoured trading status, and were allowed to maintain their own trading posts in the Black Sea and near Constantinople, whence they shipped slaves mainly to Maluka Egypt.

When Italian ships headed back to their home ports, they often carried slaves in their cargoes. The arrival of new slaves in Italy was in effect an offshoot of the more important trade conducted by Italians between the Christian and Muslim worlds. It was, however, a relatively small trade and only increased in size following the Black Death in the fourteenth century.

The movement of slaves to Italy was a fluctuating business, especially when the Genoese were left with an effective monopoly of slave trading on the Black Sea after 1261. This had the effect of changing the origins of slaves destined to Italy. Whereas between 1200 and 1275 the majority of slaves in Genoa were Muslim (from North Africa and Spain), thereafter, and continuing into the fourteenth and fifteenth centuries, most slaves originated in the Black Sea region.

Though slaves were scattered across the Italian peninsula in the late Middle Ages, slaves worked mainly in towns and cities, where they were employed in prosperous homes. They were 'Muslims, Tatars, Circassians, Russians, Bulgarians, Armenians, Albanians',[1] with others from the Mediterranean and Africa. In common with the rest of Europe, all this changed following the Black Death in the mid-fourteenth century. Of the many catastrophic consequences of the drop in Europe's population (of between one-quarter and one-third) was a revival in slavery. In Florence, the government in 1363 allowed the unrestricted importation of slaves – provided the slaves were non-Christian. And with the Black Sea cut off by the Turks, Italian merchants turned once again to North Africa and Spain for slaves. Gradually, however, this reliance on imported slaves gave way, notably in Venice, to indentured labour, with the importation of labourers who became free after a specified number of years (though even then, they had to purchase their freedom).

The story of Europe's entanglement with slavery was to

change, yet again, with developments much further afield. The
European break-out from the world of the Mediterranean, for
trade and settlement, first to the islands in the Atlantic and
later to the Americas, was to transform the story of slavery
completely.

*The buying and selling of slaves was commonplace in the major trad-
ing cities of late medieval Italy. Time and again, the letters, diaries and
ledgers of slave owners in late medieval Europe provide testimony to
a central feature of slavery: slaves were viewed much like any item of
trade and commerce. Slaves were ordered, in specific detail, like any
other item. But the supply of slaves was often uncertain, and requests
for slaves were not always easily satisfied. Here is an order for a slave
from a merchant in Genoa, in 1393.*

Pray buy me a little slave-girl, young and rustic, between eight
and ten years old, and she must be of good stock, strong enough
to Bear much hard work, and of good health and temper, so
that I may bring her up in my own way. I would have her only
to wash the dishes and carry wood and bread to the oven, and
work of that sort . . . for I have another here who is a good
slave, and can cook and serve well.[2]

The request was still not satisfied at the end of the year.

No ship has come in from Roumania with any on board: but
now it cannot be long before they come, and you and Margherita
will be provided as you wish. Those who are here now are not
worth taking, for they are second-hand wares . . .[3]

*Even when they were in the most wretched of conditions, slaves rarely
induced a human response from those who owned them.*

The slave you sent is sick, or rather full of boils, so that we find none who would have her. We will sell or barter her as best we can, and send you an account. Furthermore, I hear she is with child, two months gone or more, and therefore she will not be worth selling.[4]

Domestic slaves were often young women whose presence sometimes created sexual tension within a slave-holding household. Here is an example from the late fourteenth century. A wife complains that they have been sent an attractive young female slave.

Paparo's wife complains greatly of you and yet more of Monna Margherta, that she should suffer you to send such a young and fair slave. She says she never would do such a thing to her, and women should take heed not to do such things to each other.[5]

When a slave woman found herself pregnant, with no obvious father, the wife of the house sometimes blamed her husband, as happened in this case from 1391.

And since the father could not be found, I took it and sent it to nurse. But my Monna Lucia was seized with jealousy, and said it was mine: and though I told her it was only mine as a calf belong to a man who owns a cow, she still will not believe me, whether I vow or coax . . . And she has won the battle, and the slave has been turned out, and we now have an old woman who is more like a monkey than a female: and this is the life I lead . . .[6]

Even priests could be heartless. This was the 1392 response of a priest accused of being responsible for his former slave's pregnancy.

We spake to the chaplain to whom your slave belonged and he says you may throw her into the sea, with what she has in her belly, for it is no creature of his. And we deem he speaks the truth, for had she been pregnant by him, he would not have sent her . . . Methinks you had better send the creature to the hospital.[7]

Slaves were always alert to opportunities to escape their bondage. This example from 1409 describes how a group managed to row to freedom – but were unlucky enough to be imprisoned again in Majorca.

We hear from Ibiza that Ser Antonio delio has arrived there, with many Moorish captives on his ship, and twelve of them ran away with his rowing boat . . . But because of the weather the said Moors came here [Majorca] and for the present have been imprisoned, which has been a great piece of good fortune.[8]

Slave owners used their personal networks to secure the return of runaway slaves. This is an owner's description of slaves who escaped from Barcelona to Avignon, c.1400–1410?.

One of them is named Dmitri a big man and very handsome. His flesh is good and rosey . . . [the other] lacks a front tooth and has rather greenish skin . . . I pray you, senor, have them caught, let them be strongly fettered and send them back by boat to me.[9]

3. Slavery and Islam

Long before the establishment of African slavery in the Americas, Islamic societies were characterized by the widespread and generally unchallenged use of slavery. Indeed slavery was commonplace throughout Arabia well before the rise of Islam. But as Islam spread, between the eighth and fifteenth centuries, and especially into black Africa, it extended and confirmed the commonplace use of slavery and slave trading. At the apogee of Islamic influence, slaves were imported into Islamic societies from Africa, Europe, Central Asia and even India. At first, however, there was no link between colour or ethnicity and slavery, even though large numbers of Islamic slaves were indeed black Africans. The critical issue was the insistence that the enslaved should be non-Muslim, just as, later, Christian slave traders would not enslave fellow Christians.

From its earliest days, Islam was associated with slavery. The prophet Muhammad had owned slaves; his teachings, in the form of the Koran, contain frequent references to slaves and slavery: specifying how masters should treat their slaves, and how they might enable slaves to free themselves; and Islamic writers (holy men and legal commentators) frequently discussed the problems posed by slavery. Slavery accompanied the spread of Islam across the Mediterranean, North Africa and into sub-Saharan Africa. In the process, overland and maritime trade routes evolved to supply slave markets with captives from the further-most reaches of Islamic trade and influence. Black Africa proved to be a rich source of slaves for the major slave markets of the Mediterranean and the Near East. The slave routes across the Sahara, for example, survived from the seventh to the twentieth century, and millions of Africans were force-marched along them from their homelands to the slave markets to the north. One estimate puts the total number of slaves involved at more than seven million between 650 and 1900, though more recent calculations have revised that figure to between three and a half and four million. Even at that lower level, the trans-Saharan slave trade represents one of the largest examples of enslavement in world history. On such arduous treks, large numbers inevitably perished en route. Most appear to have been enslaved, initially, by violent raids in Africa. The trans-Saharan slave trade was only the most striking and best remembered aspect of Islamic slavery.

Though the enslavement of fellow Muslims was disapproved of, in time this came to be overlooked or ignored by Muslim slave traders. The sheer growth of slave trading on so massive a scale, across such vast geographic expanses of the Islamic world, and the ubiquity of slavery, sometimes overrode theological or moral objections. In time, it came to be assumed that black Africans were natural slaves, though this had not been the case initially. And the spread of Islam into black Africa created the risk and the lucrative temptation of enslaving fellow Muslims.

Unlike the later Atlantic slave trade, Islamic slavery was primarily female – a clear enough sign that Islamic slaves were destined for different kinds of labour, mainly for domestic and sexual services. Female slaves toiled in a range of domestic work and other tasks across the Islamic world, from Córdoba to Baghdad. Men too were enslaved, large numbers being employed as eunuchs in harems and as literate slaves in administrative and educational roles. The Caliph of Baghdad in the late tenth century was thought to have had 7,000 black and 4,000 white eunuchs in his palace. From the earliest days, of course, slaves (many of them black) were employed in hard physical labour: in mines, in salt pans and for harsh agricultural work, as well as the military. By the eighth century, slavery was flourishing throughout the Islamic world, which stretched from the Middle East to Spain, though it is unlikely that slaves ever formed more than 5 per cent of the total population.

Slaves had long been recruited from sub-Saharan Africa, and from Nubia. But why were Africans especially prone to enslavement: was there a special stigma to blackness itself? Did Islam think black Africans especially suitable for enslavement and slavery? At first Islam, like Christianity, seems to have emerged in a relatively colour-blind environment, but that changed as circumstances changed. As Islam pushed ever deeper into black Africa, and growing numbers of captives were enslaved and passed on to the overland slave traders, Arabs/Muslims began to think of black Africans as ideally suited for slavery. Gradually, a distinct racial prejudice emerged. It can be seen, for example, in a wide range of Arabic poetry (much as similar racial prejudice was later reflected in the works of major writers in English). The complex issues posed by Islamic slavery – of law, treatment, religion, colour – recur time and again in the rich literary sources of Islam.

Thus long before the rise of European maritime power, and the tentative arrival of Europeans on the West African coast, firm links had been forged between black Africa and slavery. Coffles of Africans were familiar in the slave markets of North Africa and Egypt, and the enforced movement of enslaved Africans along vast overland trade routes was commonplace, long before the European pioneers in the Americas began to consider the use of African slaves as labourers in the American settlements.

Scholars of Islamic history have discovered a wealth of literature about the complex history of slavery in Islamic societies. As in the world of classical Antiquity, slaves were a basic and largely unquestioned feature of Islamic life. Islam had a vast geography, stretching at its height from Spain to Baghdad and on into Asia, and deep into East and West Africa. We have evidence about slavery and Islam across more than a millennium. Of course, the earlier evidence is sparse and fragmentary, but revealing for all that. As the use of enslaved Africans grew, infusing Islam with a pronounced sense of racial prejudice, from as early as the seventh and eighteenth centuries, contemporary poetry addressed the joint issues of blackness and slavery.

The first three extracts are by the African-born poet Suhaym, who died in 660.

> If my color were pink, women would love me
> But the Lord has marred me with blackness.[1]

> Though I am a slave my soul is nobly free
> Though I am black of color my character is white.[2]

> I am covered with a black garment, but under it there
> Is a lustrous garment with white skirts.[3]

The following verse is by black poet Nusayb ibn Rabah, who died in 726.

> Blackness does not diminish me, as long as I have
> this tongue and this stout heart.
> Some are raised up by means of their lineage: the
> verses of my poems are my lineage!
> How much better a keen-minded, clear-spoken
> black than a mute white![4]

Also in the eighth century, a black poet wrote, after being goaded by racial insult:

> Though my hair is woolly and my skin coal-black,
> My hand is open and my honour bright.[5]

Europeans were familiar with Islamic slavery, not least because of the persistent enslavement of Christians over many centuries by various Islamic societies. Islam often acquired slaves from great distances to work *in a wide range of activities. The prime driving force behind the enslavement of women was their employment in sexual services. This account of the Sultan's harem in Cairo in the fifteenth century by Ibn Shahin offers one example.*

. . . as for the concubines, their numbers used to be forty. Each concubine had her entourage, her male and female slaves, and her eunuchs. As for the rest of the female slaves in the Noble Dwellings, they constituted a numerous group of women of all races among whom are those who have special occupations . . . for there are bath attendants, wet nurses, and special governesses.[6]

Men were often enslaved for use in the armed forces (and galleys) of various Islamic societies. Here we have an account by Ahmad al-Mansur of black slaves recruited for the Moroccan army in the sixteenth century.

. . . we selected those slaves to be made into soldiers and a channel for Islam, because of the qualities they possess to the exclusion of others: they are a race who give little trouble, they are content with simple living conditions, accepting things as they find them without being troublesome or demanding. In addition, this race of slaves has strengthened this blessed affair of guarding the *jihadist* fortresses and encompassing the Islamic lands to which they were assigned and directed. They are tougher and more long-suffering over its movements and relocations. They were suited to that and best fitted to undertake it most perfectly.[7]

When the British completely ended their own slave systems in 1838, they embarked on a global crusade against slavery, notably in Africa and Arabia, and throughout the nineteenth and twentieth centuries. British diplomacy and military power targeted the survival of slavery in Islamic societies. It concerned a number of Islamic authorities too that Islamic Africans were now falling victim to slave traders, who were thus breaking one of Islam's important conventions: that believers should not enslave a fellow Muslim. A similar distinction was to be important in the development of African slavery in the Americas, when Europeans came to justify the system on the grounds that Africans were pagans, not Christian. For many centuries, both Christians and Muslims accepted that slavery was justified if the slave was an outsider, a non-believer. The following is an Islamic protest at the enslavement of Muslim Africans in the late nineteenth century.

Thus will be apparent to you the heinousness of the affliction which has beset the lands of the Maghrib since the ancient times in regard to the indiscriminate enslaving of the people of the Sudan [Africa], and the importation of droves of them every year to be sold in the market places in town and country where men trade in them as one would trade in beasts – nay worse than that. People have become so inured to that, generation after generation, that many common folk believe that the reason for being enslaved according to the Holy Law is merely that a man should be black in color and come from those regions. This, by God's life, is one of the foulest and gravest evils perpetrated upon God's religion, for the people of the Sudan are Muslims having the same rights and responsibilities as ourselves. Even if you assume that some of them are pagans or belong to a religion other than Islam, nevertheless the majority of them are Muslims, and judgement is made according to the majority. Again, even if you suppose that Muslims are not a majority and that Islam and unbelief claim equal members there, who among us can tell whether those brought here are Muslims or unbelievers? For the innate condition of humankind is freedom and lack of any cause for being enslaved. Whoever maintains the opposite is denying the basic condition.[8]

PART II
Slavery in the Atlantic World

4. The Origins of Atlantic Slavery

The first speculative European explorations of West Africa were in search of various goods (notably gold), but not in pursuit of slaves. Europeans also wanted a route to the East, as part of their attempt to outflank Islam (which now effectively blocked Mediterranean trade to the East) by edging round Africa, thence to Asia. The voyages were dangerous, prolonged and speculative, spearheaded by the Portuguese (and largely inspired by Prince Henry the Navigator). Progress was slow, haphazard and unpredictable. But, bit by bit, it yielded tangible proof of viable and lucrative long-distance maritime trade. It also provided direct access to goods which had previously only reached Europeans via overland Arab trade routes. Henceforth, Africa's goods were exposed to direct European trade and incursion.

Using Cueta in Morocco as a base, Portuguese sailors and adventurers slowly nosed along the Moroccan coast, returning to Portugal from each voyage with African goods, including African slaves. In the 1430s and 1440s, successive voyages pressed further south along the African coast, at each point touching on internal African trade routes which yielded goods (and humanity) from deep inside Africa. The early slaves taken to Portugal were Arab, Berber and black African. In 1444 the first batch were displayed in a field outside Lagos in southern Portugal.

Early piratical raids to grab Africans as slaves were clearly of limited value, and gradually the Portuguese began to trade, rather than raid, for slaves, though then, and throughout the history of the slave trade, violence was the ultimate and main means of initial enslavement. With a base (a 'factory') on Arguin island, the Portuguese accumulated groups of slaves brought to them by Berber merchants. By the mid-fifteenth century, upwards of 800 slaves a year were being dispatched to Portugal.

By 1460 the Portuguese had reached northern Senegambia, where they exchanged horses for slaves. They still remained more interested in other items and valuable commodities (notably gold and spices), but they shipped Africans to labour in the recently settled Cape Verde Islands and in Portugal itself. As they moved further south along the African coast, in the 1460s and 1470s, the Portuguese came face to face with African gold, mined inland but available in abundance on the coast. Among the goods they were expected to offer in exchange for that gold were slaves: thus did the Portuguese begin to exchange slaves, purchased further south in the Niger delta, in Kongo and Angola for gold. And as both Spain and Portugal settled and converted the Atlantic islands – the Canaries, the Cape Verde Islands and later the small off-shore islands of Fernando Po, Príncipe and São Tomé – they began to use Africans for various tasks on those islands.

Among the produce the European settlers and their African slaves cultivated on the islands was sugar cane. Cane sugar had long been known in Europe, but its popularity was confined in the wake of the Crusades to the eastern Mediterranean. Cane sugar was brought back from the islands to western Europe – just one of a host of exotic imports which pandered to the tastes of wealthy European elites. Cane sugar cultivation spread to plantations in the Holy Land and later other suitable locations in the Mediterranean (Cyprus, Crete, North Africa, Sicily and southern Spain). But there, the labour was free and not enslaved.

As Europeans tentatively edged into the Atlantic, they discovered new trading routes, established settlements and devised new forms of local production and cultivation. The new lands – islands, trading posts, colonies – were all to bring some form of material bounty to the settler nation and its merchants. Madeira, for example, proved a good spot for sugar production (after other crops had been tried), especially with the help of slaves imported from Africa. Sugar was also planted in the Azores (unsuccessfully), and in the Canaries and the Cape Verde Islands. European markets snapped up the growing volumes of sugar: Europe's taste for sweet food and drinks was voracious. Europeans tried to cultivate other crops before resorting to slave-grown sugar – a pattern that was to be repeated in the Americas – but wherever sugar cane was produced, the link was gradually confirmed between sugar cultivation and African slave labour.

The use of African slave labour was a key change in this new form of tropical cultivation – and one which was to transform the tropical Americas. Unlike the earlier Mediterranean plantations, the new Atlantic settlements turned to nearby Africa not simply for labour but for slave labour. The formula was quickly established: sugar equals plantations equals African slavery. This was at its most striking on the islands of São Tomé and Príncipe, close to the African mainland, where the new sugar plantations filled with African slaves. These islands also became staging posts for the transit of African slaves, en route to other Atlantic islands, Portugal and later the Americas.

Portuguese traders (themselves growing in numbers) increasingly turned to Kongo for supplies of slaves. Despite efforts by African rulers to control or limit the local slave trade (with all its damaging consequences to their own and neighbouring communities), the demand set in train by the Portuguese presence proved irresistible. Whenever difficulties arose, the Europeans looked elsewhere for slaves (to Angola, for instance). This pattern was to characterize European slave trading in West Africa: a creeping zone of coastal slave trading to feed the appetite for slave labour in the Atlantic islands and Portugal itself. The Portuguese orchestrated well-established, lucrative and vast trading systems, stretching from Morocco to Angola, which depended to a marked degree on slave labour. All this, however was as nothing compared to what was to follow on the other side of the Atlantic.

Columbus's voyages to the Americas were part of the European search for maritime routes to the East. In time, the discoveries of and in the Americas were to be more valuable than anyone could have imagined. The physical problems faced by the early European settlers (led by the Spaniards in the Caribbean and Central America, and the Portuguese in Brazil) seemed tolerable when the Spaniards discovered the dazzling wealth of the Aztec and Inca empires. In the rush to find precious treasure, the initial planting schemes, including sugar, were set aside. Subsequent early efforts to grow sugar using indigenous labour highlighted a difficulty which was to face European settlers throughout the colonial history of the Americas: the reluctance or refusal of indigenous Indian peoples to bow to the harsh disciplined labour required on plantations. And this was in addition to the devastation wrought by imported diseases among the indigenous peoples. From first to last, 'Indian' labour was unsuitable for the back-breaking tasks demanded of workers by white settlers, especially in agricultural development and mining. Legions of Indians died in early experiments, while others simply disappeared, and Europeans were faced with a labour shortage. With never enough of their own kind to under-take the tasks of settlement, the Europeans soon realized that the solution to their labour shortage was readily to hand. Both Portuguese and Spaniards having had long experience of using African slave labour, in Iberia and on their Atlantic islands, once it became obvious, in the mines and fields, that native labour was inadequate, Spanish officials received early and regular demands from the colonies for African slaves to enable the colonies to flourish. From 1516 the use of imported Africans was supported by Las Casas, Bishop of Chiapas, in order to save native people, although he was later to regret his support. The drift to African slave labour in the Americas seems, in retro-spect, almost inevitable: a natural drift on the far side of Atlantic towards what the marauding Europeans had already pioneered in the eastern Atlantic.

A similar pattern unfolded in the Portuguese settlements (which were no more than toeholds at first) on the vast land-mass of Brazil, especially when trade gave way to settlement in the 1530s. Here, again, native labour proved resistant to the European demands placed on it: in mining and agricultural work, the Indians simply died out or drifted away. Enslaving Indians never answered the Europeans' labour need. When sugar plantations were developed in Bahia and Pernambuco, especially after 1575, the need for imported labour became imperative, and within forty years Brazilian sugar plantations had become dependent on African slaves. Although, like the Spaniards before them, the Portuguese had already used African slaves, henceforth they forged a new and qualitatively different link, which was to remain unbroken for the next three centuries, between sugar and African slavery. Sugar brought prosperity (to planters, merchants and their metropolitan backers) on an unprecedented scale, but at the price of acute misery to a grow-ing army of Africans, shipped across the Atlantic to serve the plantations of the Americas.

The rising volumes of Brazilian sugar shipped to Europe, pandering to the expanding social habit of sweet consumption, revealed to all other aspiring colonial powers that tropical settle-ment might be rendered highly profitable − provided, that is, that there were enough African slaves for the labour. It was a lesson later learned by the English and the French.

African slaves had arrived in the Americas as early as Columbus's second voyage in 1493, and in 1513 the Spanish Crown, through the grant of Asientos, formally licensed the Portuguese to transport African slaves to Spanish colonies. Thereafter the supply of Africans was a source of commercial, and later international, diplomatic control and licensing. Licences to trade in Africans became a lucrative form of international trade and barter. However, American demand for slaves was so expansive that most efforts at regulation broke down in the face of planters' demand. American slave owners always wanted more slaves than formal state controls or licences were able to supply and, from the first, there was a clash of economic principle: of regulation versus freer trade.

The broad slave-trading pattern of the following centuries was quickly established: a three-legged voyage, with ships sailing first from Europe to Africa, where Africans were collected, then across the Atlantic, and finally back to Europe with American produce. In time, this system became infinitely more complex, both commercially and geographically. Yet whatever the system, and even though transit times quickened, the experience for the Africans was an exercise in squalid misery. By even as early as 1600 perhaps 200,000 Africans had been shipped from West Africa.

Whatever scruples Europeans might have had about the sufferings they inflicted on growing numbers of Africans, they were never strong enough to overcome the slave trade's commercial appeal. And by the mid-sixteenth century, there were plenty of privateers and merchants keen to carve out a place for themselves in the booming world of the Atlantic slave trade.

Because the Portuguese were the initial Atlantic slave traders, they dominated the supply points in Africa. But how could they hope to keep interlopers out of so vast a geographic stretch of African coastline? What was to stop other merchants and adventurers plucking their own Africans from the coast and shipping them to eager purchasers in the Americas? This is exactly what the first English merchants did, encouraged and backed by the Crown (itself prompted in part by diplomatic disputes with the Iberian Crowns). In 1555 William Towerson was the first Englishman to break into the Atlantic slave trade, making a second voyage the year after. More famously, in 1562 John Hawkins ('Queen Elizabeth's slave trader') made his first piratical incursion into the trade, repeating it in 1564–5 and again in 1567–8. That Hawkins had royal approval and support moved this English involvement beyond the mere commercial or piratical: the English state and monarchy had made a clear declaration (however disguised) of its intention to follow the lucrative path fashioned by their Iberian rivals, and to trade in African humanity.

The English involvement (more properly 'British' after the union of the crowns in 1603) was small beer compared to the existing Portuguese licensed trade. But the British, and the French and Dutch too, were not to be deflected. What they needed was easier access to the American slave markets, rather than having to run the risk of infringing Spanish laws and controls on the importation of slaves. All was to change with the proliferation of European colonies in the Americas. The Dutch were the first major power to begin the gradual erosion of Iberian power in the Atlantic, developing their own posts in Africa and for a time displacing the Portuguese in Brazil. In the period of their 'Golden Age', Dutch commercial expertise, finance, and merchant and naval power secured the Dutch commercial and political strength on both sides of the Atlantic. In the process they were able to disrupt Portuguese dominance of the Atlantic slave trade. The Dutch also acquired vital experience of sugar cultivation in Brazil, and had the necessary finance to assist others. The British turned to this Dutch financial and technical expertise in sugar from the 1620s onwards, when they began the establishment and development of their own colonies in the Caribbean.

By 1650 upwards of 800,000 Africans had been removed from West Africa by sea. By then, the trading and commercial structure of this maritime pattern of enslavement was well established, and its benefits had become unquestioned across Europe. As the British became the dominant force in the Atlantic slave trade, however, the numbers of African victims involved in the Atlantic slave trade were to reach dizzying heights.

*

European involvement with African slaves predated the exploration and settlement in the Americas. Africans were shipped to Spain and Portugal, and to the Atlantic islands, before the first transatlantic voyages of discovery. This account describes African slaves for sale in Lagos in Portugal in 1444, fifty years before Columbus's first voyage.

On the next day, which was the 8th of the month of August, very early in the morning, by reason of the heat, the seamen began to make ready their boats, and to take out those captives, and carry them on shore, as they were commanded. And these, placed all together in that field, were a marvellous sight, for amongst them were some white enough, fair to look upon, and well proportioned; others were less white like mulattoes; others again were as black as Ethiops, and so ugly, both in features and in body, as almost to appear (to those who saw them) the images of a lower hemisphere. But what heart could be so hard as not to be pierced with piteous feeling to see that company? For some kept their heads low and their faces bathed in tears, looking one upon another; others stood groaning very dolorously, looking up to the height of heaven, fixing their eyes upon it, crying out loudly, as if asking help of the Father of Nature; others struck their faces with the palms of their hands, throwing themselves at full length upon the ground; others made their lamentations in the manner of a dirge, after the custom of their country. And though we could not understand the words of their language, the sound of it right well accorded with the measure of their sadness. But to increase their sufferings still more, there now arrived those who had charge of the division of the captives, and who began to separate one from another, in order to make an equal partition of the fifths; and then was it needful to part fathers from sons, husbands from wives, brothers from brothers. No respect was shewn either to friends or relations, but each fell where his lot took him.

O powerful Fortune, that with thy wheels doest and undoest, compassing the matters of this world as pleaseth thee, do thou at least put before the eyes of that miserable race some under-standing of matters to come, that they may receive some consolation in the midst of their great sorrow. And you who are so busy in making that division of the captives, look with pity upon so much misery; and see how they cling one to the other, so that you can hardly separate them.[1]

Initially, before the arrival of the Europeans proved disastrous for the native peoples of the Americas, with war, and above all disease, laying waste to one Indian society after another, Columbus hoped that the indigenous peoples of the Caribbean (the Taino) might be trained to be of service to the European settlers. This extract describes how in 1495 he dispatched Taino Indians to Spain to the royal couple, Ferdinand and Isabella, for education and training at the Royal Court.

. . . there are now sent with these ships some of the cannibals, men and women and boys and girls. These Their Highnesses can order to be placed in charge of persons so that they may be able better to learn the language, employing them in forms of service, and ordering that gradually greater care be given to them than other slaves . . . [To] take some of the men and women and send them home to Castile would not be anything but well, for they may some day be led to abandon that in-human custom which they have of eating men, and there in Castile, learning the language, they will more readily receive baptism and secure the welfare of their souls.[2]

As it became clear that the European presence was dramatically damag-ing the Indian peoples, churchmen began to ask for the importation of non-Christian Africans in order to spare the sufferings of the Indians. It was also thought vital that the Africans were 'heathen', which allowed Europeans to avoid enslaving fellow Christians. Here Jeronimite fathers request the importation of non-Christian Africans into the Spanish Americas, c.1516.

Especially that leave be given to them to bring over heathen [*bozales*] negroes, of the kind of which we have already experience. Wherefore here it is agreed that Your Highness should command us to grant licences to send armed ships from this island to fetch them from the Cape Verde Islands, or Guinea, or that it may be done by some other persons to bring them here. Your Highness may believe that if this is permitted it will be very advantageous for the future of the settlers of these islands, and for the royal revenue; as also for the Indians your vassals, who will be cared for and eased in their work, and can better cultivate their souls' welfare, and will increase in numbers.[3]

Demand for African slaves became so extensive, and so lucrative, that trading in them became a much sought-after commercial venture, bringing profit both to the shippers and to the royal licensees. Sometimes, it even overrode the preference for non-Christian slaves. This licence of 1518 from the King of Spain authorizes Lorenzo de Gorrevod to ship 4,000 black Christian slaves to the Americas.

The King. Our officials who reside in the city of Seville in our House of Trade of the Indies; Know ye that I have given permission, and by the present [instrument] do give it, to Lorenzo de Gorrevod, governor of Bresa, member of my Council, whereby he, or the person or persons who may have his authority therefor, may proceed to take to the Indies, the islands and the mainland of the ocean sea already discovered or to be discovered, four thousand negro slaves both male and female, provided they be Christians, in whatever proportions he may choose. Until these are all taken and transported no other slaves, male or female, may be transported, except those whom I have given permission [to take] up to the present date. Therefore, I order you to allow and consent to the governor of Bresa aforesaid or the person or persons aforesaid who may have his said authority to transport and take the four thousand slaves male and female, without molesting him in any way; and, if the said gover-

nor of Bresa or the persons aforesaid who may have his authority, should make any arrangements with traders or other persons
to ship the said slaves, male or female, direct from the isles of
Guinea and other regions from which they are wont to bring
the said negroes to these realms and to Portugal, or from any
other region they please, even though they do not bring them
to register in that house, they may do so provided that you take
sufficient security that they bring you proof of how many they
have taken to each island and that the said negroes male and
female, have become Christians on reaching each island, and
how they have paid the customs duties there, in order that those
taken be known and be not in excess of the aforesaid number.
Notwithstanding any prohibition and order that may exist to
the contrary, I require you and order you in regard to this not
to collect any duty in that house [of trade] on the said slaves
but rather you are to allow them to be taken freely and this
my cedula shall be written down in the books of that house
[of trade].

Done in Saragossa, the eighteenth day of August of the year
1518.

I THE KING,
By order of the King, FRANCISCO DE LOS COVOS.[4]

*Before Africans were loaded on to the European ships, most had been
force-marched long distances to the coast or river. There they were held
together until the Europeans arrived to negotiate a purchase. Branded
and stripped, they were ready for transfer into European hands. In the
following passage John Barbot describes what happened to Africans
prior to loading on to the Atlantic slave ships, in 1682.*

As the slaves come down to Fida from the inland country, they
are put into a booth, or prison, built for that purpose, near the
beach, all of them together; and when the Europeans are to
receive them, they are brought out into a large plain, where
the surgeons examine every part of every one of them, to the

smallest member, men and women being all stark naked. Such
as are allowed good and sound, are set on one side, and the
others by themselves; which slaves so rejected are there called
Mackrons, being above thirty five years of age, or defective in
their limbs, eyes or teeth; or grown grey, or that have the ven-
ereal disease, or any other imperfection. These being so set aside,
each of the others, which have passed as good, is marked on
the breast, with a red-hot iron, imprinting the mark of the
French, English, or Dutch companies, that so each nation may
distinguish their own, and to prevent their being chang'd by
the natives for worse, as they are apt to do. In this particular,
care is taken that the women, as tenderest, be not burnt too
hard.

The branded slaves, after this, are returned to their former
booth . . . There they continue sometimes ten or fifteen days,
till the sea is still enough to send them aboard; for very often
it continues too boisterous for so long a time . . . Before they
enter the canoes, or come out of the booth, their former Black
masters strip them of every rag they have, without distinction
of men or women; to supply which, in orderly ships, each of
them as they come aboard is allowed a piece of canvas, to wrap
around their waist . . .[5]

*The Atlantic slave ships quickly established themselves as uniquely
terrifying and dangerous places to experience, as the following description of Africans on a slave ship in 1627 makes clear. The shipboard
conditions, the filth and disease, the simple terrors of the deep and more
all took their toll of the Africans below decks.*

[The Africans are] so crowded, in such disgusting conditions,
and so mistreated, as the very ones who transport them assure
me, that they come by six and six, with collars around their
necks, and these same ones by two and two with fetters on
their feet, in such a way that they come imprisoned from head
to feet, below the deck, locked in from outside, where they see

neither sun nor moon, [and] that there is no Spaniard who dares to stick his head in the hatch without becoming ill, nor to remain inside for an hour without the risk of great sickness. So great is the stench, the crowding and the misery of that place. And the [only] refuge and consolation that they have in it is [that] to each [is given] once a day no more than a half bowl of uncooked corn flour or millet, which is like our rice, and with it a small jug of water and nothing else, except for much beating, much lashing, and bad words. This is that which commonly happens with the men and I well think that some of the shippers treat them with more kindness and mildness, principally in these times . . . [Nevertheless, most] arrive turned into skeletons.[6]

5. The Coming of the British

As we have seen, the British played no part in the origins, and little part in the early development, of the Atlantic slave trade. From the early seventeenth century onwards, however, they were to transform it. But, like that of the pioneers before them, theirs was a complex story, played out in three corners of the Atlantic: in Europe, Africa and the Americas. Before European settlement and colonies in the tropical and semi-tropical Americas began, African slaves had been important, but not vital, in the many changes undertaken in parts of Europe and the Atlantic islands. At first, even in the Americas, the Africans seemed little different from other new arrivals: useful workers in a world where Europeans, Indians and Africans worked side by side in the initial tasks of settling and securing a safe, viable grip on local life. All that changed with the coming of sugar.

The British had to learn what the Brazilians already knew: that if a tropical economy turned to sugar plantations, it needed lots of raw labour, and that labour could not be found among local Indians or immigrant Europeans. Africa, on the other hand, seemed ready to yield such labour on a vast and unending scale. Brazil had already absorbed growing numbers of Africans for its sugar plantations. Perhaps 50,000 had been transported to Brazil by 1600, another 100,000 over the next twenty-five years, and a similar number between 1625 and 1650. The British thus stepped in where others had gone before.

The British had been tempted to begin trade and exploration in the Atlantic from the late fifteenth century. Trading contacts with both Spain and Portugal had revealed the economic potential opening up in the Atlantic islands, West Africa and, eventually, the Americas. Merchants in London and Bristol financed the initial voyages of Towerson and Hawkins into the Portuguese sphere of interest in Africa. But the profits from these early English slave-trading voyages were soon overshadowed by the rich pickings to be had by preying on the Spanish fleets (and settlements) in the Caribbean. Between 1586 and 1603, for example, there were an estimated 235 privateers flitting around the Caribbean, easily hidden in the myriad island hideaways, ready to pounce on stray vessels and on the treasure fleets heading home to Spain. The damage such activity inflicted on Spain was enormous, and in the process the English developed their own experience of long-distance trade and war in the Caribbean. This piratical phase, supported by the Crown, soon gave way to a long-term interest in settlement and colonization in the region. The seizure of St Kitts (1624) and Barbados (1625) launched a new phase in regional (and British) history.

The power of Spain and Portugal in the same period was on the wane. Dutch attacks on Portuguese possessions abroad, and internal divisions in Iberia, all compounded by the devastation of the Thirty Years War in Europe (1618–48), diverted the attention and undermined the influence of those involved. The British were in effect given a relatively free hand to pursue their own interests in the Caribbean. Merchants with Atlantic experience (and ambitions), men with money and influential figures in and around the court coalesced into influential groups with a strategic and commercial interest in Atlantic trade and New World settlement, which came to be linked by the slave trade.

The early settlers in Barbados tried to develop a range of export crops, notably tobacco. The island, at first, had many more whites than slaves (18,300 white men and 5,680 slaves in 1645) and indentured labour was the dominant form of labour. When Barbados turned to sugar, after 1645, the island's history was transformed. To do this, the settlers turned to the Dutch for help, both for sugar technology and for the necessary finance, and as Barbados produced more and more sugar for the British market (output rose from 3,750 tons in 1651 to 9,525 tons in 1669), so too did the settlers import ever more African slaves. The slave population rose from 20,000 to 30,000 in the same period; by 1680 there were 38,000 slaves on the island. By then the proliferation of property owners had stopped, and there emerged a class of large plantation owners. At the same time, indentured white labour declined. Barbados was now the richest of all British colonies, and Bridgetown the most prosperous, bustling seaport in British America. Africans were imported by the boatload, and by 1700 Barbados was home to more than 50,000 slaves. It was a pattern which was replicated through all the smaller British islands in the region: St Kitts, Nevis, Montserrat and Antigua. By the end of the seventeenth century these British islands (along with Jamaica) had absorbed more than a quarter of a million African slaves.

Barbados set the pace, in the process helping to create the infamous British 'sweet tooth'. But Barbados's primacy was short-lived, for in 1655, as part of Cromwell's 'Western Design', British forces (many recruited from the eastern Caribbean) took Jamaica from the Spanish. Like Barbados earlier, Jamaica was settled by a motley bunch of ex-soldiers, free settlers, convict labour and indentured workers from Ireland and Scotland. After the initial task of settling the land, and winning it over to cultivation, the settlers, on land granted from the newly restored English Crown, turned to a variety of crops. The contrasting geography of Jamaica (larger and more varied than tiny Barbados) was suitable for a range of tropical and semi-tropical crops. But again, sugar proved the best, and the most lucrative. To grow sugar, however, Jamaica, like Barbados, needed a plentiful supply of labour. Again, the early migrants were never numerous enough, or willing to undertake the intensive labour required. As had Brazil and Barbados, Jamaica turned for its labour force to African slaves, who had no say in the matter. Less than fifty years after the British seizure of Jamaica, the enslaved population stood at 42,000; fifty years later it was 118,000. The numbers imported were even greater than these figures might suggest, for the death rate in the islands was high, while many other African arrivals were trans-shipped to other slave colonies.

This pattern was repeated on the Caribbean islands taken by the French – not surprisingly, since all the major European maritime and colonizing powers were competing for colonies, dominance and lucrative trade (and not merely in the Americas, of course, but around the world). French interest had settled on St Kitts, Guadeloupe and, the most important of the trio, Martinique. By 1670, the French had added St Domingue (Haiti) to the list. Again, the Dutch had been helpful in the initial introduction of sugar technology, and as the French islands turned to sugar, so too did they turn to Africa for labour. By 1700, some 124,000 Africans had been landed in the French islands. By then, the numbers of Africans forcefully removed to the Americas was massive: more than half a million to Brazil, some 450,000 to the non-Spanish Caribbean and almost as many again to Spanish settlements in the Americas. These figures were, by any standards, staggering: the movements of population were on a such scale, and of such an intensity (both of numbers and of human suffering), that historians have tended to recoil from the inhumanity of it all, retreating into statistical analysis. But even these figures begin to pale when set against the numbers of Africans shipped across the Atlantic in the eighteenth century.

North America's conversion to African slavery came much later, and more slowly, than in the islands. By the time Africans were imported in significant numbers into North America, slaves had already utterly transformed the economies (and become the dominant demographic feature) of societies throughout the Caribbean and large parts of South America. The first Africans had been famously imported into Jamestown by the Dutch in 1619, but the economy of the Chesapeake region was driven forwards for the best part of three-quarters of a century not by slaves but by indentured labour, mainly from Britain. As tobacco gradually transformed the region, the plantations (generally much smaller than the sugar plantations in the islands) turned to Africans. In this, they were helped by the flourishing British slave-trade fleet. As the Chesapeake disgorged ever more slave-grown tobacco (and by 1750 there were some 145,000 slaves there), it helped to dislodge Caribbean tobacco from the European market. By that date, 1750, another 40,000 slaves had been landed in South Carolina, destined mainly for the new coastal rice plantations. All these expanding economies were sustained by local slave populations which began to grow by natural increase, unlike the slave populations of most parts of the West Indies, which grew primarily through African importations. The end result was that by 1790 there were about 700,000 slaves in the newly formed United States.

Even before then, by, say, the mid-eighteenth century, slavery had become a dominant feature of life in most corners of the colonial, tropical Americas. Though slaves were few in the more northern colonies, from Maryland south through Virginia, the Carolinas and Georgia, across the great arc of West Indian islands from Cuba to Trinidad, and south along the north-east coast of South America to Brazil, in addition to the Spanish empire in Central and South America, slaves were commonplace in a range of rural, urban and domestic employments. By 1790 Brazil was home to almost one million slaves, and slaves worked in all forms of economic activities. Where there was harsh work to be done, there we find black slaves. And where there were thriving exports of tropical staples, there again we find slaves: in tobacco and rice, in sugar, rum and coffee.

What made all this possible, of course, was the enforced maritime transportation of Africans across the Atlantic. But precisely how that shipping should be arranged was from first to last a source of economic – and diplomatic – contention. As we have seen, nations argued and fought among themselves for the rights (or monopoly) to trade in African humanity. Even within individual nations, arguments flowed back and forth about the best (most profitable) means of shipping slaves. And not until the late eighteenth century did Europeans and Americans begin seriously to argue about the ethics – the humanity – of the slave ships. Not until the age of Enlightenment, and the era of massive slave unrest, did white people begin to discuss seriously the morality of treating black people as mere items of trade.

After the Restoration in 1660, the Crown shifted its allegiance from privateer slave traders to monopoly companies, its support culminating in the formation of the Royal African Company in 1672. Despite having high-placed and well-heeled backers, the company (like its contemporaries in France and the Netherlands) simply could not satisfy demand for slaves in the Americas. Moreover, private merchants and interlopers regularly broke the company's monopoly system. As monopoly gave way to free trade, it was still thought essential to keep the slave trade in British hands. This was done through various Navigation Acts, enforced by the growing might of the Royal Navy and a series of Vice-Admiralty courts in the Americas.

By the time the Royal African Company's monopoly was ended in 1713, it had shipped 120,000 Africans across the Atlantic. Yet still the planters wanted more. Again, the figures are breathtaking. By the time the British ended their own slave trade in 1807, they had shipped three and a quarter million Africans across the Atlantic. To do that, generations of British sailors and merchants trawled the vast African coastline, from Senegambia to the Congo. European nations evolved their own spheres of slaving interests. The Portuguese – with their own direct slave routes from Africa to Brazil – tended to concentrate on Angola. The British moved up and down the coast, trading wherever business was good: Senegambia, Sierra Leone, the Gold Coast, the Bight of Benin and, especially, the Bight of Biafra. The British sometimes used slaving forts, and sometimes established their own trading posts. Individual traders also slipped up and down the coast, following rumours and information, taking their ships wherever groups or cargoes of Africans could be acquired. This was often a long drawn-out and time-consuming business: small groups of Africans bought here, others elsewhere. Despite this roving trade, the British took the great bulk of their slaves from particular regions in West and Central Africa. The longer Europeans lingered on the African coast, the more the risks mounted: the risk of African hostility and violence, the risks to the health (and lives) of the slaves already below decks, and equally the risk to the lives of the white sailors. West Africa was a ferociously hostile environment for Europeans and for the slaves – all of whom had already been force-marched great distances from their homes or the point of their initial enslavement.

Europeans may seem at first sight to have been the powerful group on the African coast, with their modern sailing ships, superior firepower and economic blandishments. In fact their position and safety were always, and everywhere, tenuous. Even with the most solid of fortresses, Europeans had their backs to the sea and remained wary of being surrounded by Africans. Europeans faced local African communities they did not understand (even when they traded and lived with them for years) and whose power to surprise them was unrelenting. This was the case whether Europeans traded from their ships, from beaches, from the shore or along a river system. Slave trading was uncomfortable, dangerous and often lethal. But the fact that it persisted over such a huge span of time, stretched along so vast a stretch of African coastline and involved so many millions of Africans is, in itself, a clue to its commercial appeal and its potential profitability.

Thus did the Atlantic slave trade become a major industry, with its economic tentacles stretching far beyond the Atlantic itself. Goods from Asia (textiles from India, for example) regularly traded on the African coast. Similarly, produce from the slave plantations travelled around the globe, transforming tastes and pleasures wherever they intruded: people in all corners of the world began to demand slave-grown sweetness in food and drink, and men – especially men – the world over were won over to slave-grown tobacco.

Tobacco was perhaps the most startling example of the global impact of slave-grown produce. Men of all sorts and conditions smoked tobacco in every conceivable location, from fashionable European courts to the rough social world of sailors at sea and soldiers on the dangerous edge of empire. Even slaves, penned below decks on the Atlantic slave ships, were provided with tobacco to humour them through their sea-borne miseries. Women also smoked, though this faded in the eighteenth century, giving way to snuff-taking: men smoked, ladies took snuff. Yet both habits were possible because of African slaves labouring on tobacco plantations in the Chesapeake.

Europeans had quickly learned of the virtues and attractions of tobacco via their contacts with Indians throughout the Americas. Colonizers had tried tobacco cultivation in a host of American colonies, and it seemed especially suitable on a number of the Caribbean islands. But the rise of sugar quickly marginalized tobacco as a West Indian export crop; the process was aided by the rise of the Chesapeake tobacco industry. This was manned, initially, by indentured labour from Britain. From the 1670s, however, as labour costs increased, and as African slaves became more readily available, tobacco planters turned to slaves. It also seemed a natural progression, given what their fellow planters had achieved with slaves in the Caribbean (there were thriving cultural and economic links between the islands and the mainland colonies). By 1700 Chesapeake was dispatching 38 million pounds of slave-grown tobacco across the Atlantic.

The development of the rice plantations of South Carolina also began to draw boatloads of Africans to Charleston (some 40,000 had landed by 1750) and the fruits of their labour, notably rice, and indigo for dye, became invaluable export crops. Again, here was slave-grown produce which became part of the warp and the weft of the Western world, but who thought about the slaves when using starch (made from rice), filling their pipe or sweetening their tea?

Thus British colonies were transformed, and in a few cases made possible, by the regular provision of African slave labour, greatly assisted by the rise of the British Atlantic slaving fleet – the two went together. But the Atlantic slave trade was only one feature of a much broader, complex trading system which involved Europe, Africa and the Americas, and ought not to be separated from that system. Furthermore, it depended for its vitality – for its very being – on economic and social forces which few of those most actively involved fully comprehended. This was notably the case with Africa: slaves became available on the African coast via internal African trading systems about which coastal traders and sailors had little comprehension. To add to the complexities, the Atlantic slave trade was also influenced by much broader global patterns of trade, especially the movement of money and goods from Asia to Europe and Africa. Such complexities, however, were lost on the millions of Africans involved, who knew only the suffering the system caused, most painfully in the stinking squalor of the slave ships.

The first English slave voyages to and from West Africa entered a region already opened up to European slave trading. Tensions already existed between Europeans and Africans – the victims of what were in effect piratical raids on their people and goods – and between competing European slave traders. The accounts of the two voyages of William Towerson in 1555 and 1556 reveal all these tensions. They also tell the story of the removal of a small band of Africans to England, and their return a year later. It was a small beginning to a massive displacement of Africans.

This fellowe came aboord our shippe without feare, and as soone as he came, he demaunded, why we had not brought againe their men, which the last yeere we tooke away, and could tell us that there were five taken away by Englishmen: we made him answere, that they were in England well used, and were there kept till they could speake the language, and then they should be brought againe to be a helpe to Englishmen in this Countrey: and then he spake no more of that matter . . . we saw many boates lying upon the shoare, and divers came by us, but none of them would come neere us, being as we judged afraid of us: because that foure men were taken perforce the last yeere from this place, so that no man came to us . . .

Then we went aboord to goe from this place, seeing the Negroes bent against us, because that the last yeere M. Gainsh did take away the Captaines sonne and three others from this place with their golde, and all that they had about them: which was the cause that they became friends with the Portugales, whom before they hated, as did appeare the last yeere by the courteous intertainement which the *Trinitie* had there, when the Captaine came aboord the shippe, and brought them to his towne, and offered them ground to build a Castle in, and there they had good sales . . .[1]

This place is called Bulle, and here the Negros were very glad of our Negros, and shewed them all the friendship they could, when they had told them that they were the men that were taken away being now againe brought by us . . .

The sixteenth day I went along the shore with two pinnasses of the Frenchmen, and found a Baie and a fresh river, and after that went to a towne called Hanta, twelve leagues beyond the Cape. At this towne our Negros were well knowen, and the men of the towne wept for joy when they saw them, and demanded of them where Anthonie and Binne had bene: and they told them that they had bene at London in England, and should bee brought home the next voyage . . .

Then wee departed and went to Shamma, and went into the river with five boates well appointed with men and ordinance, and with our noises of trumpets and drummes, for we thought here to have found some Portugals but there were none: so wee sent our Negros on shore, and after them went divers of us, and were very well received, and the people were very glad of our Negros, specially one of their brothers wives, and one of their aunts, which received them with much joy, and so did all the rest of the people, as if they had bene their naturall brethren . . .²

In 1562–3 what was effectively the first English transatlantic slave voyage took place under the command of John Hawkins. He sailed with royal approval and represented a group of commercial interests in both the City of London and in his native West Country.

Master John Hawkins having made divers voyages to the Iles of the Canaries, and there by his good and upright dealing being growen in love and favour with the people, informed himselfe amongst them by diligent inquisition, of the state of the West India, whereof hee had received some knowledge by the instructions of his father, but increased the same by the advertisements and reports of that people. And being amongst other particulars assured, that Negros were very good marchandise in Hispaniola, and that store of Negros might easily bee had upon the coast of Guinea, resolved with himselfe to make triall thereof, and communicated that devise with his worshipfull friendes of London: namely with Sir Lionell Ducket, sir Thomas Lodge, M. Gunson his father in law, sir William Winter, M. Bromfield, and others. All which persons liked so well of his intention, that they became liberall contributors and adventurers in the action. For which purpose there were three good ships immediately provided: The one called the *Salomon* of the burthern of 120. tunne, wherein M. Hawkins himselfe went as Generall: The second the *Swallow* of 100. tunnes, wherein went

for Captaine M. Thomas Hampton: and the third the *Jonas* a
barke of 40. tunnes, wherein the Master supplied the Captaines
roome: in which small fleete M. Hawkins tooke with him not
above 100. men for feare of sicknesse and other inconveniences,
whereunto men in long voyages are commonly subject.

With this companie he put off and departed from the coast
of England in the moneth of October 1562. and in his course
touched first at Teneriffe, where hee received friendly inter-
tainment. From thence he passed to Sierra Leona, upon the
coast of Guinea, which place by the people of the countrey is
called Tagarin, where he stayed some good time, and got into
his possession, partly by the sworde, and partly by other meanes,
to the number of 300. Negros at the least, besides other
merchandises which that countrey yeeldeth. With this praye hee
sayled over the Ocean sea unto the Iland of Hispaniola, and
arrived first at the port of Isabella: and there hee had reasonable utterance of his English commodities, as also of some part
of his Negros, trusting the Spaniards no further, then that by
his owne strength he was able still to master them. From the
port of Isabella he went to Puerto de Plata, where he made
like sales, standing alwaies upon his guard: from thence also hee
sayled to Monte Christi another port on the North side of
Hispaniola, and the last place of his touching, where he had
peaceable traffique, and made vent of the whole number of his
Negros: for which he received in those 3. places by way of
exchange such quantitie of merchandise, that hee did not onely
lade his owne 3. shippes with hides, ginger, sugars, and some
quantities of pearles, but he fraighted also two other hulkes
with hides and the like commodities, which hee sent into
Spaine. And thus leaving the Iland, he returned and disem-
boqued, passing out by the Ilands of the Caycos, without further
entring into the bay of Mexico, in this his first voyage to the
West India. And so with prosperous successe and much gaine
to himselfe and the aforesayde adventurers, he came home, and
arrived in the moneth of September 1563.[3]

Initially, English (later British) slave traders supplied Africans to settlers in the Americas from other European nations. But the establishment of English colonies in the Caribbean from the 1620s created a new demand for Africans. Thereafter – and until abolition in 1807 – the English-speaking colonies devoured Africans in growing numbers. It was a demand which started with, and was driven forward by, Caribbean sugar plantations, as George Downing (the second graduate of Harvard) described on 26 August 1645 to John Winthrop, the Governor of Connecticut.

If you go to Barbados, you shal see a flourishing Iland, many able men. I believe they have bought this year no lesse than a thousand Negroes, and the more they buie, the better able they are to buye, for in a yeare and halfe they will earne (with God's blessing) as much as they cost . . .

A man that will settle ther must looke to procure servants, which if you could gett out of England, for 6, or 8, or 9 yeares time, onely paying their passages, or at the most but som smale above, it would do very well, for so therby you shall be able to doe something upon a plantation, and in short tim be able, with good husbandry, to procure Negroes (the life of this place) out of the encrease of your owne plantation.[4]

To satisfy the growing demand for Africans, a series of licensed trading companies were established in London. Those companies laid down specific instructions for their captains and traders: how and where they should trade, how they should trade on the African coast, and how they should treat their enslaved Africans. This letter from the Guinea Company to James Pope on 9 December 1651 provides instructions for one such slave-trading mission.

Mr James Pope.
Loveing friend, Upon receipt of your letter out of the Downes bearing date the 7th of October we dispatched away the Pinnace *Jno.*: Thomas Bluck master, without the French

Spirrets, depending upon the sale of your negers, and ladeing your ship for London, whose order and directions you are to followe untill he shall give you your dispatch for London. Wee desire you to be veary carefull in the well stoweing of your ship and that none of the goods you shall take aboard be abused, and being dispatched from thence we pray you hasten for London, and when you come int[o] our Chanell be veary vigilant and carefull for feare of surprysalls, not trusting any. And our ord'r is that all the while you lye in the River Gambra untill your Cargo be provided that you followe the directions of Mr James Pope and from all places where you shall touch send us advice of your proceedings. There is put aboard your Pinck *Supply* 30 paire of shackles and boults for such of your negers as are rebellious and we pray you be veary carefull to keepe them under and let them have their food in due season that they ryse not against you, as they have done in other ships.

When you shall come into the Downes you are to send unto Mr Thomas Waad at Dover for a case of Cristall beads w'ch he will put aboard you there w'ch you are to cary with you for Gambra and deliver with the rest of the Cargo unto Mr James Pope. So Comitting you to God's protection we rest Your loving friends.

> Row: Wilson
> Thomas Walter
> Tho: Chambrelan
> John Woods
> Maurice Thomson.[5]

With the booming of the slave trade after the Restoration of the monarchy in 1660, especially after the acquisition of the island of Jamaica, few doubted the commercial value of the sugar colonies and the transatlantic supplies of Africans to those islands. The Crown licensed monopoly companies to supply Africans, for the financial benefit of both itself and the nation at large. The following two letters from the Company of Royal Adventurers illustrate the wide acceptance of the commercial value of the Africa trade to the English nation (and others). The first is to Francis Lord Willoughby in 1662/3; the second to the King in 1663.

My Lord, The Royal Company being very sensible how necessary it is that the English Plantations in America should have a competent and a constant supply of Negro-servants for their own use of Planting, and that at a moderate Rate, have already sent abroad, and shall within eight days dispatch so many Ships for the Coast of Africa as shall by Gods permission furnish the said Plantations with at least 3000 Negroes, and will proceed from time to time to provide them a constant and sufficient succession of them, so as the Planter shall have no just cause to complain of any Want: And for the Price, and terms of Payment, they have for the present resolved, to order all their Servants and Factors not to sell any Negroes higher than is expressed in this following Resolve.

Resolved, That Orders be given to the Factors in the Plantations of the Charibee Islands, to sell all Blacks that are found in Lotts (as hath been customary) at £ 17. sterling p. head in Money (ps. of 8/8 Sivil and Mexico at 4 sh.) or Bills Exchange for England with good assurance of payment, or at 2400 *l.* of well cured Muscovado Sugar in Cask, with express condition, that no Blacks be delivered without present payment in Money, Bills, or Sugar, viewed and accepted by the Factors, or in Cotton or Indico, according to the price currant between them and Sugar.

And do desire your Lordship, that you will be pleased to communicate these Resolutions of the Company to your respective Deputies in all His Majesties American Dominions under your Lordships Government, and direct them to publish the same within their respective Limits and Jurisdictions, and to gather from the Planters and Inhabitants, and to transmit to us as soon as they conveniently can, the certain number of Negroes which they desire, and will engage to receive yearly from Us on those reasonable Terms proposed, that so we may proportion our Care for them accordingly.

And further, The Company doth desire your Lordship to order this inclosed Paper of Conditions to be declared by your respective Deputies, in the most usual manner, and to receive such Subscriptions as shall be accordingly made, and to transmit to us Authentique Copies of them by the first Passage that shall present for England, after the time of subscribing is expired.

By Order of the Royal Company:

ELLIS LEIGHTON, SECRET.[6]

1663.

Humbly represent that the trade of Africa is so necessary to England that the very being of the Plantations depends upon the supply of negro servants for their works. This trade was at the time of his Majesty's restoration managed by particular adventurers, who were so far from any possible design of having forts or asserting the honour of the nation that they were a constant prey to the Hollanders and were quite tired out of the trade by their great and frequent losses, of which they brought in clear proofs to the Court of Admiralty; so if his Majesty had not established a company the nation had probably by this time been quite driven out of it. The Company under the special management of the Duke of York sent out this last year above 160,000 *l.* in cargoes, have plentifully supplied the coast to the great satisfaction of the natives, furnished all the Plantations with negro servants, set up new manufactures at home and improved the old, vented a great many native commodities, employed above 40 ships, and doubt not they shall import very considerable quantities of gold and silver, as they have already begun. They have built forts and factories in Africa and repaired others, and have no European rivals but the Hollanders; but as to them, experience of the past gives just cause to apprehend what is intended for the future. For as the annexed extracts of letters prove, the Dutch have endeavoured to drive the English Company from the coast, have followed their ships from port to port, and hindered them coming nigh the shore to trade; they have persuaded the negroes to destroy their servants and to take their forts, have seized their boats and goods, violently taken possession of Cape Coast, and shot at his Majesty's Royal flag. To complete the former indignities, one Valckenburgh, Director-General of the West India Company in Africa, has sent a protest to their factors, in which he challenges the whole trade of Guinea as their propriety, by right of conquest from the Portuguese; of which having sought remedy by means of Sir George Downing the Company have received no satisfaction. In a word, notwithstanding a stock so considerable, and the many good ships of force and the land forces they have sent, had it not been for the countenance of some of his Majesty's ships, to give the Company a respect in the eyes of the natives and preserve their forts, the Company had ere this been stripped of their possessions and interest in Africa; Cormantin Castle itself being in extreme danger when the *Marmaduke* and *Speedwell* arrived there. The Dutch have sent a second protest, in which they say they will force the English from their forts if they do not quit them.[7]

In 1672 the Royal African Company was given the monopoly to ship slaves from Africa to the Americas. It could not satisfy the soaring demand from the plantation colonies and its monopoly was revoked in 1712. Here is its 1672 Charter.

Charles the Second by the Grace of God King of England Scotland France and Ireland, Defender of the Faith, etc., To all to whom these presents shall come, Greeting: Whereas all and singular the regions, countrys, dominions and territories, continents, coasts and places, now or at any time heretofore called or known by the name or names of Guinny, Buiny, Angola and South Barbary or by any of them, or which are or have been reputed esteemed or taken to be parcel or member of any region country dominion territory or continent called Guinny or Binny, Angola or South Barbary and all and singular ports and havens, rivers, creeks, islands and places in the parts of Africa to them or any of them belonging, and the sole and onely trade and traffic thereof, are the undoubted right of Us our heirs and successors and are and have been enjoyed by Us and by our predecessors for many years past as in right of this our Crown of England,

And whereas the trade of the said regions, countries and places is of great advantage to our subjects of this Kingdom, and for the improvement thereof divers attempts have been made and several charters granted by our Royal Progenitors to several persons with such powers and authorities, as were then conceived proper for the carrying on of the said trade, but all the said endeavours proved ineffectual untill We by Letters Patents under our Great Seal of England bearing date the tenth day of January in the fourteenth year of our reign did give and grant unto our Royal Consort Queen Katherine, Mary the Queen our Mother (since deceased), our dearest Brother James Duke of York and others therein named the propriety and government of all the said regions territories, countries, dominions, continents, coasts and places, in trust for the Company of Royal Adventurers of England, trading into Africa, And for the better managing of the Trade and traffic thereof, did create and make them and such as they should think fit to receive into their Society [a?] body politick and Corporate by the name of the Company of the Royal Adventurers of England trading into Africa, Granting to them and their Successors the sole Trade of the said Regions, Countries, Dominions, Territories, Continents, Coasts and places, with prohibition to all others, and several other liberties and priviledges as by the said Letters Patents may appear, whereby the said trade is very much advanced and improved . . . [8]

6. Slave Ships

At its simplest the Atlantic slave trade was the enforced flow of humanity between Africa and the Americas. Something like twelve million Africans were loaded on to slave ships. It is a staggering historical phenomenon, the horror of it hardly diminished by the global human tragedies of the twentieth century. Even today, however, it is difficult to recall that beneath these statistics lay the sufferings of millions of individuals. What follows is intended not to diminish that suffering by reducing it to simple statistics which can mask the human misery they represent, but rather to describe in broad outline the process by which it was ordered and brought into being by apparently impersonal forces in distant parts of the globe.

The Africans caught in this trade were the human pawns in a massive commercial system which was driven forward by the widely accepted belief that slaves were things, not people: chattels, not humanity. Grotesque to the modern mind, such a view, for all its contradictions and confusions, was the necessary philosophy which underpinned the whole Atlantic business. Concede the African's humanity, and the system unravelled. And that is exactly what began to happen, in the late eighteenth century, when voices of moral, religious (and economic) dissent began to challenge the idea of the slave as commodity, as we shall see.

What appears at first to be the relatively simple trading structure of the Atlantic slave trade – a flow of people, goods and trade linking Europe, Africa and the Americas – gave way to a remarkably complex system. The centre of economic gravity of the British trade, for instance, was London, but the focus of slave trading itself shifted from London first to Bristol, and later to Liverpool. Although large numbers of ports joined in, sending local vessels out to profit from the cornucopia that was the slave trade, the British slave trade was dominated by these major ports. Throughout, the finance, insurance and complicated flow of money, letters of credit, insurance and trading instructions passed through trading houses and banking facilities primarily in London.

The statistics of the Atlantic slave trade are now familiar, if no less remarkable for that. Of the twelve million Africans loaded on to the ships, ten and a half million survived to landfall in the Americas. There were something like 27,000 known slave voyages, of which about 12,000 were British or British colonial, mainly North American. About 5,000 slave voyages originated in Liverpool. The majority of those African captives were male, although the gender ratio on the slave ships changed over time. By the last years of the slave trade, in the mid-nineteenth century, when the last, illegal slave ships heading for Brazil and Cuba were trying to outrun the British and American anti-slavery patrols, their human cargoes were largely very young and predominantly male Africans.

There are, of course, any number of ways in which we can arrange these figures. But one particular formulation demonstrates the dominance of Africans in the population movement westwards to the Americas. Although it is tempting to think of transatlantic migrations to the Americas as European, until about 1820 the African was the typical migrant across the Atlantic. Before the 1820s, some two and a half million Europeans migrated to the Americas, but in the same period almost eight and a half million Africans were transported in the slave ships. Of the total number of Africans landed in the Americas fewer than 10 per cent were taken to North America. The great majority were shipped to Brazil and to the Caribbean for one basic reason: they were destined to work in the sugar fields. Despite the dispersal of slaves to all corners of the American economies (from jobs ranging from domestic labour to work as cowboys), it was sugar which pulled the majority across the Atlantic.

The preferred aim of the maritime slave traders was to fill their holds quickly with Africans and to leave the African coast as soon as possible. But this was often impossible. The longer the slave traders lingered on the coast, the higher the death rate among the crews (some experienced death rates of 45 per cent per month when on the coast); but the slave ships often had to linger until they acquired sufficient human cargo to make the crossing economically worthwhile. It is wrong, however, to think that slaves were the sole African export: until about 1700 the total value of other exported African goods, led by gold, was higher than slave exports. Whatever the nature of their trade, Europeans were, throughout, effectively in the hands of African coastal traders and African governing elites. They in turn were dependent on the flow of slaves and other goods from the African interior or elsewhere on the coast. Slave captains and European traders developed highly complex and ritualized methods of negotiation with African merchants, traders and local elites in search of slave cargoes, handing over by way of exchange cargoes imported from Europe or goods trans-shipped from Asia. The early casual offerings of baubles and trinkets were soon forgotten as Africans developed specific trading demands and learned the commercial value of their human commodities.

What seems like a set of simple negotiations on the coast was in fact just the most visible (to the Europeans) of hugely complex and geographically diverse trade systems which stretched from the point of contact on the African coast into the interior. The consequences of that trade were enormous, at their most extreme helping to bring down indigenous African states and encouraging violence and warfare in the search for prisoners/slaves for onward sale to traders on the coast. The selling of Africans to the slave ships was only the latest of a long sequence of transactions which had seen them enslaved and moved onwards, mainly on foot, from their homelands (often considerable distances away) to the coast. Most had almost certainly never seen white men before; nor had they ever seen the ocean or European sailing ships. All this before they were thrust into the stinking hell of the slave decks.

The slave trade was a harsh commercial business. All the people involved expected a profitable return on their risky investments. The slave traders' aim was to get their human cargoes across the Atlantic and to the American slave markets without loss or injury. Dead or sick slaves meant a financial loss. However crude, the simple point remains indisputable: slave traders (for all the brutality of the system) were anxious to deliver as many Africans as possible, and in as good a condition as possible. Whatever brutalities took place, and there were plenty of them, the aim was not to damage or harm – and certainly not to kill – the slaves, but to transport them swiftly in order to sell them at a profit. In fact, the majority of all Africans loaded on to the ships did indeed land in the Americas, though large numbers arrived sick (a fact reflected in the death rates among newly landed slaves). Nevertheless, a significant proportion did not survive the crossing.

On board the slave ships, the enslaved Africans were packed below decks, normally divided by gender, with the young often sharing the women's quarters. They were more crowded than any other comparable maritime travellers (including troops), but the degree of packing did not seem to affect the levels of shipboard mortality. There were huge variations in the percentage of deaths among Africans on board the slave ships, though over time the overall level fell. The death rates on slave ships in the late eighteenth century were half those of the early days of the slave trade. And this was true on all European ships. The key factors seem to have been the point of departure from Africa and the length of time of the voyage. What tended to reduce the death rates was the growing experience of slave trading itself. Traders developed expertise in how best to ship, load and transport large numbers of people on the African coast, and then across the Atlantic. Like other businesses, they learned from experience and they simply got better at their trade. Again, this was true of all the nationalities involved.

Slave ships were markedly smaller than other vessels plying the West Indian or American routes. It seems clear enough that the size of ship was important for the survival of the Africans. Through trial and error over a very long period, more easily navigable and swifter vessels emerged as the ships best suited to carry Africans across the Atlantic. They were not, however, best for carrying American produce back to Europe, and there thus emerged a separate leg of different ships bringing produce back to Europe. The so-called 'triangular trade' was in fact a complex criss-crossing of sailing routes: direct to and from Africa; from Europe to the Americas direct, and back; from North America to the West Indies and back. There was a similar series of routes across the South Atlantic, between Africa and Brazil.

All ships were, of course, at the mercy of the natural elements: of currents and wind systems, of storms and being becalmed. Slave traders learned the maritime tricks of the Atlantic system: how best to catch the winds and currents to get to their chosen destination, when (and when not) to leave, and when to quit the hurricane-prone Caribbean. The timing of transatlantic crossings varied hugely: the average time from Africa to Brazil was one month, to the Caribbean and North America two months. Crossing times got shorter, as traders learned how best to load and transport human cargoes. With the exception of those destined for North America (in the mid-eighteenth century carrying about 200 slaves each), European slave ships carried more Africans by the end of the eighteenth century than they had previously: the British 390, the French and Portuguese 340. The figures were even higher, in the 400s for Brazil, in the last phase of the illegal nineteenth-century slave trade to Brazil.

We do not know how many Africans died in captivity before reaching the slave ships, but we have a reasonably clear idea of the mortality levels on the slave ships. In total some one and a half million Africans died on board, to be cast overboard, their numbers (never their names) simply struck from the ship's logs like so much lost cargo. But mortality levels declined from something like 20 per cent in the early seventeenth century to half that figure a century later. Death rates rarely fell below 5 per cent. There were, of course, catastrophic examples of contagious disease sweeping away huge numbers of Africans, quite apart from the death and destruction brought about by slave insurrection or resistance. We know of shipboard insurrection on an estimated 10 per cent of Atlantic slave ships.

Most slave deaths on board were from gastrointestinal disorders, mainly the 'bloody flux'. Inevitably, untold numbers of survivors stumbled ashore in the Americas suffering from the same condition: weakened, aged (often 'bunged up' by slave traders anxious to pass them off as fit) and destined for an early grave. Slaves were shackled below, normally in small groups. They fed from communal supplies, and shuffled, in chains, to the 'necessary tubs'; but when sick, they relieved themselves where they lay, their faeces soiling and contaminating themselves and their fellow prisoners. When weather and security allowed the crew to bring the Africans on deck for exercise, they did so in small groups; sailors always feared that Africans might resort to violence or simply end their torments by leaping overboard. In bad weather they were neither cleaned nor exercised, because the crew were too busy grappling with the ship. It took a strong-stomached surgeon, or a hardened crewman, to venture into the stinking, pestilential slave holds. The Africans, on the other hand, had no choice in the matter. The conditions in which they crossed the Atlantic often defy belief and description. When Parliament began to scrutinize the slave trade in the late 1780s, the litany of maritime horror stories from men who had served on the slave ships proved a telling factor in turning opinion against the trade.

At this point we return, inevitably, to the issue of historical interpretation. How are we to capture, present and discuss suffering on such an acute and epic scale? How should we represent suffering of such a personal humiliating nature, in which private functions were public, privacy had no meaning and living quarters quickly descended into the squalor of a sea-borne stable? Statistics are clearly vital for any historical understanding of what happened, and without them we have mere guesswork. Nonetheless, it is only when we peer into the slave hold, when we try to capture the physical reality of the slave ship, to catch a whiff of a slave ship's distinctive stink (other vessels could smell them miles downwind), that we can begin to get a better sense of what the slaves actually experienced. Yet perhaps there is no certain way of imagining life below decks on the slave ships. Here perhaps is one of those historical topics (the Holocaust is surely another) which defies easy historical grasp and reconstruction.

Even when land was once again in sight and when the Africans were finally released from the holds, their agonies did not end: they merely entered another phase of what must have seemed an unending horror story. Before they went ashore for sale, they were prepared for further inspection, which was to be followed by yet more onward travel to another distant, unknown destination.

Africans were prepared for sale by ships' crews, keen to present their cargoes in the best commercial light – that is, as fit and well as they could manage. This generally involved a period of cleaning, resting and feeding on board, in an attempt to make good the wear and tear of the Atlantic crossing. For many Africans, little could be done to restore them to health (and saleability). There is perhaps nothing more revealing of the whole wretched story than the existence and fate of 'refuse slaves', those incapacitated and rendered commercially worthless by sickness, and destined to an early death soon after landfall in the Americas. Even among those who were sold, a substantial proportion carried to their new American homes the ailments and frailties acquired in the protracted period of enslavement and transportation. It is not surprising that many died within the first year of arrival.

On shore, the patterns of physical inspection were similar wherever the slave ships made landfall, repeating the Africans' humiliations in their initial encounters with slave traders on the African coast. Slaves were scrutinized and probed, handled and inspected in the most intimate, medical-like manner, to seek out their weaknesses, strengths and imperfections. After the Atlantic crossing, there were plenty of flaws to look for. In warehouses, in barracoons, on board ship, or in auction pens and markets, Africans were inspected by potential purchasers, agents, planters and merchants, all keen to acquire healthy (and therefore profitable) slaves.

For many, their oceanic travels had not ended. Hundreds of thousands of Africans were shipped on from their point of arrival, to other destinations. For instance, 200,000 were trans-shipped from Jamaica, mainly to Spanish and French possessions. Similarly, Dutch ships headed for the small Dutch island of Curaçao, from where the Africans were trans-shipped to Spanish colonies. Many Africans were then directed to Central America and Columbia; others crossed to Panama and thence to Lima. In North America, many of the Africans landing in the Chesapeake Bay region (to work on the tobacco plantations) had already been trans-shipped from the Caribbean and faced a daunting trek into the American interior.

In general the slave ships headed for those regions of the Americas that were in the full flood of slave-based development and desposited their human cargoes where labour was most wanted. Naturally, the patterns changed over time. Before 1600, Spanish America and Brazil attracted most of the Africans. After 1640, and the explosive growth of the sugar islands, the bulk of African slaves headed to the Caribbean. The numbers imported gathered pace as the plantations proliferated, and as Europe devoured increasing volumes of slave-grown commodities. Between 1640 and 1700, 1.6 million Africans were landed in the Americas. In the course of the eighteenth century some six million Africans were shipped out of Africa. Despite the British and American abolition of the slave trade in 1807, a further three million Africans crossed the Atlantic as slaves in the nineteenth century, destined primarily for Brazil and Cuba.

The end result of these massive enforced movements of people was that Africans were scattered to all corners of the Americas as slaves, though they were concentrated initially on the plantations (and mainly on the sugar plantations). Africans dominated the population of Brazil; they greatly outnumbered whites in all the West Indian slave islands; and they formed a substantial minority in the slave colonies of North America. They worked in towns and cities across the Americas; they toiled on boats and ships in all maritime and riverine trades, and as agricultural workers in all forms of labouring and skilled tasks.

Slaves were ubiquitous, appearing in all corners of the Atlantic economy, from the most distant American frontier to the dockside communities of London and Nantes. Africans and their descendants were not only integral to the evolution and prosperity of the Atlantic world but inescapable. And all had been scattered by the uniquely distressing experience of months on board the Atlantic slave ships.

For all its commercial appeal and profitability, the Atlantic slave trade was, from its inception, a highly dangerous affair. European crews died in large numbers on the African coast. Captain John Blake describes the loss of twenty-three men in his time on the River Gambia in 1651–2.

Since our Coming Into this River It hath pleased the Lord aflickt us with much Sicknes that wee have bured three and twenty men. My Chefe and my Second maites and botswaine

are three of them; both my Guneres maites and botswaines
mait, three more, Mr Dobes one of your factores foure, the rest
of them the lustiest men wee had In our Shipe, my Sellf having
bine very Sicke being taken Sick one of the first So that noe
man that see mee that did ever thincke that I should a recoverd,
but It hath pleased the Lord to raise and restore mee and many
more of us to our health againe, I hope to his glory and our
Comfortes; most part of all our men hath bine sicke and are
Sicke at present, but all upon the mending hand but vere weake
and febell. Wee have noe more well mene at present then will
man our long boat w'ch Is sum tenne; my Sellfe at present very
well and lusty and I hope with In a short tyme to see all the
rest up againe and lusty.[1]

*Trading on the coast was precarious and uncertain as well as danger-
ous. The crew died, and the Africans died (in great numbers, of course),
and all were threatened when food and water supplies ran low. This
journal kept on the Dutch ship* St Jan *in 1659 captures many of the
hazards involved.*

We weighed anchor, by order of the Hon'ble Director, Johan
Valckenborch, and the Hon'ble Director, Jasper van Heussen,
to proceed on our voyage to Rio Reael, to trade for slaves for
the hon'ble company.

March 8. Saturday. Arrived with our ship before Ardra, to take
on board the surgeon's mate and a supply of tamarinds for
refreshment for the slaves; sailed again next day on our voyage
to Rio Reael.

17. Arrived at Rio Reael in front of a village called Bany,
where we found the company's yacht, named the *Vrede*, which
was sent out to assist us to trade for slaves.

In April. Nothing was done except to trade for slaves.

May 6. One of our seamen died; his name was Claes van
Diemen, of Durgerdam.

22. Again weighed anchor and ran out of Rio Reael accompanied by the yacht *Vrede*; purchased there two hundred and nineteen head of slaves, men, women, boys, and girls, and set our course for the high land of Ambosius, for the purpose of procuring food there for the slaves, as nothing was to be had at Rio Reael.

26. Monday. Arrived under the high land of Ambosius to look there for victuals for the slaves, and spent seven days there, but barely obtained enough for the daily consumption of the slaves, so that we resolved to run to Rio Cammerones to see if any food could be had there for the slaves.

June 5. Thursday. Arrived at the Rio Cammerones and the yacht *Vrede* went up to look for provisions for the slaves. This day died our cooper, named Pieter Claessen, of Amsterdam.

29. Sunday. Again resolved to proceed on our voyage, as there also but little food was to be had for the slaves in consequence of the great rains which fell every day, and because many of the slaves were suffering from the bloody flux in consequence of the bad provisions we were supplied with at El Mina, amongst which were many barrels of groats, wholly unfit for use.

We then turned over to Adriaen Blaes, the skipper, one hundred and ninety five slaves, consisting of eighty one men, one hundred and five women, six boys, and three girls for which bills of lading were signed and sent, one by the yacht *Vrede* to El Mina with an account of, and receipts for, remaining merchandise.

July 25. Arrived at Cabo de Loop de Consalvo for water and wood.

27. Our surgeon, named Martyn de Lanoy, died of the bloody flux.

Aug. 10. Arrived the company's ship, named *Swartem Arent*, from Castle St George d'el Mina, bound for Patria.

11. Again resolved to pursue our voyage towards the island of Annebo, in order to purchase there some refreshments for the slaves.

We have lain sixteen days at Cabo de Loop hauling water and wood. Among the water barrels, more than forty had fallen to pieces and were unfit to be used, as our cooper died at Rio Cammerones, and we had no other person capable of repairing them.

Aug. 15. Arrived at the island Annebo, where we purchased for the slaves one hundred half tierces of beans, twelve hogs, five thousand cocoanuts, five thousand sweet oranges, besides some other stores.

17. Again hoisted sail to prosecute our voyage to the island of Curaçao.

Sept. 21. The skipper called the ships officers aft, and resolved to run for the island of Tobago and to procure water there; otherwise we should have perished for want of water, as many of our water casks had leaked dry.

24. Friday. Arrived at the island of Tobago and hauled water there, also purchased some bread, as our hands had had no ration for three weeks.

27. Again set sail on our voyage to the island of Curaçao, as before.

Nov. 1. Lost our ship on the Reef of Rocus, and all hands immediately took to the boat, as there was no prospect of saving the slaves, for we must abandon the ship in consequence of the heavy surf.

4. Arrived with the boat at the island of Curaçao; the Hon'ble Governor Beck ordered two sloops to take the slaves off the wreck, one of which sloops with eighty four slaves on board, was captured by a privateer.

List of the Slaves who died on board the Ship 'St Jan' from 30th June to 29th October in the year 1659:[2]

[1659]	Men	Women	Children
June 30	3	2	
July 1	2	1	
3		1	
5		2	I
6		1	
7	1		
8	2	1	
9	2		
10		2	
12		1	

Running a slave ship filled with alienated and sick Africans below decks was, from first to last, a risky exercise. But all European slave traders developed well-honed routines and quickly learned how best to pacify and control shipboard Africans. The ideal system often collapsed, however, in the face of problems – especially difficult weather, truculent Africans and widespread illness. John Barbot describes the management of Africans on board a slave ship, in Journey to the Congo River, *published in 1700.*

. . . the slaves lie in two rows, one above the other, and as close together as they can be crouded . . .

The planks, or deals, contract some dampness more or less, either from the deck being so often wash'd to keep it clean and sweet, or from the rain that gets in now and then through the scuttles or other openings, and even from the very sweat of the slaves; which being so crouded in a low place, is perpetual, and occasions many distempers, or at best great inconveniences dangerous to their health . . .

It has been observ'd before, that some slaves fancy they are carry'd to be eaten, which make them desperate; and others are so on account of their captivity: so that if care be not taken, they will mutiny and destroy the ship's crue in hopes to get away.

To prevent such misfortunes, we used to visit them daily, narrowly searching every corner between decks, to see whether they have not found means, to gather any pieces of iron, or wood, or knives, about the ship, notwithstanding the great care we take not to leave any tools or nails, or other things in the way: which, however cannot be always so exactly observ'd, where so many people are in the narrow compass of a ship.

We cause as many of our men as is convenient to lie in the quarter-deck and gun-room, and our principal officers in the great cabin, where we keep all our small arms in a readiness, with sentinels constantly at the doors and avenues to it; being thus ready to disappoint any attempts our slave might make on a sudden.

These precautions contribute very much to keep them in awe; and if all those who carry slaves duly observ'd them, we should not hear of so many revolts as have happen'd. Where I was concern'd, we always kept our slaves in such order, that we did not perceive the least inclination in any of them to revolt, or mutiny and lost very few of our number in the voyage. As to the management of our slaves aboard, we lodge the two sexes apart, by means of a strong partition at the main mast; the forepart is for the men, the other behind the mast for the women. If it be in large ships carrying five or six hundred slaves, the deck in such ships ought to be at least five and a half or six foot high, which is very requisite for driving a continual trade of slaves: for the greater height it has, the more airy and convenient it is for such a considerable number of human creatures; and consequently far the more healthy for them, and fitter to look after them. We take their meals twice a-day, at fix'd hours, that is, at ten in the morning, and at five at night; which being ended, we made the men go down again between the decks; for the women were almost entirely at their own discretion, to be upon deck as long as they pleas'd, nay even many of the males had the same liberty by turns, successively; few or none being fetter'd or kept in shackles, and that only on account of some disturbances, or injuries, offer'd to their fellow captives, as will unavoidably happen among a numerous croud of such savage people. Besides we allow'd each of them betwixt their meals a handful of Indian wheat and Mandioca, and now and then short pipes and tobacco to smoak upon deck by turns, and some coconuts; and to the women a piece of coarse cloth to cover them, and the same to many of the men, which we took care they did wash from time to time, to prevent vermin, which they are very subject to; and because it look'd sweeter and more agreeable. Toward the evening they diverted themselves on the deck as they thought fit, some conversing together, others dancing, singing, and sporting after their manner, which pleased them highly, and often made us pastime; especially the female sex, who being apart from the males, on the quarterdeck, and many of them sprightly maidens, full of jollity and good-humour, afforded us abundance of recreation, as did several fine little boys, which we mostly kept to attend on us about the ship.

We mess'd the slaves twice a day, as I have observed; the first meal was of our large beans boil'd, with a certain quantity of Muscovy lard . . . The other meal was of pease, or of Indian wheat, and sometimes meal of Mandioca . . . boiled with either lard, or suet, or grease by turns: and sometimes with palm-oil and malaguette or Guinea pepper I found they had much better stomachs for beans, and it is a proper fattening food for captives . . .

At each meal we allow'd every slave a full coconut shell of water, and from time to time a dram of brandy, to strengthen their stomachs . . .[3]

At their worst, the slave ships were like floating stables. Notable among those who bore witness to the consequent suffering of the Africans were the surgeons who worked on the ships. This account is by Alexander Falconbridge, writing in 1788.

But at the same time, they are frequently stowed so close, as to admit of no other posture than lying on their sides. Neither will the height between decks, unless directly under the grating, permit them the indulgence of an erect posture; especially where there are platforms, which is generally the case. These platforms are a kind of shelf, about eight or nine feet in breadth, extending from the side of the ship towards the centre. They are placed nearly midway between the decks, at the distance of two or three feet from each deck. Upon these the negroes are stowed in the same manner as they are on the deck underneath.

In each of the apartments are placed three or four large buckets, of a conical form, being near two feet in diameter at the bottom, and only one foot at the top, and in depth about twenty-eight inches; to which, when necessary, the negroes have recourse. It often happens, that those who are placed at a distance from the buckets, in endeavouring to get to them, tumble over their companions, in consequence of their being shackled. These accidents, although unavoidable, are productive of continual quarrels, in which some of them are always bruised. In this distressed situation, unable to proceed, and prevented from getting to the tubs, they desist from the attempt; and, as the necessities of nature are not to be repelled, ease themselves as they lie. This becomes a fresh source of broils and disturbances, and tends to render the condition of the poor captive wretches still more uncomfortable. The nuisance arising from these circumstances, is not unfrequently increased by the tubs being much too small for the purpose intended, and their being usually emptied but once every day. The rule for doing this, however, varies in different ships, according to the attention paid to the health and convenience of the slaves by the captain.[4]

Former sailors – and captains – from the slave ships also give graphic eyewitness accounts of the appalling conditions endured by Africans. This one, by John Newton, was published in the early days of abolition in 1788.

And I have known a white man sent down, among the men, to lay them in these rows to the greatest advantage, so that as little space as possible might be lost. Let it be observed, that the poor creatures, thus cramped for want of room, are likewise in irons, for the most part both hands and feet, and two together, which makes it difficult for them to to turn or move, to attempt either to rise or to lie down, without hurting themselves, or each other. Nor is the motion of the ship, especially her heeling, or stoop on one side, when under sail, to be omitted; for this, as they lie athwart, or across the ship, adds to the uncomfortableness of their lodging, especially to those who lie on the leeward, or leaning, side of the vessel.

Dire is the tossing, deep the groans.

The heat and the smell of these rooms, when the weather will not admit of the Slaves being brought upon deck, and of having their rooms cleaned every day, would be, almost, insupportable, to a person not accustomed to them. If the Slaves and their rooms can be constantly aired, and they are not detained too long on board, perhaps there are not many die; but the contrary is often their lot. They are kept down, by the weather, to breathe a hot and corrupted air, sometimes for a week: this, added to the galling of their irons, and the despondency which seizes their spirits, when thus confined, soon becomes fatal. And every morning, perhaps, more instances than one are found, of the living and the dead, like the Captives of Mezentius, fastened together.

Epidemical fevers and fluxes, which fill the ship with noisome and noxious effluvia, often break out, infect the Seamen likewise, and the Oppressors, and the Oppressed, fall by the same stroke. I believe, nearly one half of the Slaves on board, have, sometimes, died; and that the loss of a third part, in these circumstances, is not unusual. The ship, in which I was Mate, left the Coast with Two Hundred and Eighteen Slaves on board; and though we were not much affected by epidemical disorders, I find, by my journal of that voyage, (now before me,) that we buried Sixty-two on our passage to South-Carolina, exclusive of those which died before we left the Coast, of which I have no account.

I believe, upon an average between the more healthy, and the more sickly voyages and including all contingencies, One Fourth of the whole purchase may be allotted to the article of Mortality. That is, if the English ships purchase *Sixty Thousand* Slaves annually, upon the whole extent of the Coast, the annual loss of lives cannot be much less than *Fifteen Thousand.*[5]

Slave traders were very conscious that slaves in their desperation might (and did) fling themselves overboard to end their suffering. Alexander Falconbridge describes such suicides in his Account of the Slave Trade on the Coast of Africa *of 1788.*

On the coast of Angola, at the River Ambris, the following incident happened:—During the time of our residing on shore, we erected a tent to shelter ourselves from the weather. After having been there several weeks, and being unable to purchase the number of slaves we wanted, through the opposition of another English slave vessel, we determined to leave the place. The night before our departure, the tent was struck; which was no sooner perceived by some of the negroe women on board, than it was considered as a prelude to our sailing; and about eighteen of them, when they were sent between decks, threw themselves into the sea through one of the gun ports; the ship carrying guns between decks. They were all of them, however, excepting one, soon picked up; and that which was missing, was, not long after, taken about a mile from the shore.

As very few of the negroes can so far brook the loss of their liberty, and the hardships they endure, as to bear them with any degree of patience, they are ever upon the watch to take advantage of the least negligence in their oppressors. Insurrections are frequently the consequence; which are seldom suppressed without much bloodshed. Sometimes these are successful, and the whole ship's company is cut off. They are likewise always ready to seize every opportunity for committing some act of desperation to free themselves from their miserable state; and notwithstanding the restraints under which they are laid, they often succeed.

While a ship, to which I belonged, lay in Bonny River, one evening, a short time before our departure, a lot of negroes, consisting of about ten, was brought on board; when one of them, in a favourable moment, forced his way through the network on the starboard side of the vessel, jumped overboard, and was supposed to have been devoured by the sharks.

During the time we were there, fifteen negroes belonging to a vessel from Leverpool, found means to throw themselves into the river; very few were saved; and the residue fell a sacrifice to the sharks. A similar instance took place in a French ship while we lay there.

Circumstances of this kind are very frequent.[6]

In the prolonged history of collective suffering which formed the story of Atlantic slave trading, few incidents compare to those of the Zong *case of 1781. Luke Collingwood, captain of the Liverpool ship, had 133 slaves thrown overboard to their death when supplies were running short, hoping to claim for their deaths on the ship's insurance. The case came to court in London two years later, not for mass murder but as a disputed insurance claim. It is described in the* Memoirs of Granville Sharp *in 1820.*

The ship *Zong*, or *Zung*, Luke Collingwood master, sailed from the island of St Thomas, on the coast of Africa, the 6th

September, 1781, with four hundred and forty slaves (or four hundred and forty-two) and seventeen Whites on board, for Jamaica; and on the 27th November following she fell in with that island; but, instead of proceeding to some port, the master, either through ignorance or a sinister intention, ran the ship to leeward, alleging that he mistook Jamaica for Hispaniola.

Sickness and mortality had by this time taken place, which is almost constantly the case on board slave-ships, through the avarice of those most detestable traders, which induces them to crowd, or rather to pack, too many slaves together in the holds of their ships; so that on board the *Zong*, between the time of her leaving the coast of Africa and the 29th of November 1781, sixty slaves and upwards, and seven White people, died; and a great number of the remaining slaves, on the day last mentioned, were sick of some disorder or disorders, and likely to die, or not to live long.

These circumstances of sickness and mortality are necessary to be remarked, and also the consequences of them – *viz*. that the dead and dying slaves would have been a dead loss to the owners, and, in some proportion, a loss also to the persons employed by the owners, unless some pretence or expedient had been found to throw the loss upon the insurers, as in the case of Jetsam or Jetson – *i.e.* a plea of necessity to cast over-board some part of a cargo to save the rest. These circumstances, I say, are necessary to be remarked, because they point out the most probable inducement to this enormous wickedness.

The sickness and mortality on board the *Zong*, previous to the 29th November 1781 (the time when they began to throw the poor Negroes overboard alive), was not occasioned by the want of water; for it was proved that they did not discover till that very day, the 29th November (or the preceding day) that the stock of fresh water was reduced to two hundred gallons: yet the same day, or in the evening of it, 'before any soul had been put to short allowance', and before there was any present or real want of water, 'the master of the ship called together a

few of the officers, and told them to the following effect: –
that, if the slaves died a natural death, it would be the loss of
the owners of the ship; but if they were thrown alive into the
sea, it would be the loss of the underwriters': and, to palliate
the inhuman proposal, he the said Collingwood pretended, that
'it would not be so cruel to throw the poor sick wretches
(meaning such slaves) into the sea, as to suffer them to linger
out a few days under the disorders with which they were
afflicted, or expressed himself to the like effect.' To which
proposal the mate (whose name is Colonel James Kelsal)
objected, it seems, at the first, and said 'there was no present
want of water to justify such a measure': But 'the said Luke
Collingwood prevailed upon the crew, or the rest of them, to
listen to his said proposal; and the same evening, and two or
three or some few following days, the said Luke Collingwood
picked, or caused to be picked out, from the cargo of the same
ship, one hundred and thirty-three slaves, all or most of whom
were sick or weak, and not likely to live; and ordered the crew
by turns to throw them into the sea; which most inhuman
order was cruelly complied with.' I am informed, by a memo-
randum from the deposition of Kelsal the chief mate (one of
the murderers), that fifty-four persons were actually thrown
overboard alive on the 29th of November; and that forty-two
more were also thrown overboard on the 1st December. And
on this very day, 1st December, 1781, before the stock of water
was consumed, there fell a plentiful rain, which, by the confession of one of their own advocates, 'continued a day or two,
and enabled them to collect six casks of water, which was
full allowance for eleven days, or for twenty-three days at half-
allowance'; whereas the ship actually arrived at Jamaica in
twenty-one days afterwards – *viz.* on the 22d December, 1781.
They seem also to have had an opportunity of sending their
boat for water no less than thirteen days sooner, *viz.* on the 9th
December, when they 'made the west end of Jamaica, distant
two or three leagues only,' as I am informed by a person who

was on board: and yet, notwithstanding this proof of a possibility that they might perhaps obtain further supplies by rain, or that they might be able to hold out with their new-increased stock of water till they might chance to meet with some ship, or be able to send to some island for a further supply, they nevertheless cast twenty-six more human persons alive into the sea, even after the rain, whose hands were also fettered or bound; and which was done, it seems, in the sight of many other unhappy sufferers that were brought up upon deck for the same detestable purpose, whereby ten of these miserable human creatures were driven to the lamentable necessity of jumping overboard, to avoid the fettering or binding of their hands, and were likewise drowned.[7]

PART III

The Americas

7. Slaves at Work

The sole aim of the Atlantic slave trade was to provide labour for the plantations of the Americas. The great majority of all imported Africans were destined for work in the fields, primarily in sugar, though in time, Africans and their descendants born in the Americas would be found in most corners of the colonial Americas, even in regions were slavery was marginal or unimportant. So huge were the numbers of transported Africans that it was inevitable that some would find their way into roles and places (even distant societies) which might seem to have no use for slaves. By the late eighteenth century, slavery had become so pervasive that Africans were cast into the most unlikely (for them) of social and economic roles. They were to be found from the first penal settlement in Australia to the docksides of Europe, from fashionable European aristocratic homes to the very edges of frontier exploration and adventure. The slave York, for example, proved to be a vital member of Lewis and Clark's epic trek across North America in 1803. Today, the ubiquitous black presence in the Atlantic world has become an accepted historical fact. At its core, however, there lay a simple, brutal fact: Africans were only in the Americas for the betterment of their colonial and European masters. The overwhelming majority of enslaved Africans were turned over to back-breaking labour on plantations, and to tap the potential of fruitful lands, stretching from the Chesapeake and South Carolina, and embracing the myriad islands of the Caribbean and the barely touched vastness of Brazil.

The first slaves, imported by the Spanish, mostly via the Atlantic islands, worked on crude sugar plantations in the Caribbean, though in the early days of pioneering settlement they also worked on any task which came to hand. There was no clear labouring (or social) divide between black, white and local Indian. Faced with the daunting task of hacking back the wilderness, securing a viable habitat and turning land over to cultivation and animal husbandry, settlers used whatever labour was available: free, enslaved, indentured or Indian. For black and white, life was largely a matter of personal (and collective) survival: work together or die together. Most of the initial settlers quickly realized that they could not survive without the help of each other. They also needed the help of Indian people. For their part, Indians faced a different set of problems: the closer their involvement with the invaders (black and white), the more precarious their own future. For almost four centuries, with local variations, the fate of Indian peoples was similar across the Americas. From the first European landfall to the last Indian wars on the Great Plains in the nineteenth century, contact between Indians and invaders spelled suffering, disease and death for the Indians – sometimes on a cataclysmic scale. Yet without the Indians, the new arrivals would not, in many places, have survived at all.

Slavery in the Americas really took off with the growth of the trade in Brazilian sugar in the sixteenth century. More and more Africans were imported to work on Brazilian sugar plantations which, from crude beginnings, developed into complex and sophisticated human and social systems. The process of converting luxuriant but wild tropical lands into sugar cane was completed by an industrial factory system which processed raw cane into sugar and rum, which was then loaded and dispatched for further refinement and sale to the distant ports of Europe. Sugar plantations were, in their mature form, a unique mix of interdependent agricultural and industrial processes, both of which were lubricated by a new form of labour. Slavery, as it emerged on the sugar plantations first of Brazil and later of the Caribbean, was highly regimented and disciplined. The discipline was not that of older slave systems (say in the Roman mines, or the slave galleys of various slave societies): what emerged on the American sugar plantations was an unusual mix of brute force and violence, blended with more subtle incentives and encouragement. Punishment and brutality existed in abundance on the sugar plantations. Leather whips and crops were standard pieces of managerial equipment, appearing in almost every contemporary picture of sugar slaves at work. Visitors often remarked that the crack of the whip was a regular sound among the work gangs. Even so, and as planters came to appreciate, brute force alone was never enough to persuade sugar slaves to bend to their tasks.

The key element was the organization of sugar slaves. They were divided into gangs, the strongest, first, gang undertaking the heaviest work: cutting and hacking, planting and manuring. A second gang retrieved the cane and passed it to a third gang for bundling and loading on to carts destined for the factory. There, the cane was crushed, boiled, distilled and barrelled by other slaves, many of them skilled in the specialized technology of converting cane into sugar. Each sector of labour, whether in the fields or factory, had its elite: gang leaders, drivers, foremen, each with their own managerial role, and each responsible to a superior (often a white person). These elite slaves, who were overwhelmingly men, were rewarded differently and given better homes, clothing and food allowances. They also received bonuses and rewards, all designed to bind them to their task of keeping the slaves in their charge hard at work and up to their own various tasks.

Work in the sugar fields developed its own distinctive routines, especially in the six months of the year when the crop was being harvested and replanted. There were, as with all agricultural work, slack periods when fewer hands were needed, and when the pace and pressure of work were less severe. In cropping time, roughly the period from January through to July, the gangs' toil was at its most severe, and their working days stretched from dawn to dusk. Even then, it was customary for slaves to be allowed a day of rest, when they could recover, work on their own plots or indulge in whatever they fancied: drink, music, religion or the mundane routines of family and community life. Out of season, slave life was different: less pressured, less rigorous. For a start, the factory was not working, and no longer needed constant replenishment of sugar cane from the fields. In these slacker months sugar slaves were given more free time, and more freedom to move around. Occasionally they absented themselves – absent slaves were sometimes tolerated by planters, provided they returned home eventually.

It was different in tobacco plantations, which were smaller than sugar plantations, and where black and white worked more closely together. The regime imposed by tobacco's natural growth was more extended and less physically punishing on the labour force. Slaves were not organized in gangs, as in sugar, and their work lacked the intensity, and hence many of the physical brutalities, of life on sugar plantations, though it nonetheless remained arduous. Rice plantations, on the other hand, were much closer to sugar in the physical demands made on slaves, in part because of the hostile (sometime dangerous) physical environment necessary for rice cultivation. The rice industry in South Carolina was dominated by task work, with slaves given specific duties and goals. Their work finished when their tasks were completed. They could, to a degree, fashion their own pace of work.

North American slavery is best remembered for its role in cotton growing. But cotton slavery came relatively late, from the 1790s onwards, long after the mature development of slavery in sugar, tobacco and rice. Cotton became a massive industry, and the cotton plantations of the South, which spread along the slave frontier as the United States rapidly expanded, saw the transfer of slavery to new tracts of North America, and as far west as the Texas border with New Mexico. The plantations were populated by slaves brought from the old slave states in the east, and from the natural increase in the US slave population.

Numerically, US slavery soon became the largest of all the slave economies. At American Independence in 1776 there were about half a million slaves in North America, and on the eve of the Civil War (1860) there were four million slaves in the US, of which 60 per cent worked in cotton. The US was home to the largest slave population in the Americas, even though it had imported the smallest proportion of Africans from the Atlantic slave ships.

Whatever the crop – sugar, tobacco, rice, cotton – each one created myriad jobs for slaves in addition to field work. Hard manual labour in the fields was paralleled by skilled labour in testing and assessing the growing crops, and knowing when to harvest, how to process the crop, and when and how to pack and load. There were, in addition, slaves responsible for the material infrastructure of plantation life: masons, joiners, coopers, metalworkers, transport slaves, all in addition to the armies of domestic slaves in all slave societies. Slaves also moved out of the plantations into urban areas, serving all aspects of local life, from dockside and shipboard loading (and some worked as inshore or oceanic sailors) through to food production and marketeering, and from the very edges of frontier exploration (York on the Lewis and Clark expedition) through to the gentility of European fashionable society (where black domestic labour became a symbol of social status for their owners). Others appeared in what we might, today, think of as the most unlikely of circumstances, from New York City to domestic service in rural Yorkshire. Nonetheless, slaves' prime purpose was to form a labouring army, tackling the harshest of tasks throughout the tropical and semi-tropical Americas.

Domestic slavery was a striking feature of slave societies everywhere. Although domestic slaves were spared the harshest of outdoor labours, it was a standard punishment to transfer troublesome/errant slaves to field work, and domestic labour itself possessed its own dangers and risks, as when, for instance, slaves found themselves under the relentless gaze of owners and their

families. Disputes between domestic slaves and white women
were common, and the frictions of living and working in close
proximity added to the tensions. Visitors were amazed by how
many slaves seemed to be required in and around white house-
holds. Slaves were on hand for each and every aspect of
domestic life, from cleaning and cooking to child care and
sexual services. Domestic slaves were also an important conduit
for news and gossip, and for the transfer of goods, from white
life into the local slave quarters. Old clothes and food passed
from owners to slave domestics, and thence to the slave cabins.
Owners regularly complained of slave theft, and of later finding
missing items in slave hands. But it was perhaps the transfer
of information which was most important. Table talk, and over-
heard conversations among whites, quickly found their way
back to slave quarters. News from the ships newly arrived from
Europe, Africa or the Americas instantly passed, via attentive
(though generally silent) domestic servants, back to the slaves
in other corners of the plantations. Rumour was a potent force
in all slave societies, and it seeped effortlessly from the master
or mistress into the slave quarters, courtesy of domestic slaves.

Everywhere, slave systems were designed to secure the best
returns from all slaves: to ensure that owners got the best from
their human property, whatever the slave's age, sex or condition. With this in mind, slaves were allocated to the various
tasks according to age and strength, moving up or down the
scale of operations as age and skills determined, or as their
strength and capabilities diminished with the passage of time.
The young and the old mingled in the simplest tasks; men and
women in their physical prime were mixed for the most
demanding of work; and the most promising were instructed
in skilled work (often following a father or mother).

Over each form of slave work there lurked the crucial presence of white (sometimes black) owners, each with their own
personal style of control. Slaves everywhere had to accommo-
date disciplines of labour which were at once part function of

the local crop and environment, and part reflection of the
owner's or the driver's individual approach to slave management. This was as true for the field gangs as it was for domestic
slaves. From the freshly arrived African, struggling to survive in
a new habitat and weakened by sickness, through to the young
local-born slave, needing to heed the warnings of older family
members and workmates, labour discipline had to be learned
and adhered to.

In the course of their working lives, all slaves inevitably
encountered a range of different men charged with their supervision: some more benign, some brutal to the point of sadism.
However we measure the chances that slaves would attract
physical punishment, it was the inescapability of the threat, the
cavalier way it was often administered and the randomness of
violence in the workplace which characterized slave labour.
Even though the cycle and calendar of local work differed from
crop to crop, and contained periods of less intense activity, the
slave's working life remained harsh and generally unrelenting.
And the threat of physical punishment – to goad slaves to work,
to satisfy the driver or master's whims – was rarely far away.

Punishment – especially the whip – was never enough, in
itself, to persuade the slaves to work or to keep them in order.
This was especially true in sugar, where the slave gangs greatly
outnumbered the drivers, and where, in crop time, slaves went
to work armed with a fearful array of implements (machetes,
hoes, bills, spades), all of which could be turned angrily against
their persecutors. Throughout the Americas, the discipline of
slave labour, to be effective, required incentives too. Free time,
access to land (for private cultivation and animal rearing),
bonuses for good or productive work and behaviour, and material benefits (more food, clothing, gifts and hand-me-downs)
all formed part of the complicated discipline of keeping slaves
in place and at work.

When Africans were shipped to the Americas to work, their
local-born descendants inherited the obligation of labouring,

against their will, at whatever task their owners thought fit. Though numbers were freed, emancipation was an exception rather than the rule, and their labours lasted a lifetime, for little or no return. The most significant material rewards came not from the owners but from the slaves' own efforts, in their free time. Yet such rewards were sparse and hard-won, and for all the examples we can cite of slaves able to adorn themselves and their meagre homes with a few extra items (clothing, furnishings, small luxuries) there were many more whose enslaved lives were bleak and devoid of material comforts.

It is also true that not all slave owners were prosperous. As slave owning became a way of life in Brazil, the Caribbean and the southern US, slave ownership spread far beyond the large planters and major property owners. The humblest of people owned slaves, including non-whites; poorer white and 'coloured' people normally used slaves as domestics. Slaves also worked on the Atlantic ships, landing in Europe as enslaved sailors or the enslaved domestics to captains and officers. It was not clear, legally, if slavery could exist in England, but, slaves could be bought and sold in Europe. But what economic purpose could they serve in Europe, where labour was already plentiful and cheap? The very fact that black slavery existed in Europe, where indigenous slavery had long since died out, is a clear sign of the importance of slavery in the broader world of the Atlantic. It had spilled out from its major locations, from the sugar, tobacco, rice and cotton fields, into all corners of Atlantic econ- omy and society. Slave labour had become indispensable in the Americas, and the Western economy came to rely on slavery for a range of tropical and semi-tropical staples which the West consumed in ever-increasing volumes.

Slave labour was an alien institution when Europeans made their first tentative explorations across the Atlantic. Within a century and a half it had become a vital means of settling and developing key regions of the Americas. Few doubted that what- ever economic development had taken place in the slave colonies of the Americas could not have been achieved without slavery. In the process slave labour had itself been transformed from an outdated, almost forgotten institution into a vital force. Europeans had devised new forms of African slavery to tap the economic potential of the Americas. Without Africans, it is hard to see how the Western world could have prospered from its tropical American colonies.

The great majority of all Africans shipped into the Americas were destined, initially at least, for the sugar fields. In their mature form, the sugar plantations were highly complex organizations, harnessing disciplined and regimented field work with sugar production in an adjoining factory, although there were other, much smaller plantations, of course. The account here, by Thomas Roughley in 1823, offers a classic account of slaves working in sugar.

The great gang. Nothing animates the planting system more than the wellbeing of this admirable effective force, composed of the flower of all the field battalions, drafted and recruited from all the other gangs, as they come of an age to endure severe labour. They are drilled to become veterans in the most arduous field undertakings, furnish drivers, cattlemen, mulemen, boilers, and distillers. They are the very essence of an estate, its support in all weathers and necessities; the proprietor's glory, the overseer's favourite, directed by him. Brigaded by its chief field-officer, the head driver, they inspire confidence, and command respect. This gang, composed of a mixture of able men and women, sometimes amounting to an hundred, should always be put to the field work, which requires strength and skill in the execution; such as making lime-kilns, digging cane-holes, making roads through the estate, trenching, building stone walls, planting canes and provisions, trashing heavy canes, cutting and tying canes and tops in crop time, cutting copper-wood, feeding the mill, carrying green trash from the mill to

the trash-house, and repairing the public roads, when allot-
ments are to be worked out. They should always be provided
with good hoes, bills, a knife, and axes, to those men who
know how to make use of them. They should have these tools
kept in the most serviceable order. They should be made to
work in a parallel line as they are set in. The head-driver, his
assistant-driver, and bookkeeper, should visit each row, and see
that they do their work well. An animating inoffensive song,
struck up by one of them, should be encouraged and chorused
while at work; for they are thought good composers in their
own way. No punishment should be inflicted, but what is
absolutely necessary, and that with mercy. In bad weather, a
glass of good rum should be given to each; and when making
lime-kilns, roads, and digging cane-holes, a small proportion
of rum and sugar likewise to each. Their cook should be regular with their breakfast by nine o'clock in the morning, and
their salt provisions constantly served to them. Keeping them
in heart, they will work accordingly.

Second gang. This gang should be composed of people, who
are thought to be of rather weakly habits, mothers of sucking
children, youths drafted from the children's gang, from twelve
to eighteen years of age, and elderly people that are sufficiently
strong for field-work. They should have a competent driver to
follow and direct them. Their strength and abilities should be
ascertained and assimilated to field-work of the second order,
such as cleaning and banking young canes, turning trash on
ratoon pieces, threshing light canes, chopping and heaping
manure, planting corn, cleaning grass pieces, carrying dry trash
in crop time to the stokeholes, and such work, requiring no
great strength. The mothers of sucking children should be
provided with nurses to take care of the infants, while they are
at work in the fields, and a hut made in a convenient place, to
retire to, in case of stress of weather. One mother out of every
four in the field should be allowed to go and suckle her child
for a quarter of an hour, then succeeded by others, and so on,

that the infants should not want, and those mothers should not be obliged to turn out to work before sunrise, or be detained to work after sunset. They should have a weekly allowance, of a pint of flour or meal, with a proportion of sugar for each child. The mothers and infants should be kept clean, and free from chegoes. A yard or two of flannel and check, should be given to each infant, for a frock and cover, besides their usual allowance of clothing . . .

The Third or Weeding Gang. This corps, forming the rising generation, from which, in progress of time, all the vacancies occurring in the different branches of slave population are filled up, comes next to be considered. Their merits are great in their sphere. The expectations formed of them are still greater, when contemplated in a future point of view. They are drivers, cattlemen, mulemen carpenters, coopers, and masons, as it were in embryo . . .

Negro children, after they pass five or six years of age, if free from the yaws, or other scrophula, and are healthy, should be taken from the nurse in the negro houses, and put under the tuition of the driveress, who has the conducting of the weeding gang . . . An experienced negro woman in all manner of field work, should be selected to superintend, instruct, and govern this gang of pupils, armed with a pliant, serviceable twig, more to create dread, than inflict chastisement. I should prefer a woman who had been the mother of, and reared a number of healthy children of her own, to a sterile creature, whose mind often partakes of the disposition of her body . . . Each child should be provided with a light small hoe, with a proportionate handle to it well fixed. These little implements should always be ground for them, when out of order, by a carpenter or cooper, and kept wedged; they should be furnished with a small knife, and small basket each, calculated to carry dung. They should be accustomed, in planting time, with those baskets to attend the great gang, and throw dung before them in the cane-holes, which they can do expertly; and by this they will be taught to observe the mode of planting, and putting the cane in the ground. They should be encouraged when they do their work well, and when the sun is unusually powerful, with a drink made of water, sugar, and lime-juice, such being cooling and wholesome for them. They should be minutely examined and cleaned from chegoes; their heads and bodies from itch or scrophula; which last, when discovered, they should immediately be put under the care of the hothouse doctor, physicked and rubbed with proper ointment, and not sent to work till they are cured. Their cleanliness should be exemplary, their meals always strengthened with a small quantity of salt pork or fish, and some kind of garden-stuff, such as peas or beans . . . When any of these children become twelve years old, and are healthy, they are fit subjects to be drafted into the second gang, going on thus progressively from one gang to the other.[1]

Work in the sugar fields is widely recognized as being among the most arduous form of slave work in the Americas. So too was slave-based rice cultivation in South Carolina. This account by Basil Hall, from 1820, describes the process and the strenuousness of the work involved.

After dinner we strolled over the plantation, under our friend Solomon's direction, and a most intelligent and agreeable guide he proved – more so, indeed, than it had ever occurred to us any slave-driver could possibly be. The imagination pictures such a character flourishing his whip, and so far it is true, for this symbol of office is never laid down – but he made no use of it during our stay, and he appeared to be any thing but stern or tyrannical in his deportment, to the people under his orders. We found the principal body of the negroes making a dam to keep back the waters of an adjacent river, which had invaded some of the rice fields. The negroes were working in a long string, exactly like a row of ants, with baskets of earth on their heads, under the superintendence of two under drivers, likewise blacks. This labour appeared to be heavy, and as the day declined, some of the poor people, especially the women, looked tired enough.

This plantation, at the time of our visit, consisted of 270 acres of rice, 50 of cotton, 80 of Indian corn, and 12 of potatoes, besides some minor plots for vegetables; the whole being cultivated by eighty working hands. A shovel plough is used at certain seasons for weeding; but all the essential and laborious work of preparing the soil, as well as that of sowing and reaping the crops, is done exclusively by hand.

Next day we left our hospitable friend's plantation, and proceeded to the southward. We had no difficulty in again finding shelter, for the considerate people of Charleston had supplied us amply with introductions, enjoining us, at the same time, to consider every house we came to, as open to receive us, if we had any wish to occupy it. An experienced traveller on this road, had given us a hint where we should be best entertained, and we accordingly drove up to a very promising establishment, which fully answered the description given of it. The master of the place was walking about the grounds, but the servants had orders, they said, to receive us, and begged us to walk in.

The day being hot and calm, all the doors and windows were thrown open, and we walked through the house to a pleasant garden, overhanging the Combahee River, flowing majestically past, in a direction from the sea. Our host, who soon joined us, explained that the current we saw, was caused by the flood tide, though the sea was distant full 30 miles. This ebb and flow of the rivers intersecting the level parts of South Carolina, is of the greatest consequence to the rice growers, as it enables them to irrigate their fields at the proper season, and in the proper quantity; an advantage which leads to the production of those magnificent crops, with which all the world is familiar.

During our stay at this extensive and skilfully managed plantation, we had an opportunity of being initiated into the mysteries of the cultivation of rice, a staple of Carolina. This grain is sown in rows, in the bottom of trenches made by slave labour entirely. These ridges lie about seventeen inches apart, from centre to centre. The rice is put in with the hand, generally by women, and is never scattered, but cast so as to fall in a line. This is done about the 17th of March. By means of flood-gates, the water is then permitted to flow over the fields, and to remain on the ground five days, at the depth of several inches. The object of this drenching is to sprout the seeds, as it is technically called. The water is next drawn off, and the ground allowed to dry, until the rice has risen to what is termed four leaves high, or between three and four inches. This requires about a month. The fields are then again overflowed, and they remain submerged for upwards of a fortnight, to destroy the grass and weeds. These processes bring matters to the 17th of May, after which the ground is allowed to remain dry till the 15th of July, during which interval it is repeatedly hoed, to remove such weeds as have not been effectually drowned, and also to loosen the soil. The water is then, for the last time, introduced, in order that the rice may be brought to maturity – and it actually ripens while standing in the water. The harvest commences about the end of August, and extends into October. It is all cut by the male slaves, who use a sickle, while the women make it up into bundles. As it seems that no ingenuity has yet been able to overcome the difficulty of thrashing the grains out by machinery, without breaking them, the whole of this part of the process is done with hand flails in a courtyard.

The cultivation of rice was described to me as by far the most unhealthy work in which the slaves were employed; and, in spite of every care, that they sank under it in great numbers. The causes of this dreadful mortality, are the constant moisture and heat of the atmosphere, together with the alternate floodings and dryings of the fields, on which the negroes are perpetually at work, often ankle-deep in mud, with their bare heads exposed to the fierce rays of the sun. At such seasons every white man leaves the spot, as a matter of course, and proceeds inland to the high grounds; or, if he can afford it, he travels northward to the springs of Saratoga, or the Lakes of Canada.[2]

The tobacco plantations of the Chesapeake region, where slavery in the North American colonies took root, tended to be much smaller than sugar plantations. Initially, as in the West Indian plantations, tobacco slaves increased via imports from Africa and the Caribbean. In time, however, their numbers grew naturally, and by the time of American Independence in 1776 North America had no further need of new Africans. This passage by Hugh Jones describes the tobacco plantations of Virginia in 1724.

The whole country is a perfect forest, except where the woods are cleared for plantations, and old fields, and where have been formerly Indian towns, and poisoned fields and meadows, where the timber has been burnt down in fire-hunting or otherwise; and about the creeks and rivers are large rank morasses or marshes, and up the country are poor savannahs.

The gentlemen's seats are of late built for the most part of good brick, and many of timber very handsom, commodious, and capacious; and likewise the common planters live in pretty timber houses, neater than the farm houses are generally in England; with timber also are built houses for the overseers and out-houses; among which is the kitchen apart from the dwelling house, because of the smell of hot victuals, offensive in hot weather.

The Negroes live in small cottages called quarters, in about six in a gang, under the direction of an overseer or bailiff; who takes care that they tend such land as the owner allots and orders, upon which they raise hogs and cattle, and plant Indian corn (or maize) and tobacco for the use of their master; out of which the overseer has a dividend (or share) in proportion to the number of hands including himself; this with several privileges in his salary, and is an ample recompense for his pains, and encouragement of his industrious care, as to the labour, health, and provision of the Negroes.

The Negroes are very numerous, some gentlemen having hundreds of them of all sorts, to whom they bring great profit; for the sake of which they are obliged to keep them well, and not overwork, starve, or famish them, besides other inducements to favour them; which is done in a great degree, to such especially that are laborious, careful, and honest; though indeed some masters, careless of their own interest or reputation, are too cruel and negligent.

The Negroes are not only encreased by fresh supplies from Africa and the West India Islands, but also are very prolific among themselves; and they that are born there talk good English, and affect our language, habits, and customs; and though they be naturally of a barbarous and cruel temper, yet are they kept under by severe discipline upon occasion, and by good laws are prevented from running away, injuring the English, or neglecting their business.

Their work (or chimerical hard slavery) is not very laborious; their greatest hardship consisting in that they and their posterity are not at their own liberty or disposal, but are the property of their owners; and when they are free, they know not how to provide so well for themselves generally; neither did they live so plentifully nor (many of them) so easily in their own country, where they are made slaves to one another, or taken captive by their enemies.

The children belong to the master of the woman that bears them; and such as are born of a Negroe and an European are called Molattoes; but such as are born of an Indian and Negroe are called Mustees.

Their work is to take care of the stock, and plant corn, tobacco, fruits, etc. which is not harder than thrashing, hedging, or ditching; besides, though they are out in the violent heat, wherein they delight, yet in wet or cold weather there is little occasion for their working in the fields, in which few will let them be abroad, lest by this means they might get sick or die, which would prove a great loss to their owners, a good Negroe being sometimes worth three (nay four) score pounds sterling, if he be a tradesman; so that upon this (if upon no other account) they are obliged not to overwork them, but to cloath and feed them sufficiently, and take care of their health.

Several of them are taught to be sawyers, carpenters, smiths, coopers, etc. and though for the most part they be none of the aptest or nicest; yet they are by nature cut out for hard labour and fatigue, and will perform tolerably well; though they fall much short of an Indian, that has learned and seen the same things; and those Negroes make the best servants, that have been slaves in their own country; for they that have been kings and great men there are generally lazy, haughty, and obstinate; whereas the others are sharper, better humoured, and more laborious.[3]

Slave society consisted of much more than the armies of field labourers. Plantations, and the local communities they sustained, required a host of skills for their orderly and profitable functioning. This description of George Mason's slave craftsmen in eighteenth-century Virginia offers a glimpse of the diversity of slave skills in the Americas.

My father had among his slaves carpenters, coopers, sawyers, blacksmiths, tanners, curriers, shoemakers, spinners, weavers and knitters, and even a distiller. His woods furnished timber and plank for the carpenters and coopers, and charcoal for the blacksmith; his cattle killed for his own consumption and for sale supplied skins for the tanners, curriers, and shoemakers, and his sheep gave wool and his fields produced cotton and flax for the weavers and spinners, and his orchards fruit for the distiller. His carpenters and sawyers built and kept in repair all the dwelling-houses, barns, stables, ploughs, barrows, gates &c., on the plantations and the out-houses at the home house. His coopers made the hogsheads the tobacco was prized in and the tight casks to hold the cider and other liquors. The tanners and curriers with the proper vats &c., tanned and dressed the skins as well for upper as for lower leather to the full amount of the consumption of the estate, and the shoemakers made them into shoes for the negroes . . . The blacksmiths did all the iron work required by the establishment, as making and repairing ploughs, harrow, teeth chains, bolts &c., &c. The spinners, weavers and knitters made all the coarse cloths and stockings used by the negroes, and some of finer texture worn by the white family, nearly all worn by the children of it. The distiller made every fall a good deal of apple, peach and persimmon brandy . . . All these operations were carried on at the home house, and their results distributed as occasion required to the different planta-tions. Moreover all the beeves and hogs for consumption or sale were driven up and slaughtered there at the proper seasons, and whatever was to be preserved was salted and packed away for after distribution.[4]

Everywhere in the enslaved Americas, slaves had a price on their heads.
They were valued – sold, bought, bartered, inherited – like other forms
of property. Their commercial value depended on age, health and skill.
Here is a list of slaves advertised for sale in the Virginia Gazette *in*
1768.

PRIZES	VALUE	CONTENTS OF PRIZES
1 of	£180	A Negro man named Ralph, about 22 years old, an exceeding good finer.
1 of	£220	A Negro man named Isaac, about 20 years old, an exceeding good hammerman and finer.
1 of	£250	A Negro man named Sam, about 26 years old, a fine chaffery man; also his wife Daphne, a very good hand at the hoe, or in the house.

1 of	£200	A Negro man named Abraham, about 26 years old, an exceeding good forge carpenter, cooper, and clapboard carpenter.
1 of	£150	A Negro man named Bob, about 27 years old, a very fine master collier.
1 of	£90	A negro man named Dublin, about 30 years old, a very good collier.
1 of	£90	A negro man named London, about 25 years old, a very good collier.
1 of	£90	A negro man named Cambridge, about 24 years old, a good collier.
1 of	£90	A Negro man named Harry, a very good collier.
1 of	£100	A Negro man named Toby, a very fine master collier.
1 of	£120	A Negro man named Peter, about 18 years old, an exceedingly trusty good waggoner.
1 of	£190	A Negro man named Dick, about 24 years old, a very fine blacksmith; also his smith's tools.
1 of	£80	A Negro man named Sampson, about 32 years old, the skipper of the flat.
1 of	£70	A Negro man named Dundee, about 38 years old, a good planter.
1 of	£85	A Negro man named Caroline Joe, about 35 years old, a very fine planter.
1 of	£110	A Negro woman named Rachel, about 32 years old, and her children Daniel and Thompson, both very fine.
1 of	£70	A Negro woman named Hannah, about 16 years old.
1 of	£75	A Negro man named Jack, a good planter.
1 of	£75	A Negro man named Ben, about 25 years old, a good house servant, and a good carter, &c.

1 of	£120	A Negro man named Robin, a good sawer, and Bella his wife.
1 of	£70	A Negro girl named Sukey, about 12 years old, and another named Betty, about 7 years old, children of Robin and Bella.
1 of	£75	A Negro man named York, a good sawer.
1 of	£80	A Negro woman named Kate, and a young child called Judy.
1 of	£60	A Negro girl (Aggy) and boy (Nat) children of Kate.
1 of	£75	A Negro named Pompey, a young fellow.
1 of	£110	A fine breeding woman named Pat, lame of one side, with child, and her three children, Let, Milley, and Charlotte.
1 of	£60	A fine boy named Phil, son of Patty, about 14 years old.
1 of	£50	A Negro man named Tom, an outlandish fellow.
1 of	£280	A Negro man named Caesar, about 30 years old, a very good blacksmith; and his wife, named Nanny, with two children, Tab and Jane.
1 of	£110	A Negro man named Edom, about 23 years old, a blacksmith, who has served four years to the trade.
1 of	£160	A Negro man named Moses, about 23 years old, a very good planter; and his wife Phebe, a fine young wench, with her child, Nell.[5]

8. Slave Resistance

Atlantic slavery was a system defined by violence. Africans were enslaved by force, they were transported brutally, and, as we have seen, they were kept at their lifetime's toil by an aggressive slave management which made lavish use of physical punishment. It might seem that in the teeth of such persistent and ubiquitous violence, or threats of violence, slaves would simply succumb. Many of course did. But the story of slavery is also one of resistance. It was not simply a straightforward triumph for the slave-owning classes.

Slaves resisted their bondage throughout the history of slavery. This was true from the classical world to the last days of Atlantic slavery. But the concept of slave resistance can be misleading, if only because it embraces a very wide range of responses by slaves to the world around them.

From first to last, slaves sought to put a physical or social distance between themselves and slavery: to resist it by whatever means seemed most appropriate or to insulate themselves from its most troublesome consequences. They resisted at one extreme through acts of violence and rebellion, and at the other extreme by simple foot-dragging or by feigning stupidity. Resistance began from the moment of enslavement in Africa. Given the opportunity, Africans fled their captors long before reaching the Atlantic coast, but the further they were from their point of enslavement, the further they were from accessible safety. In Africa and in the Americas, escaping slaves faced the basic problem of surviving in a strange and hostile environment.

Even in the shackled and cowed environment of the slave ships, Africans tried to escape. Alert to the ever-present risk of slaves jumping overboard, alone or in batches, slavers rigged safety nets around the ship, and kept a close eye on slaves as they were exercised. However vigilant, though, slavers simply could not prevent desperate acts of slave suicide. Nor, despite the guns, the shackles and the formalized brutality of life on board, could they totally prevent Africans from trying to harm or overthrow the slave ship's crew. We know of at least 400 revolts on slave ships, which ranged from minor outbursts of violence to the complete overthrow – and destruction – of the crew, and even of the ship itself. Perhaps 10 per cent of all slave voyages experienced some sort of revolt among the Africans. Not surprisingly, a mixture of vigilance and fear pervaded slavers' reactions to the Africans throughout the time at sea.

Fear of slaves continued in the Americas and remained a pre-eminent feature of life throughout all American slave societies, shaping the broad legal and social contours. It fashioned (and periodically enhanced) slave owners' powers and determined the restrictions on slaves' personal and communal lives. Slave owners everywhere worried that slaves were dangerous, apt to respond violently, likely to run away or revolt, and always and everywhere in a state of permanent truculence: lazy, mendacious and stupid. Each and every aspect of slave life was regulated and controlled by law and conventions founded on a fundamental distrust of the slaves.

Slaves ran away from their owners, and from the slave plantations. This was perhaps one of the most persistent features of slave societies, but they ran away for many different reasons. The most striking slave runaways were the 'maroon' communities which developed in a number of American societies. These were runaways who had freed themselves to create free societies in remote, inaccessible regions of colonial lands: in the rugged interior of Jamaica's 'Cockpit' country, in the tropical forests of Surinam, in the inaccessible interior of Bahia. Some of these communities survived throughout the history of slavery, to emerge, in days of freedom, as independent-minded communities which persist to this day. Others ended in violent conflict or mass suicide. They were initially African-dominated, often guerrilla-like, and always separatist, and they were always viewed as a threat by colonial authorities, though some ultimately came to an agreement with colonial governments, allowing them to continue as independent communities.

More common was the simple act of slaves running away on their own. Some, not willing to tolerate any more cavalier physical (and sexual) violence, ran to escape brutality. Just as many (more, perhaps) were heading for loved ones: partners, children, parents, family and friends. Since slaves were scattered to the four winds by crude economics (owners splitting and dividing up families) or had married/settled with partners who belonged to and lived with distant slave owners, this was hardly surprising. Occasionally (odd as it may seem), planters even connived in their slaves' absenteeism: if work was slack, and/or food was in short supply, slave owners were sometimes happy to let slaves slip away, but always on the understanding that they would return as and when required. Colonial newspapers were peppered with advertisements seeking runaway slaves, asking for their return or requesting information on their whereabouts. Slave owners often had some idea of where the runaway might be found, normally close to a relative or loved one, or hiding near a previous home.

Slave holders' greatest fear was of physical violence. There were universal fears that domestic slaves might strike in the night, that young men (always a problem to slave holders) might rear up in unrestrained youthful anger after one insult or blow too many. Harsh words or a slave owner's assault could, and did, easily lead to slave anger and a physical response. There was, too, the fear of sexual attack, although as far as we can tell slave sexual attacks on white women were few and far between, and scarcely registered on the same scale as the widespread predatory sexual assaults of white men on slave women.

The vast panoply of colonial laws, and local usage, that

emerged to head off slave violence provided exemplary and
vicious retribution for any slave offender. Slave colonies had
penal codes more bloody than any comparable code in Europe.
Corporal legally prescribed punishments were commonplace,
providing readily available solutions to all sorts of slave trans-
gressions (much to the alarm of visitors – themselves no strangers
to violent penal policy). These were, of course, in addition to
whatever personal, ad hoc blows and lashes individuals felt free
to rain down on their slaves. Whites feared black retribution in
proportion to the violence they meted out, on a daily and generally unregulated basis, to their human possessions. The worst fear
must have been that slaves might behave like slave owners.

Occasionally, slaves fulfilled the owners' nightmares. They
hurt, sometimes killed, owners and their children, they struck
back when assaulted, they damaged and destroyed property, they
plotted and revolted. In the Caribbean, slave revolts were a regular event. Small islands (Antigua 1735–6, Grenada 1795–6), big
islands (Jamaica 1760, 1831–2) and even tiny Barbados (1816)
periodically erupted into slave violence. Sometimes the planters
and their colonial military scarcely held the line against insur-
gent slave rebels. The causes of such outbursts were varied and
confusing: a mix of local grievances, magnetic slave leadership,
unsettling outside news, frustrated ambitions or thwarted hopes.
But everywhere the result was the same: slave violence answered
by massive and violent plantocratic and colonial repression. The
bloodletting to repress slave upheavals got worse and worse. It
seemed, by the early nineteenth century, that only violence on
an almost medieval scale could keep the slaves in their place.
And, if that was true, outsiders began to ask, was it really worth
it? How could such retribution and slaughter be justified (particularly to an increasingly sceptical European constituency)?
The violent excesses of the slave-owning classes, especially in
the Caribbean, ultimately proved counter-productive and helped
to swing opinion towards black freedom.

Slave rebellion was less common in North America than in

the West Indies or Brazil. Nonetheless, there were major upheavals or conspiracies: at Stono, South Carolina in 1739, at Pointe Coupee in Louisiana in 1796, Denmark Vesey's conspiracy in 1822 and Nat Turner's rebellion in 1831. Again, retribution followed on an ugly and sickening scale. In common with all slave societies, revolt was followed by a tightening of the local slave code. Slaves not involved in revolts invariably suffered for the failure of the rebels.

Although revolts littered the Americas, in only one case – the epic revolution in Haiti (unleashed by the French Revolution) – did slave revolt succeed in overthrowing a slave society (1791–1804). The emergence of independent Haiti, the first black republic outside Africa, sent shock waves throughout the enslaved Americas. Refugees (black and white) scattered to neighbouring islands and to North America. Most troublesome of all, however, was the example of successful black revolt, and Haiti's simple message of black equality. This struck the most telling blow. Even though it remained the only slave revolt to overthrow slavery completely, Haiti was a threat to slavery and slaveholders in all corners of the Americas.

It was followed by a string of revolts in the British Caribbean. In addition, on the back of massive imports of Africans into Brazil between 1807 and 1835, large numbers of local revolts erupted there. The most remarkable and largest was the Male, among Islamic slaves in 1835.

Slave rebellions (especially in the British West Indies in the early nineteenth century) helped to undermine the slave system, and to persuade British opinion that slavery was damned and ought to be abolished. Haiti aside, however, slave revolts did not succeed. But that fact begs a simple question: what did slaves want from their acts of resistance? What were slave aspirations? What are we to read into this account of slave resistance against their owners?

The major point to make is that revolt was perhaps untypical of the way most slaves responded to their condition in slave societies in the Americas. Over the whole history of Atlantic slavery, revolts were relatively few and involved only a small proportion of slaves. Most slaves lived out their lives untouched by revolt.

Slave plots, however, were more common than revolts. Rumours of plots abounded. Planters and their friends, who lived physically isolated, far from other whites, and were surrounded by legions of hostile slaves, readily believed the rumours and gossip which swirled around all slave communities. They always feared the worst, and assumed that their slaves were dangerous and threatening, even when they had known them for years (even as lovers). Sudden death and illness (commonplace in the pre-modern world, and an everyday event in the tropics) were put down to slave malevolence. When put under pressure (that is, tortured), suspect slaves were likely to tell slave owners what they wanted to hear. Thus did rumours and whispers harden into evidence of betrayal and plots.

Most slaves clearly did not plot, even though most slaves were obviously deeply miserable with their lives. But we cannot assume that because the majority failed to associate themselves with open resistance they merely accepted their fate. There were, after all, many different ways of responding to the condition of slavery. Slaves quickly learned the tricks of the trade: the lessons of survival and accommodation, how to get by, doing what was asked of them but not too eagerly or assiduously, going through the motions at work, labouring in a listless fashion, doing just enough to go unnoticed without too much effort and without attracting too much attention. Foot-dragging and misunderstanding, deception and ignorance: all came together to produce that slavish mentality and style which infuriated slave owners yet made life and work a little more tolerable for the slaves themselves. Orders half-understood and half-complied with, instructions partly followed, time drawn out and tasks lingered over: all this characterized slave work. Often, of course, such behaviour provoked anger and punishment. More often it prompted resigned helplessness, helping to confirm all the deepest prejudices in the minds of slave owners and their white associates that they were dealing with very stupid people. To their minds, only the restraints of slavery could be guaranteed to exact the required effort from slaves.

There was also the question of language and comprehension. Africans needed an intermediary at first (even among themselves), while local-born slaves acquired Creole languages which were not always fully understood by Europeans. But the slaves' apparent lack of comprehension was not simply a linguistic matter. It was often a strategy by which slaves imposed their own pace and style on work and life in general. It was, quite simply, a form of resistance: a refusal to accept the world as their owners saw it.

In this they were not always successful. Sometimes they incurred the wrath of their superiors. Yet, in all quarters of the enslaved Americas, the pattern was much the same, whatever the local variants: slaves tried as far as possible to make a world for themselves. And that involved a pervasive reluctance to live and to work at the pace, and in pursuit of the demands, of those in control of their lives. Here, perhaps, was the most successful and universal form of slave resistance in the wider story of slavery in the Atlantic world.

Violence was the lubricant of the entire slave system, though on its own it could never hope to maintain the stability and functioning of slavery. More curious still, the men who administered violence were often cultured and sophisticated individuals who found no confusion in blending their refinement with brutal violence, as William Byrd of Westover, Virginia, illustrates in diary entries from 1709.

8 [February 1709]. I rose at 5 o'clock this morning and read a chapter in Hebrew and 200 verses in Homer's *Odyssey*. I ate milk for breakfast. I said my prayers. Jenny and Eugene were whipped. I danced my dance. I read law in the morning and Italian in the afternoon . . .

22 [*February 1709*]. I rose at 7 o'clock and read a chapter in Hebrew and 200 verses in Homer's *Odyssey*. I said my prayers, and ate milk for breakfast. I threatened Anaka with a whipping if she did not confess the intrigue between Daniel and Nurse, but she prevented by a confession. I chided Nurse severely about it, but she denied, with an impudent face, protesting that Daniel only lay on the bed for the sake of the child. I ate nothing but beef for dinner . . .

17 [*April 1709*] . . . Anaka was whipped yesterday for stealing the rum and filling the bottle up with water . . .

10 [*June 1709*]. I rose at 5 o'clock this morning but could not read anything because of Captain Keeling, but I played at billiards with him and won half a crown of him and the Doctor. George B—th brought home my boy Eugene . . . In the evening I took a walk about the plantation. Eugene was whipped for running away and had the [bit] put on him. I said my prayers and had good health, good thoughts, and good humor, thanks be to God Almighty.[1]

Slaves periodically reacted to their fate and their sufferings with violence of their own. But they knew what terrible fates awaited them if they were unsuccessful. This account from Virginia in 1769 describes an outburst of slave violence – and its suppression.

Sometime about Christmas last, a tragical affair happened at a plantation in North Wales, Hanover county, belonging to Bowler Cocke, Esq; the particulars of which, according to the accounts we have received, are as follow, viz. The Negroes belonging to the plantation having long been treated with too much lenity and indulgence, were grown extremely insolent and unruly; Mr Cocke therefore had employed a new Steward. The Steward's deputy (a young man) had ordered one of the slaves to make a fire every morning very early; the fellow did not appear till sunrise; on being examined why he came not sooner, he gave most insolent and provoking answers, upon which, the young man going to chastise him, the fellow made a stroke at him with an axe (or some such weapon) that was in his hand, but happily missed him. The young man then closed with him, and having the advantage, a number of other slaves came to the Negro's assistance, and beat the young man severely. At last the ringleader (a very sensible fellow) interceded for him, on which they desisted. The young man then made off as fast as he could, to procure assistance to quell them. Whilst he was gone, they tied up the Steward, and also a poor innocent, harmless old man, who overlooked a neighbouring quarter, and on hearing the uproar ... [illegible] across the creek to know the ... [illegible] they whipped [them] till they were raw from the neck to the waistband. In some time the young man returned, with about twelve white men, and two little boys carrying each a gun. They released the two unhappy sufferers, and then proceeded to a barn, where they found a large body of the Negroes assembled (some say forty, some fifty) on whom they tried to prevail by persuasion, but the slaves, deaf to all they said, rushed upon them with a desperate fury, armed with clubs and staves; one of them knocked down a white man, and was going to repeat the blow to finish him, which one of the boys seeing, levelled his piece, discharged its contents into the fellow's breast, and brought him to the dust. Another fellow having also knocked down another of the Whites, was in the same manner, shot by the other boy. In short, the battle continued sometime desperate, but another of the Negroes having his head almost cut off with a broad sword, and five of them being wounded, the rest fled. The accounts vary; some say three were killed upon the spot, and five wounded, others that two were killed, and five wounded, one of whom died soon after. It is said they had threatened to kill the Steward as soon as he came to the plantation. The ringleader was one of the slain.[2]

Every slave society was plagued by slave runaways. They ran away for a host of reasons. The following examples of advertisements for their return, from Virginia, South Carolina and Jamaica, provide revealing insights into the nature of local slavery – and capture personal details of the people involved.

Chesterfield, December 15, 1772

RUN away from the Subscriber on *Sunday* the 22nd of *November*, a new Negro fellow of small Stature, and pitted with the Smallpox; he calls himself BONNA, and says he came from a place of that Name in the *Ibo* country, in *Africa*, where he served in the Capacity of a Canoe Man.

RICHARD BOOKER[3]

RUN away from the Subscriber about the 1st of *September*, in the upper End of *King William* [County], two new Negro Men, of the *Ibo* country, named CHARLES and FRANK, who have been in the Province about twelve Months, and it is supposed cannot tell their Master's Name. *Charles* is a large Fellow, with his Country Marks in his Face, and has lost or broke off one or two of his fore Teeth, which he says was done by a Cow in his Country. Frank is a smaller Fellow, well set, and has sharp Teeth. They carried with them a *Dutch* Blanket, had each a coarse hat, and other usual Summer clothes.

JOSEPH HILLYARD[4]

TAKEN up, about one Mile from my Plantation, in St Matthew's Parish, Berkley County, two NEGRO-FELLOWS of the Guiney Country, who call themselves POMPEY and SAMBO: they are about five Feet ten Inches high, speak but very little English. They say that their Master's Name is JAMES BUTLER, and lives by the side of a River, and that their old Master lives on the other Side. By what I can learn by a Guiney fellow of mine, they have been run away ever since the Spring before last. They are entirely naked, and their Feet and Legs are swelled very much by lying in the Cold, on which Account I thought it would not be prudent to send them to the Work-House. If the Owner of the above Fellows, should find any Difficulty in conveying a Letter to me, they may write to Mr JAMES COURTONE, jeweller, in CHARLES-TOWN.

WILLIAM HEATLY[5]

RUN away some time in *September* last, from *James Armstrong of Fauquier* County, a Negro man named AYRE, belonging to the estate of the late Mr *Allen Macrae*, deceased, about 35 years of age, 5 feet 7 inches high, rather slim made, and of a yellowish complexion, has a remarkable twist with his mouth when he speaks, and although an *African*, affects to pronounce the *English* language very fine, or rather to clip it. As he can both read and write, it is more than presumable he may have forged a pass and by that means may have travelled where he pleased as a free man. His common wearing apparel was of striped country cloth, and had on half worn hat, and country made shoes, all of which he may doubtless have had the address to alter or change, long e'er now. Whoever apprehends and so secures the said runaway Negro, so as to be had again, shall receive ten dollars if taken within 20 miles of his home, and if at a greater distance, or out of the State of *Virginia* 20 dollars, if delivered to the aforesaid *James Armstrong*, his overseer, or brought to the *Neabsco Furnace*, all reasonable charges will be thankfully paid, by

THOMAS LAWSON[6]

RUN AWAY from the Subscriber on the 31st ult., an African Negro named JASPER, by trade a carpenter, speaks very plain English as he came young into the country. He is about 50 years of age, and I think about 5 feet 5 or 6 inches in height, short limb'd and well made for strength; he can read tolerably well, and is both sensible and very artful; he has a surly countenance, especially if offended, and is of a morose temper, fond of liquor, and when drunk is very turbulent; has had the small pox, for which he was innoculated, and is a little marked with it in his face; he has also a remarkable scar above half-round his neck, given by a knife in a scoffle he had with another Negro some time past – The dress he went off in is uncertain; he took with him two coats, one with short skirts, a drab coloured duffle; the other a white Virginia cloth, long skirted; whatever other articles is unknown. I make no doubt but he will endeavour to pass for a free man, and is most probable will endeavour to get into some of the northern states, in order to facilitate his escape; I believe he has procured some forged pass or writing – Any person who will apprehend the said runaway within the state . . . shall receive a reward of TEN POUNDS – and if without the state TWENTY.

FRANCIS JERDONE
Louisa county, April 3, 1793.[7]

Passage Port, June 2, 1790

ABSCONDED

From John Munro's wharf at this place, the 30th ultimo, a NEGRO SAILOR MAN, of the Coromantee nation; he is about 5 feet 5 inches high, his face furrowed with the small pox marks, he has no brand mark, his back has got several lumps which in some manner resemble a bunch of grapes; this fellow is well acquainted in and with all the different islands to Windward; he has been on the Continent of America; came to this island from Rhode Isle in the sloop Amphion, Captain Oliver Berry, who sold him lately to Mr Munro; he had on when he went off an osnaburgh frock and a pair of India Dungaree trowsers; supposed to be lurking in or about Kingston; he is artful, speaks the English, French, Dutch, Danish and Portugese languages; of course it is thought he may endeavour to pass for a free man, and may thus impose on foreigners and other seafaring gentlemen.

    A suitable reward will be given to any person who will lodge

him in any gaol or workhouse in this island, or conduct him
to this wharf.[8]

Berkshire Hall,
St Thomas in the Vale
July 4, 1790

ABSCONDED the 9th ult. from this estate
FOUR NEW NEGRO MEN
stout made, marked on the shoulder E. W., cannot speak much
English. Whoever apprehends and lodges them in any of the
gaols or workhouses, or delivers them to this Estate, shall be
handsomely rewarded by the subscriber.

EDW. YOUNG WOODCOCK[9]

RAN AWAY
From her owner, about the month of Sept. last, a short creole
wench named
DILIGENCE alias JUNK
has a large scar on her breast, occasioned by a burn, with a toe
off each foot, and is troubled with the crab yaws, for which
she wears slippers. Speaks very slow and artful; she has been in
the possession of a free brown woman in Clarendon, from
whose property she frequently travels to Colbeck's Estate (where
she has a husband called Chester) and from thence to Old
Harbour. Fifty shillings reward will be paid for taking her up
and lodging her in any gaol or workhouse. Any person prov-
ing to conviction by whom she is harboured will be suitably
rewarded on notice being given at this office.[10]

RUN AWAY FROM OXFORD PLANTATION
in the parish of Saint Mary, a NEGRO MAN native of Guadaloupe,
named PIERRE,
a stout, young fellow of a yellow complexion, has a scar on
his throat where he formerly cut it; speaks good English and
may attempt to pass for a free man. He has some relations and

countrypeople in the neighbourhood of Montego Bay, where
there is some reason to suspect he is now gone.

Two Pistoles Reward will be given on lodging the above
Negro in any of the gaols of this island, or on delivering him
at the above estate, or to the subscriber in Kingston.

J. SYMES[11]

19 August 1780

*'Maroon' communities — of slaves who managed to escape from their
tormentors completely and, wherever the habitat allowed, formed independent communities of their own — plagued slave holders everywhere.
This description of 1729, from a letter from Lieutenant Governor Sir
William Gooch to the Board of Trade, Williamsburg, outlines a maroon
community in Virginia.*

MY LORDS:

. . . Sometime after my Last a number of Negroes, about
fifteen, belonging to a new Plantation on the head of James
River formed a Design to withdraw from their Master and to
fix themselves in the fastnesses of the neighbouring Mountains.
They had found means to get into their possession some Arms
& Ammunition, and they took along with them some Provisions,
their Cloaths, bedding and working Tools; but the Gentleman
to whom they belonged with a Party of Men made such diligent pursuit after them, that he soon found them out in their
new Settlement, a very obscure place among the Mountains,
where they had already begun to clear the ground, and obliged
them after exchanging a shot or two by which one of the Slaves
was wounded, to surrender and return back, and so prevented
for this time a design which might have proved as dangerous
to this Country, as is that of the Negroes in the Mountains of
Jamaica to the Inhabitants of that Island. Tho' this attempt has
happily been defeated, it ought nevertheless to awaken us into
some effectual measures for preventing the like hereafter, it
being certain that a very small number of Negroes once settled

in those Parts, would very soon be encreas'd by the Accession of other Runaways and prove dangerous Neighbours to our frontier Inhabitants. To prevent this and many other Mischiefs I am training and exercising the Militia in the several counties as the best means to deter our Slaves from endeavouring to make their Escape, and to suppress them if they should.[12]

For slaves who rebelled and failed, torture and death in its most excru-ciating forms were the standard fate. These two accounts, from Surinam in 1790 and Jamaica in 1832, tell of the gruesome death of executed rebels.

The Negro Joosje shall be hanged from the gibbet by an Iron Hook through his ribs, until dead; his head shall then be severed and displayed on a stake by the riverbank, remaining to be picked over by birds of prey. As for the Negroes Wierai and Manbote, they shall be bound to a stake and roasted alive over a slow fire, while being tortured with glowing Tongs. The Negro girls, Lucretia, Ambia, Aga, Gomba, Marie and Victoria will be tied to a Cross, to be broken alive, and their heads severed, to be exposed by the riverbank on stakes.[13]

At first shooting was the favourite mode of execution and many were thus disposed of. But when the novelty of this had ceased the gallows was put in requisition . . . The gibbet erected in the public square in the centre of the town was seldom with-out occupants, during the day, for many weeks. Generally four, seldom less than three, were hung at once. The bodies remained stiffening in the breeze . . . Other victims would then be brought out and suspended in their place, and cut down in their turn to make room for more; the whole heap of bodies remaining just as they fell until the workhouse Negroes came and took them away, to cast them into a pit dug for the purpose, a little distance out of the town.[14]

9. Slave Communities

Africans landed in the Americas alone. They were purchased and transported not in family groups but as individuals. On the ships they formed important links with each other (the concept of 'shipmate' remained precious in the years after landfall) but they landed bereft of family and friends. All had been deracinated from their African homes and familiar environments by a process of regular selling and reselling – within Africa, into the slave ships – that would continue in the Americas from the slave ship to new owners. At each point the slave's identity was changed. Names were dropped and exchanged for numbers (on the ships), brand marks were often added when slaves settled on a plantation, and then new names were allocated. Often, they were allowed to keep their African name, but often too they were given an utterly different name – for example, a classical name. It was a name chosen by the owner, not by the slave; this renaming was, of course, part of the broader process of recasting slaves in the planters' mould and removing as far as possible all traces of Africa. The slave we meet in the planters' formal documentation (ledgers, sale transactions, diaries) is the slave as he or she had been recast by slave traders and by his or her new owners. It is not, however, the person as seen by other slaves. Slaves lived a double life: they were one thing to their owners, but quite another among their fellow slaves.

Gradually, as local economic and social life matured, Africans and their descendants born in the Americas coalesced into their own communities. These were quite unlike the societies they had left in Africa. Of course that was also true of white settlers, whose communities were quite unlike their European backgrounds. Africans, however, faced utterly different circumstances. They were, obviously, reluctant migrants, dumped in the Americas – they knew not where – alone or in small groups: the human property of white people whose language they did not even comprehend. Many, perhaps most, were sick on arrival yet they were soon turned over to field work (often using implements they could not understand). As pioneer settlers, working with local Indians or white settlers, or as newcomers on an established plantation or farm, Africans were expected to play their part. Slaves lived apart from their owners but close enough to be gathered and called to work, grouped into family units. On the sugar plantations, where the slave labour force was large, slaves lived in villages (often described as 'African villages'), but on smaller properties they resided in smaller gatherings, close to the place of work, often close to white homes. Domestic slaves lived in the yards and sometimes in the homes of their employers/owners. This was also true of slaves living and working in towns, especially in the ports which formed the vital link between the developing colonies and the distant world of Africa and Europe.

Moving between the rural and the urban slaves were peripatetic slaves: specialized (and trusted) slaves who travelled back and forth, by land or water, riding, walking or rowing between plantations, to local towns and to distant properties on business and errands, bringing goods to and from the plantations, organizing the transit of new Africans from the dockside to the plantations, driving beasts and carts, sugar wains and barrels of tobacco from the plantation down to the nearest dockside for loading and transit, and collecting supplies from ships or agents and hauling them back to their rural place of work. This movement of slaves was in addition to those gaggles of slaves who travelled in their own free time, on their day of rest, carrying home-grown produce and driving their own animals to local markets, towns, river crossings or road junctions, where they haggled and bartered, bought and sold, exchanging goods and cash. They also swapped news and gossip with other slaves, from distant plantations and even from the ships freshly arrived from Africa, Europe and other colonies.

Some slaves took off on their own without permission, and had to be sought out and returned. But there were many other slaves who travelled with authorization: who were given approval to visit family and friends, normally on high days and holidays, or in family crises, and returned at the appointed time.

There was, however, another, darker, more sinister side to the story of slave mobility. Slaves were shifted around, often great distances, against their will. Africans, who had already endured enforced transit across vast distances, both within Africa and across the Atlantic, often travelled huge distances before settling in their final workplace. Even for local-born slaves, people who knew no other world but the one they had been born into, there was no guarantee that life would be fixed, permanent or unchanging. They could, and often were, uprooted and shifted to new locations, at a moment's notice, to suit their owners' interests or changed economic fortunes. It is here that we see those distressing scenes of slave family break-up which haunt the history and public memory of black life throughout the era of slavery. These were especially common in the US in the nineteenth century. The boom in slave-grown cotton, the spread south and west of the cotton plantations and the rapid expansion of US slavery saw millions of slaves forced out of their original homes and dragooned towards the new cotton plantations. Slaves found themselves uprooted for a variety of reasons. Sometimes owners wanted to get rid of troublesome, nonproductive or surplus slaves (the accountancy of slavery transmuting humanity into ciphers in the ledgers). Sometimes they allowed slaves to join loved ones elsewhere. Much more likely, though, was a heartless uprooting. The death of an owner meant that property (including the slaves) was bequeathed to relatives who might live far away from the slaves' home base.

Economic decline or collapse might also lead to the sale of land and slaves. All these transactions and more saw slaves removed from what they had assumed was their home, their family and community, and relocated elsewhere, often many miles distant. In the world of slavery, where the victims were deemed to be property, like other forms of property they could be shifted around at will. In this, as in so much besides, the slaves had little say and little control.

The scenes of terrible personal and communal grief behind the enforced resettlement of slaves – the nineteenth-century story of US slavery is blighted with accounts of slaves wailing and weeping for loved ones lost to a departing river boat or driven away by slave agents keen to sell slaves to distant plantations – provide important evidence of slaves' deep attachment to family life. This is surprising only because Africans had arrived alone, their original family ties lost over the horizon in Africa. By the nineteenth century African families had once again become important, but this time in the Americas. The slave family was, then, integral to slavery. At one level this is – and was – obvious. At another, it needs to be reaffirmed, not least because of a persistent scholarly trend of suggesting the contrary. True, the slave family faced enormous tensions and difficulties. As well as being buffeted by the destructive forces of plantation economics and by masters' capricious relocation of slaves hither and yon, slave families were permanently threatened by random violence and, above all perhaps, by the predatory sexuality of white men towards slave women. What did all this do to the slave family? The knowledge, for instance, that white males took their sexual pick of slave wives and partners, slave mothers and daughters, without the least regard for the feelings of slave women and men must have been corrosive of family relations. Nevertheless through all the danger and confusion it seems clear that the slave family was not destroyed.

The slave family was important at a number of critical levels.

Above all it was where slave affection and emotions developed: the grounding for everything that individuals held dear from one generation to another. And, of course, it was the prime site for slave culture and socialization. Within the family, young slaves learned the lessons to equip them for the harsh life of a mature slave: what to do, what not to do, how to listen and watch, how they should respond to the snares and dangers waiting for them in the fields and even, closer to home, in their owners' homes. Slaves needed to know how far they could go, what not to do, how far they might respond to provocation, how much they might get away with before incurring the wrath and assaults of owners and drivers. Such lessons were learned initially within the home, and within the slave communities, from mothers, grandmothers, fathers, older siblings and workmates. Slaves learned their personal and social skills just as they learned their labouring skills: not from whites but from other slaves.

The slave family was part of a much broader social network of slave communities, notably the immediate slave quarters in and around the plantations. Whatever the community's form, small or large, closely linked or dispersed, slaves invariably sought out each other. Even in the strange and sometimes hostile environment of European cities, slaves and free blacks gathered together for company, security and social pleasure. Dr Johnson's manservant Francis Barber had black friends visit him in Johnson's London home. Certain London pubs became favourite haunts for black customers in the late eighteenth century. And this black communal sociability took place thousands of miles away from the great concentrations of slaves in the tropical Americas.

There was, of course, no single slave community, but certain broad patterns were familiar: of slaves living close to each other, in family groups, seeking out each other for pleasure and relaxation at the end of the working day, exchanging stories, making their own entertainments, welcoming visitors (sometimes on the run, often fresh from the slave ships), working at those myriad domestic and communal tasks common to all communities. The slave yard, the communal cooking space, the gardens and plots, the regular local markets, the sheds and huts hard by the owner's house, all these and more provided slaves with a communal space in which social life evolved.

The origins of these varied slave communities began long before arrival in the Americas. The 'African villages' were dominated by Africans, though that changed over time as local-born slaves began to outnumber Africans. Africans brought the varied and complex memories of Africa into the slave quarters: the languages, the skills and military experiences, the familial and religious customs, the folk ways, from clothing to belief systems and religions, which blended into the social mix that was the local slave community. And this was in addition to the cultural patterns which evolved from the slaves' contact with the dominant local European-American *mores*.

From this remarkable mix of peoples and cultures there emerged distinctive local Creole cultures which marked one slave community from another. Other differences in slave life emerged via the contrasting patterns of local work and economies. Working in sugar was very different from labour at higher altitudes in coffee cultivation, and different again from work on smaller tobacco holdings or in swampy rice fields. Domestic or urban slavery was quite unlike working as a slave sailor. The particular nature of work imposed is own features on the slave experience. Such distinctions caution against any bold generalization about slave society and community.

This diversity of experience in lifestyle may cause one to question the purpose or value of speaking about 'community' when it was so fractured. Yet the sharp distinctions between slave experiences were overridden by a number of factors which bound slaves together. First, and obviously, slaves were all victims and survivors of a complex and prolonged system of violent incarceration and transportation. The process of enslavement – especially the horrors of the slave ships, the reality and threat of daily violence and the fear of family separations – bound slaves together like no other force. 'Shipmates' were especially close. In addition, and unlike other slave systems in the past (and later), slavery in the Americas was completely racialized. Only black people could be slaves: to be black was to be enslaved, and to be enslaved was to be uniquely unequal and disadvantaged – excluded from the formal fabric of social life. Slaves knew that they had their status and their colour (ethnicity) in common – all of them. Whatever frictions, disputes and rivalries existed within any slave community, they were as nothing compared to the common interests and identities which bound slaves together.

Slaves were also lumped together in the eyes of white people. Slaves saw themselves as a group, and were regarded as such by outsiders. Whatever the obvious distinctions of origins, age, gender and skills, slaves were viewed primarily as a racial whole by white slave-owning society. And what added cohesion to that view was fear. As we have seen, perhaps above all else, whites in slave societies feared the slaves. They posed a permanent and inescapable series of threats. They ran away and resisted, they disobeyed and dragged their feet, they feigned ignorance and they lied. They were, to a man and woman, unreliable and untrustworthy. But slaves were also essential – they were a necessary evil, without whom the entire fabric of economic life in the slave societies would simply collapse – and both blacks and whites knew it.

For all the obvious fissures and local distinctions, what emerged throughout the enslaved Americas was a highly racialized, polarized world, with black/enslaved on one side and white/free on the other. There had been nothing like it before, and it was to bequeath its malignant racial inheritance to later generations. There were, of course, myriad slave communities – a mosaic of African poeples and their descendants. But there was also a stark divide which separated black from white and

which formed the immutable core of slave self-awareness and
the heart of the slave community.

*Whichever slave colony we care to examine, some remarkable transfor-
mations took place in the slave quarters, as from the most wretched
and depressing of beginnings (isolated sick Africans landing alone in
the Americas) distinctive slave family and community structures emerged.
The centre of slave life was the simple home – a 'little habitation' –
with attached gardens and communal yards. This informative account
by Isaac Weld of a North American slave community is from the
1790s.*

The slaves on the large plantations are in general very well
provided for, and treated with mildness. During three months,
nearly, that I was in Virginia, but two or three instances of ill
treatment towards them came under my observation. Their
quarters, the name whereby their habitations are called, are
usually situated one or two hundred yards from the dwelling
house, which gives the appearance of a village to the residence
of every planter in Virginia; when the estate, however, is so large
as to be divided into several farms, then separate quarters are
attached to the house of the overseer on each farm. Adjoining
their little habitations, the slaves commonly have small gardens
and yards for poultry, which are all their own property; they
have ample time to attend to their own concerns, and their
gardens are generally found well stocked, and their flocks of
poultry numerous. Besides the food they raise for themselves,
they are allowed liberal rations of salted pork and Indian corn.
Many of their little huts are comfortably furnished, and they
are themselves, in general, extremely well clothed. In short, their
condition is by no means so wretched as might be imagined.
They are forced to work certain hours in the day; but in return
they are clothed, dieted, and lodged comfortably, and saved all
anxiety about provision for their offspring. Still, however, let

the condition of a slave be made ever so comfortable, as long as he is conscious of being the property of another man, who has it in his power to dispose of him according to the dictates of caprice; as long as he hears people around him talking of the blessings of liberty, and considers that he is in a state of bondage, it is not to be supposed that he can feel equally happy with the freeman. It is immaterial under what form slavery presents itself: whenever it appears, there is ample cause for humanity to weep at the sight, and to lament that men can be found so forgetful of their own situations, as to live regardless of the feelings of their fellow creatures.[1]

Family life was central: the crucible for slave society and for the cultivation of slave mores *and culture. The planter Edward Long (no friend to the slaves) explains the importance of family life in his account of slaves in Jamaica in 1774.*

They are all married (*in their way*) to a husband, or wife, *pro tempore*, or have other family connexions, in almost every parish throughout the island; so that one of them, perhaps, has six or more husbands, or wives, in several different places; by this means they find support, when their own lands fail them; and houses of call and refreshment, whenever they are upon their travels. Thus, a general correspondence is carried on, all over the island, amongst the Creole Blacks; and most of them become intimately acquainted with all affairs of the white inhabitants, public as well as private. In their houses, they are many of them very neat and cleanly, piquing themselves on having tolerably good furniture, and other conveniencies. In their care for their children; some are remarkably exemplary. A Negroe has been known so earnest and sincere in the tuition of his child, as to pay money out of his own pocket for smith's work, to keep a truant son employed, during his apprenticeship to that business, that he might not become remiss in acquiring a proper knowledge of it, for want of work. They exercise a kind of sovereignty over their children, which never ceases during life; chastizing them sometimes with much severity; and seeming to hold filial obedience in much higher estimation than conjugal fidelity; perhaps, because of the whole number of wives or husbands, one only is the object of particular steady attachment; the rest, although called wives, are only a sort of occasional concubines, or drudges, whose assistance the husband claims in the culture of his land, sale of his produce, and so on; rendering to them reciprocal acts of friendship, when they are in want. They laugh at the idea of a marriage, which ties two persons together indis-solubly. Their notions of love are, that it is free and transitory.[2]

That the cultural life of slaves was heavily African is registered in Edward Long's description of slave names and language patterns of 1774.

The Africans speak their respective dialects, with some mixture of broken English. The language of the Creoles is bad English, larded with the Guiney dialect, owing to their adopting the African words, in order to make themselves understood by the imported slaves; which they find much easier than teaching these strangers to learn English. The better sort are very fond of improv-ing their language, by catching at any hard word that the Whites happen to let fall in their hearing; and they alter and misapply it in a strange manner; but a tolerable collection of them gives an air of knowledge and importance in the eyes of their brethren, which tickles their vanity, and makes them more assiduous in stocking themselves with this unintelligible jargon. The Negroes seem very fond of reduplications, to express a greater or less quantity of any thing; as *walky-walky, talky-talky, washy-washy, nappy-nappy, tie-tie, lilly-lilly, fum-fum: so bug-a-bugs* (wood-ants); *dab-a-dab* (an olio, made with maize, herrings, and pepper); *bra-bra* (another of their dishes); *grande-grande* (augmentative size, or grandeur), and so forth. In their conversation, they confound all the moods, tenses, cases, and conjugations, without mercy: for example; *I*

surprize (for, I am surprized); *me glad for see you* (*pro*, I am glad
to see you); *how you do* (for, how d'ye do?); *me tank you; me ver
well*; &c. This sort of gibberish likewise infects many of the white
Creoles, who learn it from their nurses in infancy, and meet with
much difficulty, as they advance in years, to shake it entirely off,
and express themselves with correctness.

Many of the plantation Blacks call their children by the
African name for the day of the week on which they are born;
and these names are of two genders, male and female; as for
instance:

Male.	Female.	Day.
Cudjoe,	Juba,	Monday.
Cubbenah,	Beneba,	Tuesday.
Quâco,	Cuba,	Wednesday.
Quao,	Abba,	Thursday.
Cuffee,	Phibba,	Friday.
Quamin,	Mimba,	Saturday.
Quashee,	Quasheba,	Sunday.[3]

*Observers of slave communities – local whites and visitors – rarely
failed to comment on the slaves' social life. Despite the arduousness of
their lives, slaves made the most of their time of rest. Foremost among
those impressions were slaves' musical pleasures, described here in two
accounts from North America, the first by John Smith in 1784 and
the second by Nicholas Cresswell in the 1770s*

Instead of retiring to rest, as might naturally be concluded he
(the slave) would be glad to do, he generally sets out from
home, and walks six or seven miles in the night, be the weather
ever so sultry, to a negroe dance, in which he performs with
astonishing agility . . . until he exhausts himself, and scarcely
has time, or strength, to return home before the hour he is
called to toil next morning.[4]

... went to see a Negro Ball. Sundays being the only days these poor creatures have to themselves, they generally meet together and amuse themselves with Dancing to the Banjo. This musical instrument (if it may be so called) is made of a Gourd something in the imitation of a Guitar, with only four strings and played with the fingers in the same manner. Some of them sing to it, which is very droll music indeed. In their songs they generally relate the usage they have received from their Masters or Mistresses in a very satirical stile and manner. Their poetry is like the Music – Rude and uncultivated. Their dancing is most violent exercise, but so irregular and grotesque. I am not able to describe it. They all appear to be exceedingly happy at these merry-makings and seem as if they had forgot or were not sensible of their miserable condition.[5]

In 1774 Edward Long, like most other commentators on the slave colonies, was especially impressed by the remarkable attachment of slaves in Jamaica to music and music making.

They have good ears for music; and their songs, as they call them, are generally *impromptus*, without the least particle of poetry, or poetic images, of which they seem to have no idea. The tunes consist of a *solo* part, which we may style the recitative, the key of which is frequently varied; and this is accompanied with a full or general chorus. Some of them are not deficient in melody; although the tone of voice is, for the most part, rather flat and melancholy. Instead of choosing panegyric for their subject-matter, they generally prefer one of derision, and not unfrequently at the expence of the overseer, if he happens to be near, and listening: this only serves to add a poignancy to their satire, and heightens the fun. In the crop season, the mill-feeders entertain themselves very often with these *jeux d'esprit* in the nighttime; and this merriment helps to keep them awake.

Their *merry-wang* is a favourite instrument, a rustic guitar, of four strings. It is made with a calibash; a slice of which being taken off, a dried bladder, or skin, is spread across the largest section; and this is fastened to a handle, which they take great pains in ornamenting with a sort of rude carved work, and ribbands.

The *goombah*, another of their musical instruments, is a hollow block of wood, covered with sheep-skin stripped of its hair. The musician holds a little stick, of about six inches in length, sharpened at one end like the blade of a knife, in each hand. With one hand he rakes it over a notched piece of wood, fixed across the instrument, the whole length, and crosses with the other alternately, using both with a brisk motion; whilst a second performer beats with all his might on the sheep-skin, or tabor.

Their tunes for dancing are usually brisk, and have an agreeable compound of the *vivace* and *larghetto*, gay and grave, pursued alternately. They seem also well-adapted to keep their dancers in just time and regular movements. The female dancer is all languishing, and easy in her motions; the man, all action, fire, and gesture; his whole person is variously turned and writhed every moment, and his limbs agitated with such lively exertions, as serve to display before his partner the vigour and elasticity of his muscles. The lady keeps her face towards him, and puts on a modest demure look, which she counterfeits with great difficulty. In her paces she exhibits a wonderful address, particularly in the motion of her hips, and steady position of the upper part of her person: the right execution of this wriggle, keeping exact time with the music, is esteemed among them a particular excellence; and on this account they begin to practise it so early in life, that few are without it in their ordinary walking. As the dance proceeds, the musician introduces now and then a pause or rest, or dwells on two or three *pianissimo* notes; then strikes out again on a sudden into a more spirited air; the dancers, in the mean while, corresponding in their movements with a great correctness of ear, and propriety of attitude; all which has a very pleasing effect.[6]

No less elaborate were slave funerals, described here by Edward Long, again from Jamaica in 1774.

The Negroe funeral calls to mind the *late-wake* of the high-lands in Scotland, thus described by Mr Pennant. The evening after the death of any person, the relations and friends of the deceased meet at the house, attended by bag-pipe and fiddle. The nearest of kin, be it wife, son, or daughter, opens a melan-choly ball, dancing and greeting (*i.e.* crying violently) at the same time. This continues till day-light, but with such gambols and frolics among the younger part of the company, that the loss which occasioned them is often more than supplied by the consequences of that night. If the corpse remains unburied for two nights, the same rites are renewed. Thus, Scythian-like, they rejoice at the deliverance of their friends out of this life of misery. The *coranich*, or singing at funerals, is still in use in some places. The songs are generally in praise of the deceased, or a recital of the valiant deeds of him or his ancestors.[7]

Slaves created a remarkable social life for themselves from the meagre rewards they were able to scrape from the world around them. Most remark-able of all perhaps was their determination to secure the basics of literacy (a process hastened by the coming of Christianity). To be literate was to be able to engage in personal and collective struggles on terms which their white owners recognized. This letter from a Virginian slave to the Bishop of London in 1723 provides moving testimony to slave aspirations.

[first page]
A [cancellation]

August the forth 1723
to The Right ~~Righ~~ Raverrand father in god my Lord arch Bishop of Lonnd
this coms to sattesfie your honour that there is in this Land of verJennia a Sort of people that is Calld molatters which are Baptised and brouaht up in the way of the Christian faith ~~and~~

~~the~~ and followes the wayes and Rulles of the Chrch of England
and sum of them has white fathars and sum white mothers and
there is in this Land ~~a L~~ a Law or act which keeps and makes
them and there seed SLaves forever –

and most honoured sir a mongst the Rest of your Charitabell
acts and deed wee ~~humbly~~ your humbell and ~~pou~~ poore
partishinners doo begg Sir your aid and assisttance in this one
thing which Lise as I doo understand in your LordShips brest
which is that ~~yr honour~~ your honour will by the help of our
Suff~~er~~vering [i.e., sovereign] Lord King George and the Rest
of the Rullers will Releese us out of this Cruell Bondegg and
this wee beg for Jesus Christs his ~~of~~ Sake who has commaded
us to seeke first the kingdom of ~~god~~ god and all things shall
be addid ~~un~~ un to us

and here it is to bee noted that one brother is a SLave to
another and one Sister to an othe which is quite out of the
way and as for mee [cancellation] my selfe I am my brothers
SLave but my name is Secrett

and here it is to be notd againe that wee are commandded to
keep holey the Sabbath day and wee doo hardly know when
it comes for our [cancellation] task mastrs are has hard with us
as the Egypttions was with the Chilldann of Issarall god be
marcifll unto us

[second page]

here follows our ~~hard service~~ Sevarity and Sorrowfull Sarvice
we are hard used up on Every account ~~wee f~~ in the first place
wee are in Ignorance of our Salvation and in the next
place wee are kept out of the Church ~~and~~ and matrimony is
deenied us

and to be plain they doo Look no more up on us then if wee
ware dogs which I hope when these Strange Lines comes to
your Lord Ships hands will be Looket in to

and here wee beg for Jesus Christs his Sake that as your honour
do hope for the marcy of god att the day of death and the

Redemtion of our Savour Christ that when this comes to your
Lord Ships hands your honour wll Take Sum pitty of us who
is your humble butt Sorrowfull portitinors and Sir wee your
humble perticners do humblly beg the favour of your Lord
Ship that your honour will grant and Settell one thing upon
us which is that our ~~ch~~ childarn may be broatt up in the way
of the Christtian faith and our desire is that they may be Larnd
the Lords prayer the creed and the ten commandements and
that they may appeare Every Lord's day att Church before the
~~C~~ Curatt to bee Exammond for our desire is that godllines
Shoulld abbound amongs us and wee desire that our Childarn
be putt to Scool and and Larnd to Reed through the Bybell

[third page]
which is all att prasant with our prayers to god for itts good
Success
before your honour these from your humbell Servants in the
Lord
my Riting is vary bad I whope yr honour will take the will
for the deede
I am but a poore SLave ~~th~~ that writt itt and has no other ~~tinme~~
time butt Sunday and hardly that att Sumtimes

September the 8th 1723
To the Right Reverrand father in ~~d~~ god
my Lord arch bishop of J London
these with care
wee dare nott Subscribe any mans name to this for feare of
our masters ~~if~~ for if they knew that wee have Sent home to
your honour wee Should goo neare to Swing upon the gallass
tree[7]

*The slave community was both local and yet international. Slaves —
and freed blacks — criss-crossed the world of Atlantic slavery, carrying
with them news and gossip from one side of the Atlantic to the other.*

For example, news of the Somerset case in London in 1771–2, which revolved around the issue of black freedom in England, quickly passed to the slave quarters in Virginia. American slaves clearly believed that slavery had been abolished in England: the following account from the Virginia Gazette *tells of one who tried to secure his freedom by fleeing from Virginia to England.*

Augusta, June 18, 1774

Run away the 16th Instant, from the Subscriber, a Negro Man named BACCHUS, about 30 Years of Age, five Feet six or seven Inches high, strong and well made; had on, and took with him, two white *Russia* Drill Coats, one turned up with blue, the other quite plain and new, with white figured Metal Buttons, blue Plush Breeches, a fine Cloth Pompadour Waistcoat, two or three thin or Summer Jackets, sundry Pairs of white Thread Stockings, five or six white Shirts, two of them pretty fine, neat Shoes, Silver Buckles, a fine Hat cut and cocked in the Macaroni Figure, a double-milled Drab Great Coat, and sundry other Wearing Apparel. He formerly belonged to Doctor *George Pitt, of Williamsburg*, and I imagine is gone there under Pretence of my sending him upon Business, as I have frequently heretofore done; he is a cunning, artful, sensible Fellow, and very capable of forging a Tale to impose on the Unwary, is well acquainted with the lower Parts of the Country, having constantly rode with me for some Years past, and has been used to waiting from his Infancy. He was seen a few Days before he went off with a Purse of Dollars, and had just before changed a five Pound Bill; most, or all of which, I suppose he must have robbed me off, which he might easily have done, I having trusted him much after what I thought had proved his Fidelity. He will probably endeavour to pass for a Freeman by the Name of *John Christian*, and attempt to get on Board some Vessel bound for *Great Britain*, from the Knowledge he has of the late Determination of *Somerset's* Case. Whoever takes up the said Slave shall have 5 l. Reward, on his Delivery to GABRIEL JONES.[8]

10. Abolishing the Slave Trade

In the last quarter of the eighteenth century, the British slave trade thrived. In the 1780s alone, British (or British colonial) ships transported more than 300,000 Africans, though only 276,100 arrived. In the process, more than 1,000 slave ships cleared British and British colonial ports bound for the slave coasts of Africa. There is little evidence from the numbers the British slave trade generated (of ships, Africans transported), to say nothing of the obvious commercial optimism of its backers and activists, that here was a system with poor prospects, a system uncertain about its economic future. If anyone involved in slave trading felt that their commercial activities were doomed, they kept their worries secret. At every geographic and commercial point of the Atlantic slave trade, those most actively involved were confident of their business future. Shippers, merchants, financial backers, African middlemen, American planters and their agents all continued to act and to plan for the continuing commercial success of the Atlantic slave trade. Yet even as they did so, a small band of well-meaning people began to plot their downfall. And within twenty years, the British (and American) slave trade had been brought to an end. The founding fathers of abolition faced a daunting task, but even they could scarcely have imagined how relatively quickly success would come. Nor could they have imagined the far-reaching consequences that would flow from their planned attack on the Atlantic slave trade.

Quakers, especially American Quakers in Philadelphia, led the way from the mid-eighteenth century. They drew upon anti-slavery sentiment of an even older vintage. On both sides of the Atlantic, Quakers had edged towards open hostility to slavery and the slave trade from as early as the 1670s, when George Fox famously denounced it. Their collective doubts began to resurface in the 1750s and 1760s. At the same time, powerful mid-eighteenth-century criticisms of slavery began to appear in the works of Enlightenment writers in France, Scotland and North America. Such voices, however, were marginal and at first were largely ignored in the continuing rush to profit from what Anthony Benezet called 'the Negro Trade'. Most churches, for example, like most contemporary secular states, simply accepted slavery as an uncontested aspect of life.

Benezet was the key figure in abolition. A prominent Philadelphia Quaker, he was a friend and visitor to British Quakers, and he maintained a prolific correspondence with kindred spirits on both sides of the Atlantic. His tracts against the slave trade, dispatched throughout the English-speaking world, were designed to persuade others to confront the brutal realities of that trade and to recognize the immorality of western reliance on African slaves. He urged fellow Quakers to 'endeavour to keep their Hands clean of this Unrighteous Gain of Oppression'. Thanks to his personal and religious links throughout the American colonies and in London, Benezet's words quickly spilled out into a broader readership. John Wesley, for example, was prompted to draft his own *Thoughts upon Slavery* (1774) by his contact with Benezet, in the process swinging his own growing band of Methodists into the abolitionist camp. Similarly, Benjamin Franklin used Benezet's writing in the abolitionist articles he published in the London press in 1770–72. Benezet was in regular contact with Granville Sharp, the man who from the 1760s had focused attention on the legal and social state of black people in Britain. Discussing the best tactic they might use to secure black freedom, Sharp and Benezet agreed on the usefulness of sending petitions from the colonies to both Parliament and to the monarch. Although this debate was about colonial issues, the principle of petitioning (a well-oiled and accepted political convention) stuck in the minds of those early abolitionists. Years later, it was to become a vital element in recruiting abolitionist sentiment and a means of expressing public opinion to Parliament.

Benezet was at the centre of a widening literary debate and increasing pamphleteering about abolition in North America. Even slave holders (most notably Thomas Jefferson) turned against the slave trade, though it is true that North America no longer needed new Africans, thanks to the natural increase of the local slave population. Even before American Independence in 1776, the issue of slavery was firmly at the centre of political debate in North America. The breakaway of the northern colonies from British control helped to focus attention on the interlaced issues of the Atlantic slave trade and African slavery. The American War of Independence threw North American slavery into turmoil. Both sides (the British and the Americans) sought to rally slaves to their side. The British did this by offering freedom. Those slaves who joined what proved to be the losing side were eventually scattered – to Canada, Britain and eventually to Sierra Leone. It seems deeply ironic that America's founding fathers, the architects of independence and the framers of the modern democratic state, were insistent on maintaining slavery. This is not surprising, given that many (including Jefferson, Washington and Madison) were slave holders. One major hope of the small band of both British and American abolitionists – that slavery would be ended in North America – was dashed by the decision to accept slavery into the new United States of America. But in the very year, 1787, that slavery was incorporated into the new American state, London-based abolitionists began their own agitation against the slave trade.

The point of departure for the British campaign was the Somerset case in 1771–2, the core of which concerned the legality of slavery in England. That case stimulated a transatlantic correspondence about slavery in general. After 1776 the

American War of Independence helped to focus attention more
closely on the issue of the slave trade and slavery, and in the
course of that conflict the question of slavery, previously
marginal to political debate, shifted to the centre of the political stage. For its part, the American Republic instantly inherited
a string of difficult legal and moral issues about slavery. The
defeated British were equally soon caught up in an increasingly
fraught debate about the Atlantic slave trade.

The key figure in London was Granville Sharp, long-time
correspondent of Benezet and, since the 1760s, steadfast friend
of British blacks in their protracted struggle for legal and social
freedom. The English legal system had long wrestled with
conflicting legal principles about slavery in England, and local
blacks found themselves pawns in a legal/political debate in
which the West India lobby (of planters and merchants) wielded
great power and influence. Sharp, initially the sole defender of
English blacks, was indefatigable in mounting a number of legal
defences of blacks threatened by enforced repatriation from
England to the slave colonies. He also publicized the scarcely
believable details of the *Zong* case.

This was a story that was shocking even to a society generally unmoved by the widespread sufferings of Africans. Luke
Collingwood, captain of a Liverpool slave ship, the *Zong*, had
ordered 133 slaves to be thrown overboard in order to help the
survival of the rest, when the ship ran short of supplies towards
the end of its Atlantic voyage. Collingwood hoped to recoup
the loss of the murdered Africans as an insurance claim.
When the case (described in more detail in Chapter 6) surfaced
in an English court in 1783, it took the form of a legal debate
about an insurance claim. 'Though it shocks one very much,'
intoned the judge, Lord Chief Justice Mansfield, 'the case of
the slaves was the same as if horses or cattle had been thrown
overboard.'[1]

It was in that same year, 1783, that Quakers first petitioned
both Parliament and the American Continental Congress against

the slave trade, and Quakers in London decided to publish anti-slavery literature. This was the small beginnings of what was to become a remarkable Quaker outpouring of abolitionist literature. Over the next fifty years, millions of tracts and articles about the slave trade and slavery were published and distributed throughout the English-speaking world. From the shadow of the *Zong* affair, there emerged a massive and hugely successful propaganda campaign which managed, by providing facts and figures, and by mixing polemic and measured argument, to generate widespread public and parliamentary support, first against the slave trade and later against slavery itself.

British Quakers had a national organization at their disposal. Theirs was a well-run national machine with important links to North America. Quakers were literate, and prided themselves both on their culture and on their efficient business-like way of managing their affairs. They also had access to sympathetic writers and publishers scattered across the country. From 1783 onwards they began to place suitable abolitionist literature in local newspapers throughout Britain, selecting articles from the whole gamut of anti-slavery literature: work by Enlightenment authors, classic texts, legal commentary and contemporary journalism. All this was in addition to 'official' tracts approved by the central Quaker committee.

This show of objections to the slave trade denounced it for its inhumanity, its commercial inefficiencies, for its immorality and its offence to religious sensibilities. It was not simply a sectarian or a religious assault on the slave trade but a widely based humanitarian onslaught, which caught the public's attention.

In 1786 the campaign was joined by the man who was to prove the catalyst for the rallying of British feeling against the slave trade. Thomas Clarkson, a young graduate and newly appointed deacon, had won a prize at Cambridge for an essay, published in 1786 as *Essay on the Slavery and Commerce of the Human Species*. This essay helped to win over William Wilberforce,

a Yorkshire MP and rising political star, to the abolition cause
(and at the same time to Evangelicalism). The two men, Clarkson
and Wilberforce, agreed to collaborate on abolition, and the
Quakers agreed to publish Clarkson's essay. Thus was a key
pioneering partnership forged: Wilberforce the parliamentary
leader of abolition, and Clarkson the public propagandist and
indefatigable researcher, campaigning the length and breadth of
Britain – and both working with the invaluable help provided
by Quakers and their well-oiled national organization. In May
1787, a small group of men, dominated by Quakers but now
including Evangelical Anglicans, and reflecting a range of political interests, formed the Committee for the Abolition of the
Slave Trade (afterwards the Abolition Committee).

Declaring the slave trade to be 'both impolitick and unjust',
the committee planned to procure 'such Information and
Evidence, and for distributing Clarkson's Essay and such other
Publications, as may tend to the Abolition of the Slave Trade'.
From the first, the decision was made to concentrate not on
slavery but on the more manageable and practical political goal
of ending the Atlantic slave trade. The committee left the more
daunting target of abolishing colonial slavery to a later date:
Clarkson wrote, 'to aim at the removal of both would be to
aim at too much, and . . . by doing this we might lose all'. The
campaigners hoped that stopping the import of Africans would
force West Indian planters to treat their slaves better, for the
simple reason that they would no longer be able to replace lost
slaves by buying new Africans. Yet even this limited ambition
– of abolishing the slave trade – involved a monumental task.
Moreover, the campaign was launched at the very time that the
British slave trade was thriving.

British abolition began with a massive propaganda campaign,
through the dispatch of tens of thousands of tracts to friends
and sympathizers throughout Britain, using Quaker contacts
and networks. It was immediately apparent that abolition struck
a popular chord among armies of people, among all religious

groups and even more broadly, among people the abolitionists had not specifically targeted (notably women and working people). They also found supporters in the US, and even in France, though France, unlike Britain and the US, was never to develop a thoroughly 'popular' base to abolition.

Despite the presence of a black community in Britain, for the British, slavery was an alien and distant institution – notwithstanding the periodic local slave case in English courts. In North America, however, the debate about the slave trade and slavery took place cheek by jowl with slavery itself. Since the Atlantic slave trade to North America was no longer important for the US, the American debates were primarily about the principle of black freedom versus the changing economic demand for slave labour in different states. Most Americans, even slave holders, could agree about the Atlantic slave trade. But they were deeply divided about slavery itself, and the debate was to be utterly recast in the early years of the nineteenth century by the rapid expansion of slave-grown cotton across huge areas of the South. In Britain in the meantime, it was the Atlantic slave trade that remained the dominant political issue. Whereas in North America a single petition against the slave trade, from Pennsylvania, was delivered to the Constitutional Convention, in London, Parliament received more than 100 abolition petitions. By the early 1790s petitioning had rapidly established itself as the key method of marshalling British public opinion in any locality or institution and of directing abolitionist demands to Parliament.

The abolitionist campaign adopted certain iconic images which remain in the public memory to this day. Wedgwood's famous cameo plaque of a supplicant slave ('Am I not a man and a brother?') and the plan and cross-section of the slave ship *Brookes* (one of the few visual images stern Quakers allowed themselves as domestic wall decorations) joined thousands of tracts and essays in helping to saturate the country with abolitionist propaganda. Old publications (notably Benezet's) jostled for attention alongside new tracts written specially to capture and enhance the new abolitionist mood of the 1780s and 1790s. The Abolition Committee was also quick to draw on the experience of men who, though once involved in the slave trade, had now seen the abolitionist light and were anxious to lend their voice to the cause. John Newton, once a slaver, published *Thoughts upon the African Slave Trade*, and Alexander Falconbridge, formerly a doctor on a slave ship, issued his *Account of the Slave Trade* (both in 1788). Their ghastly first-hand accounts of the routine horrors on board the slave ships helped to dispel any lingering doubts any readers might have had about the brutal reality of the slave trade.

A string of Nonconformist churches added their voices to the abolitionist clamour. Even the King took notice, while remaining unsympathetic to abolition. Parliament was unable to resist the mounting abolitionist pressure. In May 1788, it considered, but postponed, a debate on the abolitionist petitions it had received. Such public pressure managed to bring about some important changes, however. Dolben's Act of 1788, for example, restricted the number of Africans allowed to be carried on to British slave ships (by specifying the maximum number of Africans per ton). It also stipulated that all slave ships should carry a doctor and offered financial incentives for lowering the death rate among transported Africans.

Through this welter of activity it was the abolitionist petitions that caught the eye and that provide the best evidence for the extraordinary popularity of the abolitionist cause between 1787 and 1792. In 1788, 102 petitions arrived at Parliament from across the country. Even more – 519 – descended on Westminster in 1792. Petitioning was a tactic that reached even dizzier heights in the later phases of the campaign against slavery itself, between 1824 and 1833. In fact, historians now accept that abolitionist petitions were the most striking form of public opinion in any political campaign between 1788 and 1838. The number of signatories to abolitionist petitions far outnumbered those on other petitions to Parliament. The 1787 Manchester petition, for example, attracted 10,700 signatures from a town of 50,000. A year later 60,000 names were attached to abolitionist petitions. A generation later the figures were even more impressive: the 1833 emancipationist petitions contained more signatures than either the petitions for parliamentary reform in 1831–2 or those for Catholic emancipation in 1829. Few doubted the integrity of the petitions, and the people most closely involved (abolitionists, MPs and government ministers) simply accepted that they were a genuine expression of public opinion on the matter.

The abolition movement was soon renowned for the size and enthusiasm of its public meetings. Although abolition began life as a small caucus (a committee of Quakers and sympathizers), it soon attracted a much broader constituency. Local abolitionist committees proliferated across Britain, each in their turn convening public meetings. These were often simply an opportunity to listen to a visiting abolitionist speaker, the lecture normally being followed by the signing of an abolitionist petition. Abolition attracted unprecedented numbers of very large crowds. Thomas Clarkson led the way, travelling 35,000 miles around Britain between 1787 and 1794, lecturing and agitating wherever he went, normally to packed audiences, and establishing a punishing routine which characterized the activities of abolitionists until full emancipation in 1838. Speaking in a church in Manchester in 1787, Clarkson noted, 'When I went into the church it was so crowded that I could scarcely get to my place.'[2] The abolitionists viewed the lecture audience, the sympathetic crowd, the attentive listener, as a basic element of their tactics and of their success. After 1793, however, the use of the public meeting was a tactic which incurred growing hostility from an increasingly worried propertied society.

The first rush of abolitionist enthusiasm was soon checked by the fear of revolution. By 1792, the French Revolution had lurched into violent extremism, the slave upheaval in Haiti was threatening instability throughout the Caribbean, and British radical societies were expressing open sympathy for French revolutionary ideals. At this point, public meetings of any kind began to worry the government and its propertied supporters. What had been tolerable in the 1780s as a simple gathering of people to express abolitionist support (the coming together of friends of abolition in large meetings) was now viewed as yet another aspect of encroaching French influence, 'Jacobinism'. Even the mild-mannered Wilberforce found himself damned as a Jacobin. Throughout the rest of the 1790s, the abolitionist movement was tarred with a Jacobinical brush. By the time war broke out with France in 1793, public politics in Britain had become increasingly suspect. On the one hand, popular radical societies, led by the London Corresponding Society (LCS), had embraced abolition as one aspect of their demands for the rights of man. On the other, their opponents viewed abolition with growing suspicion for precisely the same reasons. Thomas Hardy, founder of the LCS, asserted that the rights of man 'are not confined to this small island, but are extended to the whole human race, black and white, high or low, rich or poor.'[3]

From the first, abolition was a highly literate movement which aimed at a popular readership. The founding London Abolition Committee set out to publish abolitionist literature 'as may tend to the Abolition of the Slave Trade'.[4] Though spreading propagandist literature was a well-established English radical tradition, abolition pushed it to new levels of participation. In the first year alone, more than £10,000 was spent on publishing and distributing literature. Fifteen thousand copies of Clarkson's first tract were published. Poems, letters to the press, articles and essays in local newspapers, in London's major periodicals all provided a means of giving voice and coverage to the campaign against the slave trade. Abolitionist writers were, naturally, challenged at every step of the way by the powerful West India lobby, itself able to recruit writers, planters and other West Indians to contest abolitionist claims.

But abolition had the advantage that its printed, literate campaign to end the slave trade ran parallel with large public gatherings. The advancing of the case through the spoken word and the creation of thousands of abolitionist petitions was a combination of tactics which the West India slave lobby simply could not match.

Abolition was also very unusual in attracting sizeable and important female support. Indeed, female abolitionists became a major constituency in the broader campaign. They lent their numbers and collective voice to the cause, and brought a distinctive agitation and role to it locally and nationally. Of course there had been a rich (though often overlooked) female literature prior to the rise of the abolitionist movement in 1787. There was also an established tradition, stretching back to the seventeenth century, of women petitioning Parliament. Abolition, however, had created an utterly new political cause which quickly attracted large numbers of women, who placed themselves at its centre, particularly within the petitioning campaign. In addition, a number of female writers (most famously Hannah More, whose 'Slavery, A Poem' was hurriedly written in 1787) picked up their pens in the abolitionist cause, helping to catch the abolitionist mood and to pressure Parliament on the issue. Female support was to make itself felt most dramatically in the abolitionist campaigns of the 1820s and 1830s.

The man who came to personify the abolition campaign, and who to this day is best remembered for the campaign against slavery, is of course William Wilberforce. From first to last, for almost half a century, he was the central parliamentary figure who wooed fellow MPs, peers, ministers and officials. But the public campaign – the popular agitation in the country at large – was inspired and led by Thomas Clarkson, abolition's indefatigable foot soldier: lecturer, traveller and researcher. Clarkson was the man who helped to transform the public's vague and general sense that there was something wrong with the Atlantic slave trade into a powerful and focused national voice of widespread and strident opposition. Clarkson stirred up, and then channelled, this voice.

Parliament's debate on the abolition petitions formally began in May 1789. Wilberforce's speech, presenting his now-famous twelve abolitionist propositions, lasted for three and a half hours. A mountain of evidence and a queue of witnesses ensured that the debate was protracted over two whole years. Abolitionists rallied every conceivable influential group to their side. Poets, scientists churchmen, local Africans and social critics all argued against each and every aspect of the slave trade, which was, by turns, denounced as immoral, unchristian and even uneconomic.

Wilberforce's early parliamentary efforts were defeated in 1791, stimulating further, renewed abolitionist efforts. In 1792 his abolitionist proposals passed through the Commons by 230 to 85 votes, only for the bill to be rebuffed in the Lords (where West India interests exercised great influence). By then, however, external events had begun to play a role. The pro-slave trade lobby found its case strengthened by events in the French slave colony of St Domingue (Haiti), the most prized French possession in the West Indies. St Domingue was a commercial threat to the British islands because as a new settlement it could produce better and cheaper tropical staples. But it was also a political and racial powder keg, more volatile than any other slave island in the region. Sugar and coffee from St Domingue helped to swell the coffers of merchants in Bordeaux and Nantes, but their prosperity was bought at the cost of great suffering among the brutalized ranks of African slaves, a large proportion of whom were recent imports. The revolutionary turmoil of 1789 and the impact of revolutionary ideals (notably the concept of 'the rights of man') struck a sympathetic chord with the slaves in St Domingue and sparked an explosion. Violence between black and white, between enslaved and free, and between colonial and imperial laid waste to the slave-based economy and its social infrastructure. The consequent collapse of French control also tempted the British (and the Spanish, who occupied the other half of that mountainous island) to invade, seize possession and make it their own. It was a disastrous miscalculation that cost the British unprecedented military losses (mainly through disease).

The British invasion of St Domingue was of course part of the broader conflict against revolutionary France after 1793, but it also had unforeseen consequences for the British campaign against the slave trade. Planters had simply to point to the violence in St Domingue, and to the destruction of the Haitian sugar economy, as evidence of everything they had been warning against; they had long said that freedom for slaves would bring only anarchy and bloodshed. Fear of contagion of revolution from Haiti swept through the Americas, as refugees, black and white, free and enslaved, fled from Haiti to neighbouring islands, Louisiana and South Carolina. The British Prime Minister, William Pitt, formerly a stout supporter of Wilberforce, now sided with the planters against the slaves.

Slave revolts erupted across the Caribbean in the 1790s, in Grenada, St Vincent, St Lucia, Jamaica. The French Revolution and revolutionary wars, and, above all else, the Haitian slave revolt, suggested to many that now was a bad time to discuss any sort of major change in the Atlantic slave system. The turmoil in Haiti, and the terrible loss of British military life there, hardened the hearts of many in Britain against slaves everywhere, and against abolitionists who spoke up for them. British abolitionists took comfort from the fact that in 1794 the French Convention outlawed slavery throughout French colonies and extended French citizenship to all men irrespective of colour. Their opponents, however, took a different view: such acts seemed to be precursors of further violence and destruction.

In this increasingly hostile climate, British abolitionists continued to campaign against the slave trade. They made effective use of boycotts of slave-grown sugar, in which women, again, played a prominent role, as they continued to do in the petitioning campaigns. But after 1793 abolition was clearly on the back foot, forced into a defensive posture by events in the Caribbean, and by political alarm in Britain, expressed in Parliament and by London's vocal West India lobby, that abolition of the slave trade involved a dangerous tampering with the wider slave system that could only lead to disasters on the Haitian model.

The continuing abolitonist debate managed to produce some positive results, including proposals for the better supervision and treatment of slaves in the colonies, and demands that they should have access to formal Christianity and education. These ideas were best and most comprehensively expressed by Edmund Burke, who, despite his fierce opposition to the French Revolution, drafted a comprehensive and enlightened *Sketch of a Negro Code* (1792). Burke's ideas had been greatly influenced by Montesquieu, whose work Burke had translated, and were clearly designed as a step towards full slave emancipation. But it is also revealing that even a man of the harshest anti-revolutionary persuasion had been won over to the slaves' cause, despite hostile political circumstances.

Parliament, however, continued (between 1794 and 1799) to reject Wilberforce's annual motions against the slave trade. By the mid-1790s, some leading abolitionists had begun to despair of ever persuading Parliament to abolish the slave trade. For a start, the war and domestic social unrest (hunger, for example, was widespread in 1795) made abolition seem distant and unimportant. In the mid- and late 1790s, even the most dedicated abolitionists found it difficult to maintain their spirits and their activities. To add to their woes, and despite their apparent lack of progress, abolitionists continued to have damaging accusations thrown at them. They were accused, for example, of fermenting slave rebellion, a charge notably levelled by Bryan Edwards, a prominent planter and campaigner, in *A History of Santo Domingo*. Wilberforce's dogged parliamentary pursuit of abolition was denounced because it could lead to Caribbean slave insurrection. In the words of Bryan Edwards, slaves would

> Murder their masters, and plant the tree of
> Liberty on their graves . . .[5]

Abolition simply could not shake off the stigma of Haiti. When an abolition motion failed in Parliament, again, in 1798 (by 83 to 87 votes), Wilberforce resolved not to press on until the climate had improved.

At the turn of the century, with the nation locked into the interminable French war, and with social distress on all sides, the abolitionist cause faltered. Even the normally resolute Quakers were distracted (by internal wrangles within the Society of Friends). Radical politics in general simply withered in the face of hostile government legislation and intimidation. But the short break in the war (confirmed by the Peace of Amiens in 1802) was soon followed by renewed hostilities, this time against a Napoleonic France that had reintroduced slavery into the French colonies (1802). In February 1804 Wilberforce promised once again to bring his motion for the abolition of the slave trade before Parliament. The old faces, organizations and well-tried tactics quickly resurfaced and reasserted themselves in Parliament and in public. Yet again, abolitionists bombarded the public with facts and figures, arguments and accusations about the slave trade, through a revived proliferation of tracts and pamphlets. Despite overwhelming support for abolition in the Commons, the Lords remained as obstructive as ever. Now the whole campaign was driven forward by Wilberforce's Evangelical friends in the Clapham Sect. Clarkson, once again traversing the country as he had in the 1790s, reported general support for the cause wherever he spoke. Everywhere he visited, he found a revival of local abolitionist committees.

Six months before his death in January 1806, Pitt agreed to ban the slave trade in newly captured territories (by then, trade to those territories accounted for a substantial share of the total British slave trade). It was Pitt's death, however, and the return of the Fox–Grenville government, that paved the way for complete abolition: Clarkson wrote in a letter, 'We have many more Friends to Abolition in the Cabinet than under the Old Administration.'[6]

Abolition moved quickly through Parliament, now presented as a government measure, and in May 1806 the Foreign Slave Trade Act was passed. A month later Fox gave notice that he would bring a resolution for the final abolition of the slave trade. Appropriating the language of the abolitionist pioneers, and paying fitting tribute to his late opponent, William Pitt, he proposed: 'That this House, conceiving the African Slave Trade to be contrary to the principles of justice, humanity, and sound policy, will, with all practicable expedition, proceed to take effectual measures for abolishing the said trade.'

Abolition was now guaranteed, even after Fox's own death in September 1806. At the resulting general election, abolition was a major issue, with newspaper coverage and local constituency pressures all forcing the pace of abolition. MPs across the country were obliged to state to their constituents their support for, or opposition to, abolition. Though the new Grenville administration had only a small minority, an Abolition Act was presented in the New Year 1807, quickly passing through the Lords. Opponents complained of the strident public campaign against the slave trade (and against its supporters). 'Every measure that invention or artifice could devise to create a popular clamour was resorted to on this occasion. The Church, the theatre, and the press, had laboured to create a prejudice against the Slave Trade.'[7]

The public mood had clearly changed once again, and many of the new (and younger) MPs spoke out against the slave trade, many of them having promised their constituents that they would support abolition if returned to Parliament. In the event, the Commons voted by 283 to 16 that the slave trade was 'Contrary to the principles of humanity, justice and sound policy', and ought therefore to be abolished. This grand-sounding prologue was greatly revised in the Act itself, but in March 1807 the Bill had passed all its parliamentary stages and received royal assent. The British had abolished the slave trade.

To this day, however, a great deal of mystery and speculation remains about precisely why they had done so. They had, after all, abolished a form of trade that had gone virtually unchallenged for almost two centuries, which continued to profit large numbers of people and which had made possible the development of critical areas of European settlement in the tropical Americas. That it was ended, so quickly, so comprehensively and to such public acclaim remains a historical curiosity. Had it become unprofitable, even though those people most actively involved wished to continue with the trade? Had the British people changed: had they developed a previously unknown sensibility about the slave trade and its inherent cruelties? Was it largely (or simply) the work of Wilberforce and Clarkson and their unrelenting agitation? Or was it – and this more likely – a complexity of all these and more? And what role had the slaves played in this transformation – notably those involved in the insurrection in Haiti? It is difficult to offer a satisfactory answer. And in any case, in 1807 the campaign was only half-finished. The slave trade was ended. But slavery itself survived.

The complex legal and intellectual debate about slavery which subsequently merged into the abolitionist movement first effectively appeared, in England, in the 1760s. The initial campaign was concerned with slavery in England and was led with unflagging energy and persistence by Granville Sharp. Sharp had been shocked in 1765 when he encountered the brutalization of a black slave in London and thereafter he launched what was initially a one-man campaign against slave holding in England. His first major (and influential) published attack was his Representation of the Injustice and Dangerous Tendancy

of Admitting the Least Claims of Private Property in the Persons
of Men in England, *in 1769. This extract illustrates his much-repeated
emphasis on the essential humanity of the enslaved, a view which
clashed, of course, with the slave lobby's attachment to the idea of the
slave as property.*

Thus it must appear, that the plea of *private property* in a Negro,
as in *a horse or a dog*, is very insufficient and defective. But I
will now shew, that the comparing of a man to a beast, at any
rate, is unnatural and unjust; as well as the seizing, and detain-
ing him as such, is dangerous to the pretended proprietors. For
they cannot be justified, unless they shall be able to prove, that
a Negro Slave is neither man, woman nor child: and if they are
not able to do this, how can they presume to consider such a
person as a mere *'chose in action'*? or *thing* to be demanded in
action?

The Negro must be divested of his humanity, and rendered
incapable of the King's protection, before such an action can
lawfully take place.

But how is he to be divested of his *human nature?* or of his
just right to the King's protection?

A man may, indeed, be said to be divested of his *humanity*,
1st, in a moral sense, by his own action, in stooping to any kind
of baseness beneath the dignity of a *man*. And 2dly, By the
execution of the laws, in punishment of some particular kinds
of baseness, for which a man may *lawfully* be divested of his
humanity by a *civil death:* that is; may be *'disabled to hold any
office or franchise, &c.' 'as if such person was naturally dead'*. This is
one of the penalties expressed in a Statute (2 Geo. II. ch. 24).
against bribery and corruption in Parliamentary Elections,
whereby, not less the *Briber* than the *Bribed*, (whether the offence
be committed *'by himself, or any person employed by him'*) is
subjected to the divesture abovementioned. But the vilest and
most ignorant Negro Slaves are not so *inhumanly* base and
degenerate as these Time-servers, who offend against God! the

thoughtful of those people, that we look upon them as a lower race, not worthy of the same care, nor liable to the same rewards and punishments as ourselves. Nevertheless it may with truth be said, that both amongst those who have obtained their freedom, and those who remain in servitude, some have manifested a strong sagacity and an exemplary uprightness of heart. If this hath not been generally the case with them is it a matter of surprise? Have we not reason to make the same complaint of many white servants, when discharged from our service, though many of them have had much greater opportunities of knowledge and improvement than the blacks; who, even when free, labour under the same difficulties as before: having but little access to, and intercourse with, the most reputable white people, they remain confined within their former limits of conversation. And if they seldom complain of the unjust and cruel usage they have received, in being forced from their native country, &c. it is not to be wondered at; it being a considerable time after their arrival amongst us, before they can speak our language; and, by the time they are able to express themselves, they have great reason to believe, that little or no notice would be taken of their complaints: yet let any person inquire of those who are capable of reflection, before they were brought from their native land, and he will hear such affecting relations, as, if not lost to the common feelings of humanity, will sensibly affect his heart. The case of a poor Negroe, not long since brought from Guinea, is a recent instance of this kind. From his first arrival, he appeared thoughtful and dejected, frequently dropping tears when taking notice of his master's children, the cause of which was not known till he was able to speak English, when the account he gave of himself was, 'That he had a wife and children in his own country; that some of these being sick and thirsty, he went in the night time to fetch water at a spring, where he was violently seized and carried away by persons who lay in wait to catch men, from whence he was transported to America. The remembrance of his family, friends, and other connexions, left behind, which he never expected to see any more, were the principal cause of his dejection and grief.' . . . And doubtless the case of many, very many of these afflicted people, upon inquiry, would be found to be attended with circumstances equally tragical and aggravating. And if we inquire of those Negroes, who were brought away from their native country when children, we shall find most of them to have been stolen away, when abroad from their parents on the roads, in the woods, or watching their cornfields. Now, you that have studied the book of conscience, and you that are learned in the law, what will you say to such deplorable cases? When, and how, have these oppressed people forfeited their liberty? Does not justice loudly call for its being restored to them? Have they not the same right to demand it, as any of us should have, if we have been violently snatched by pirates from our native land? Is it not the duty of every dispenser of justice, who is not forgetful of his own humanity, to remember that these are men, and to declare them free? Where instances of such cruelty frequently occur, and are neither inquired into, nor redressed, by those whose duty it is, *to seek judgment, and relieve the oppressed*, Isaiah i. 17. what can be expected, but that the groans and cries of these sufferers will reach Heaven, and what shall we do *when* God *riseth up? And when he visiteth*, what will ye answer him? *Did not he that made them, make us; and did not one fashion us in the womb?* Job xxxi. 14.[9]

These initial attacks on slavery were largely inspired by a sense of moral and religious outrage. But there was also an early economic critique, most notably, and best remembered, by Adam Smith's argument of 1776 that slavery, far from being cheap, was actually the most costly form of labour.

If little improvement was to be expected from such great proprietors, still less was to be hoped for from those who occupied

the land under them. In the ancient state of Europe, the occu-
piers of land were all tenants at will. They were all or almost
all slaves; but their slavery was of a milder kind than that known
among the ancient Greeks and Romans, or even in our West
Indian colonies. They were supposed to belong more directly
to the land than to their master. They could, therefore, be sold
with it, but not separately. They could marry, provided it was
with the consent of their master; and he could not afterwards
dissolve the marriage by selling the man and wife to different
persons. If he maimed or murdered any of them, he was liable
to some penalty, though generally but to a small one. They were
not, however, capable of acquiring property. Whatever they
acquired was acquired to their master, and he could take it from
them at pleasure. Whatever cultivation and improvement could
be carried on by means of such slaves was properly carried on
by their master. It was at his expense. The seed, the cattle, and
the instruments of husbandry were all his. It was for his benefit.
Such slaves could acquire nothing but their daily maintenance.
It was properly the proprietor himself, therefore, that, in this
case, occupied his own lands, and cultivated them by his own
bondmen. This species of slavery still subsists in Russia, Poland,
Hungary, Bohemia, Moravia, and other parts of Germany. It is
only in the western and south-western provinces of Europe
that it has gradually been abolished altogether.

But if great improvements are seldom to be expected from
great proprietors, they are least of all to be expected when they
employ slaves for their workmen. The experience of all ages
and nations, I believe, demonstrates that the work done by
slaves, though it appears to cost only their maintenance, is in
the end the dearest of any. A person who can acquire no property, can have no other interest but to eat as much, and to
labour as little as possible. Whatever work he does beyond what
is sufficient to purchase his own maintenance can be squeezed
out of him by violence only, and not by any interest of his
own . . . [10]

The early stirrings of British conscience about the slave trade and slavery were prompted in part by the issue of slavery in English courts. Legal cases, culminating in the 1772 Somerset case, often contained examples of outrageous cruelties, not on slave ships but in England. At the same time, a small band of black writers began to remind their British readers of the broader problems posed by slavery. Most famous of all, perhaps, are the letters of Ignatius Sancho, most dispatched from his grocer's shops in Westminster to a number of prominent contemporaries and friends. Sancho's celebrity, as a former slave who by good fortune and hard work turned himself into an educated man of sensibility, was confirmed by the publication of his letters in 1782 and by his portrait, painted by Gainsborough. Today, scholars recognize Sancho's writing as an important contribution to the emerging unease about Britain's slave empire. His letters – and life – also confirmed the potential of and possibilities for Africans once they were freed from the punitive restraints of slavery. In this letter of 1778 he attacks the British Empire.

I am sorry to observe that the practice of your country (which as a resident I love – and for its freedom – and for the many blessings I enjoy in it – shall ever have my warmest wishes – prayers – and blessings); I say it is with reluctance, that I must observe your country's conduct has been uniformly wicked in the East – West-Indies – and even on the coast of Guinea. – The grand object of English navigators – indeed of all christian navigators – is money – money – money – for which I do not pretend to blame them – Commerce was meant by the goodness of the Deity to diffuse the various goods of the earth into every part – to unite mankind in the blessed chains of brotherly love – society – and mutual dependence: – the enlightened Christian should diffuse the riches of the Gospel of peace – with the commodities of his respective land – Commerce attended with strict honesty – and with Religion for its companion – would be a blessing to every shore it touched at. – In Africa, the poor wretched natives – blessed with the most fertile

and luxuriant soil – are rendered so much the more miserable
for what Providence meant as a blessing: – the Christians' abom-
inable traffic for slaves – and the horrid cruelty and treachery
of the petty Kings – encouraged by their Christian customers
– who carry them strong liquors – to enflame their national
madness – and powder – and bad fire-arms – to furnish them
with the hellish means of killing and kidnapping. – But enough
– it is a subject that sours my blood – and I am sure will not
please the friendly bent of your social affections. – I mentioned
these only to guard my friend against being too hasty in
condemning the knavery of a people who bad as they may be
– possibly – were made worse – by their Christian visitors. –
Make human nature thy study – wherever thou residest – whatever the religion – or the complexion – study their hearts. –
Simplicity, kindness, and charity be thy guide – with these even
Savages will respect you – and God will bless you![11]

*A more direct attack on slavery came from the pen of Ottobah Cugoano.
Born in Ghana, c.1757, and enslaved around 1770, he had toiled in
the Caribbean before being brought to England as a servant. Also
known as John Stewart/Stuart, by the late 1780s Cugoano was a free
man working for Richard Cosway, the fashionable court painter.
Cugoano was active in the small band of London-based Africans who
began to agitate against the slave trade in the mid-1780s. A friend of
Olandan Equiano, a more famous contemporary African in London,
Cugoano was clearly influenced in his writing by a number of contemporary abolitionist writers, and there are signs that Equiano had a hand
in revising or editing his pamphlet* Thoughts and Sentiments on
the Evil and Wicked Traffic of the Slavery and Commerce of
the Human Species *(1787). This formed a more severe assault on
slavery than Sancho's earlier criticism and pointed the way to the abolitionists' demands for a total cessation of Atlantic slave trading. Here
Cugoano describes his experience of being loaded on to a slave ship
and transported to Grenada.*

But when a vessel arrived to conduct us away to the ship, it was a most horrible scene; there was nothing to be heard but rattling of chains, smacking of whips, and the groans and cries of our fellow-men. Some would not stir from the ground, when they were lashed and beat in the most horrible manner. I have forgot the name of this infernal fort; but we were taken in the ship that came for us, to another that was ready to sail from Cape Coast. When we were put into the ship, we saw several black merchants coming on board, but we were all drove into our holes, and not suffered to speak to any of them. In this situation we continued several days in sight of our native land; but I could find no good person to give any information of my situation to Accasa at Agimaque. And when we found ourselves at last taken away, death was more preferable than life, and a plan was concerted amongst us, that we might burn and blow up the ship, and to perish all together in the flames; but we were betrayed by one of our own countrywomen, who slept with some of the head men of the ship, for it was common for the dirty filthy sailors to take the African women and lie upon their bodies; but the men were chained and pent up in holes. It was the women and boys which were to burn the ship, with the approbation and groans of the rest; though that was prevented, the discovery was likewise a cruel bloody scene.

But it would be needless to give a description of all the horrible scenes which we saw, and the base treatment which we met with in this dreadful captive situation, as the similar cases of thousands, which suffer by this infernal traffic, are well known. Let it suffice to say, that I was thus lost to my dear indulgent parents and relations, and they to me. All my help was cries and tears, and these could not avail; nor suffered long, till one succeeding woe, and dread, swelled up another. Brought from a state of innocence and freedom, and, in a barbarous and cruel manner, conveyed to a state of horror and slavery: This abandoned situation may be easier conceived than described.

From the time that I was kidnapped and conducted to a factory, and from thence in the brutish, base, but fashionable way of traffic, consigned to Grenada, the grievous thoughts which I then felt, still pant in my heart; though my fears and tears have long since subsided. And yet it is still grievous to think that thousands more have suffered in similar and greater distress, under the hands of barbarous robbers, and merciless task-masters; and that many even now are suffering in all the extreme bitterness of grief and woe, that no language can describe. The cries of some, and the sight of their misery, may be seen and heard afar; but the deep sounding groans of thousands, and the great sadness of their misery and woe, under the heavy load of oppressions and calamities inflicted upon them, are such as can only be distinctly known to the ears of Jehovah Sabaoth.[12]

In 1787 a small band of ex-slaves met together in London to work against the slave trade. They were anxious to promote the arguments for abolition and were clearly part of the broader groundswell of abolition generated by the initial formation of the Abolition Committee. But they were very different from other abolitionists, not least for having emerged as free men from the agonies of slavery. As such, their voice carried conviction. They were also conscious of the debt they owed Granville Sharp – the man who had carried the abolitionist torch longer than most, and who had campaigned fiercely (and often alone) on behalf of distressed blacks in England. Calling themselves 'The Sons of Africa', in 1787 they drafted this petition of thanks to Granville Sharp for his work.

Honourable and Worthy Sir,　　　　　　　December 15, 1787.
　　Give us leave to say, that every virtuous man is a truly honourable man; and he that doth good hath honour to himself: and many blessings are upon the head of the just, and their memory shall be blessed, and their works praise them in the gate.
　　And we must say, that we, who are a part, or descendants,

of the much-wronged people of Africa, are peculiarly and greatly indebted to you, for the many good and friendly services that you have done towards us, and which are now even out of our power to enumerate.

Nevertheless, we are truly sensible of your great kindness and humanity; and we cannot do otherwise but endeavour, with the utmost sincerity and thankfulness, to acknowledge our great obligations to you, and, with the most feeling sense of our hearts, on all occasions to express and manifest our gratitude and love for your long, valuable, and indefatigable labours and benevolence towards using every means to rescue our suffering brethren in slavery.

Your writings, Sir, are not of trivial matters, but of great and essential things of moral and religious importance, worthy the regard of all men; and abound with many great and precious things, of sacred writ, particularly respecting the laws of God, and the duties of men.

Therefore, we wish, for ourselves and others, that these valuable treatises may be collected and preserved, for the benefit and good of all men, and for an enduring memorial of the great learning, piety, and vigilance of our good friend the worthy Author. And we wish that the laws of God, and his ways of righteousness set forth therein, may be as a path for the virtuous and prudent to walk in, and as a clear shining light to the wise in all ages; and that these and other writings of that nature, may be preserved and established as a monument or beacon to guide or to warn men, lest they should depart from the paths of justice and humanity; and that they may more and more become means of curbing the vicious violators of God's holy law, and to restrain the avaricious invaders of the rights and liberties of men, whilever the human race inhabits this earth below.

And, ever honourable and worthy Sir, may the blessing and peace of Almighty God be with you, and long preserve your valuable life, and make you abundantly useful in every good word and work! And when God's appointed time shall come, may your exit be blessed, and may you arise and for ever shine in the glorious world above, when that Sovereign Voice, speaking with joy, as the sound of many waters, shall be heard, saying, 'Well done, thou good and faithful servant: enter thou into the joy of thy Lord!' It will then be the sweetest of all delights for ever, and more melodious than all music! And such honour and felicity will the blessed God and Saviour of his people bestow upon all the saints and faithful servants who are redeemed from among men, and saved from sin, slavery, misery, pain, and death, and from eternal dishonour and wrath depending upon the heads of all the wicked and rebellious.

And now, honourable Sir, with the greatest submission, we must beg you to accept this memorial of our thanks for your good and faithful services towards us, and for your humane commiseration of our brethren and countrymen unlawfully held in slavery.

And we have hereunto subscribed a few of our names, as a mark of our gratitude and love. And we are, with the greatest esteem and veneration, honourable and worthy, Sir, your most obliged and most devoted humble servants.

OTTOBAH CUGOANO.	JASPER GOREE.
JOHN STUART.	GUSTAVUS VASA.
GEORGE ROBERT MANDEVILLE.	JAMES BAILEY.[13]

These disparate voices against slavery came together in 1787 in the form of a Committee for the Abolition of the Slave Trade. Appropriately, its inspiration was largely Quaker, and Quakers dominated the first committee. The formation of the committee is described here by Thomas Clarkson, in an account written twenty years later.

While such conversation was passing, and when all appeared to be interested in the cause, Mr Langton put the question, about the proposal of which I had been so diffident, to Mr Wilberforce, in the shape of a delicate compliment. The latter replied, that he had no objection to bring forward the measure in parliament, when he was better prepared for it, and provided no person more proper could be found. Upon this, Mr Hawkins Browne and Mr Windham both said they would support him there. Before I left the company, I took Mr Wilberforce aside, and asked him if I might mention this his resolution to those of my friends in the city, of whom he had often heard me speak, as desirous of aiding him by becoming a committee for the purpose. He replied, I might. I then asked Mr Langton, privately, if he had any objection to belong to a society of which there might be a committee for the abolition of the Slave-trade. He said he should be pleased to become a member of it. Having received these satisfactory answers, I returned home.

The next day, having peviously [sic] taken down the substance of the conversation at the dinner, I went to James Phillips, and desired that our friends might be called together as soon as they conveniently could, to hear my report. In the interim I wrote to Dr Peckard, and waited upon lord Scarsdale, Dr Baker, and others, to know (supposing a society were formed for the abolition of the Slave-trade) if I might say they would belong to it? All of them replied in the affirmative, and desired me to represent them, if there should be any meeting for this purpose.

At the time appointed, I met my friends. I read over the substance of the conversation which had taken place at Mr Langton's. No difficulty occurred. All were unanimous for the formation of a committee. On the next day we met by agreement for this purpose. It was then resolved unanimously, among other things, That the Slave-trade was both impolitic and unjust. It was resolved also, That the following persons be a committee for procuring such information and evidence, and publishing the same, as may tend to the abolition of the Slave-trade, and for directing the application of such moneys as have been already, and may hereafter be collected for the above purpose.

Granville Sharp	Thomas Clarkson
William Dillwyn	Richard Phillips
Samuel Hoare	John Barton
George Harrison	Joseph Hooper
John Lloyd	James Phillips
Joseph Woods	Philip Sansom

All these were present . . . on the twenty-second of May, 1787 . . . After the formation of the committee, notice was sent to Mr Wilberforce of the event, and a friendship began, which has continued uninterruptedly between them, from that to the present day.[14]

At the same time, and under pressure from the pioneering abolitionists, ministers also turned their attention to the slave trade. By 1788, even the Prime Minister, William Pitt, was persuaded of the principle of abolition (even though in the event politics, war and revolution were to alter his attachment to it), as is clear from this extract from a letter from him to Lord Hawkesbury of 30 January 1788.

The subject of the papers enclosed in your letter which I have just received is one on which I shall be very glad to converse with your Lordship. The stopping a practice which has subsisted so long as the slave trade, and which is connected with so many other objects, may certainly lead to very serious consequences; and if the measure should take place, it will be a very serious and anxious part of our duty to endeavour to diminish the inconvenience. I own however that whatever that inconvenience might be, I am at a loss to find arguments which can justify the admitting such a plea against the measure itself. I will not trouble you by going into more particulars till we have an opportunity of talking over the subject, which I wish to do very fully before it is discussed.[15]

After 1787 the abolition campaign proceeded on two fronts. In Parliament Wilberforce rallied support and led the (virtually annual) debate for abolition, while in the country at large Thomas Clarkson drummed up public support. Clarkson explains his advocacy of the ending of the slave trade in this passage from his tract of 1788, An Essay on the Impolicy of the African Slave Trade.

If the slave trade were abolished, it is evident that many mild and salutary regulations would immediately take place; that the slave would be better fed; that his hours of labour would be reduced to fewer in the day; that his person would be more secure; that he would have the power of appeal; and that every spur, that could promote population, would be administered. These then, or similar regulations, unavoidably taking place, we should see a material change in his situation. We should see him in possession of a little time to himself, and devoting it either to his own amusement, or in the improvement of his little spot, to his future advantage and support. We should see him, not chilled with horror at the sight of his proprietor as before, but smiling with gratitude and joy. We should see him *legally* engaging in the bands of connubial happiness; while his wife would have time to nurse and enjoy her child, not regretting that she had brought it into the world to inherit a life of perpetual misery and woe, but to be a witness of her new situation, and to share the change. Thus experiencing, on one hand, a diminution of their former rigours, and raised to positive advantages on the other, they would both *immediately* be admitted to a certain portion of *happiness*, and their condition be considerably *improved*.

This change having once taken place, and great benefit having necessarily arisen to the planter from the adoption of it, there can be no difficulty in anticipating the *future* situation of the slave; for it is natural to suppose, that if advantages should have been found to accrue to the planter in proportion to his humanity, he would still proceed; and when that system, which was the consequence of the abolition of the slave trade, had had its due operation, he would adopt a second still more lenient and equal. Every new indulgence of this kind would advance the slave in the scale of social life, and improve his condition. Every improvement of his condition would qualify him the more for the reception of *Christianity and freedom*; and if ever these glorious events were to be brought to pass, then would be the aera, in which happiness would be the most extensively diffused in the colonies, and the estate of the planter be productive of the greatest gain.[16]

Of the remarkable outpouring of abolitionist literature in the 1780s and 1790s, most persuasive of all were the words of men who had had first-hand experience of slavery. James Ramsay, quoted here from a tract of 1784, was a cleric who had lived and worked among slaves in the West Indies. Here he attacks the assumption that blacks were, by nature, destined for slavery. He also disputes the idea of 'the divine right of European domination'.

Had nature intended negroes for slavery, she would have endowed them with many qualities which they now want. Their food would have needed no preparation, their bodies no covering; they would have been born without any sentiment for liberty; and possessing a patience not to be provoked, would have been incapable of resentment or opposition; that high treason against the divine right of European dominion. A horse or a cow, when abused, beaten, or starved, will try to get out of the reach of the lash, and make no scruple of attempting the nearest inclosure to get at pasture. But we have not heard of their withdrawing themselves from the service of an hard master, nor of avenging with his blood the cruelty of his treatment.

To suppose different, especially superior and inferior races, supposes different rules of conduct, and a different line of duty necessary to be prescribed for them. But where do we find traces of this difference in the present case? Vice never appeared in

Africa in a more barbarous and shocking garb, than she is seen every day in the most polished parts of Europe. Europe has not shewn greater elevation of sentiment than has shone through the gloom of Africa. We can see cause why the nations, into which for the purposes of society mankind has been divided, should have characteristic marks of complexion and features, (and almost the whole of the present subject of discussion may be resolved into these) to tie, by the resemblance, fellow-citizens more closely and affectionately together. And, be it remarked, that these signs are mere arbitrary impressions, that neither give nor take away animal or rational powers; but, in their effect, are confined to the purpose for which they appear to have been impressed, the binding of tribes and families together. Farther, climate, mode of living, and accidental prevalence of particular customs, will account for many national characteristics.

But the soul is a simple substance, not to be distinguished by squat or tall, black, brown, or fair. Hence all the difference that can take place in it is a greater or less degree of energy, a more or less complete correspondence of action, with the circumstances in which the agent is placed. In short, we can have no idea of intellect, but as acting with infinite power and perfect propriety in the Deity, and with various degrees of limited power and propriety, in the several orders of intelligent created beings; so that there is nothing to distinguish these several created orders, but more or less power; and nothing to hinder us from supposing the possible gradual advancement of the lower into the higher ranks of created beings. But we cannot, in like manner, speak of the change of a bull into an horse, or of a swine into an elephant. The annihilation of the one is included in the transmutation into the other, because in it that is lost which constituted the specific difference.

We can plainly see the propriety of different pursuits, and different degrees of exertion of the reasoning energetic powers in the several individuals that compose a community, for carrying on the various purposes of society. But there is not, therefore, a necessity to have recourse to different species of souls, as if the peasant had one sort, the mechanic a second, the man of learning a third; yet whatever concludes for the propriety of races differing in point of excellence, will conclude also for a difference in these. And we see, in contradiction to all such reveries, that communities flourish in proportion as the less of any other difference takes place, than that in which society naturally disposeth of its members for their mutual or joint benefit. The soul is versatile, and being simple in itself takes its manner and tincture from the objects around it; it universally appears to be fitted only for that character in which it is to act: but that this is not an indelible character appears plainly in every page of the history of mankind.[17]

Other black writers who had been victims of the slave trade to make their views known – from Sancho to Equiano – found a sympathetic British readership in Britain in the 1780s and 1790s. Equiano's autobiography, Narrative, *of 1789 reached a remarkably wide audience. Here, in his petition to the Queen in 1788, he seeks to win over royalty to oppose the slave trade.*

To the QUEEN's *most Excellent*
Majesty.

MADAM,

Your Majesty's well known benevolence and humanity emboldens me to approach your royal presence, trusting that the obscurity of my situation will not prevent your Majesty from attending to the sufferings for which I plead.

Yet I do not solicit your royal pity for my own distress; my sufferings, although numerous, are in a measure forgotten. I supplicate your Majesty's compassion for millions of my African countrymen, who groan under the lash of tyranny in the West Indies.

The oppression and cruelty exercised to the unhappy negroes there, have at length reached the British legislature, and they are now deliberating on its redress; even several persons of property in slaves in the West Indies, have petitioned parliament against its continuance, sensible that it is as impolitic as it is unjust – and what is inhuman must ever be unwise.

Your Majesty's reign has been hitherto distinguished by private acts of benevolence and bounty; surely the more extended the misery is, the greater claim it has to your Majesty's compassion, and the greater must be your Majesty's pleasure in administering to its relief.

I presume, therefore, gracious Queen, to implore your interposition with your royal consort, in favour of the wretched Africans; that, by your Majesty's benevolent influence, a period may now be put to their misery; and that they may be raised from the condition of brutes, to which they are at present degraded, to the rights and situation of freemen, and admitted to partake of the blessings of your Majesty's happy government; so shall your Majesty enjoy the heartfelt pleasure of procuring happiness to millions, and be rewarded in the grateful prayers of themselves, and of their posterity.

And may the all-bountiful Creator shower on your Majesty, and the Royal Family, every blessing that this world can afford, and every fulness of joy which divine revelation has promised us in the next.

> I am your Majesty's most dutiful and
> devoted servant to command,
> GUSTAVUS VASSA,
The Oppressed Ethiopean.
No. 53, Baldwin's Gardens.[18]

Newspapers noted, and approved of, the early female political voice that was among the more striking innovations of the abolitionist movement to emerge. Here is an example from the York Courant *in 1792.*

It has been said that a *Petition from the Ladies* to Parliament, for an Abolition of the Slave-Trade, would have a good effect.

The idea is certainly a proper one – for, as *Female Misery* is included in the wretched Allotment of the Africans, an Appeal in their Behalf from the same Sex must carry great Weight with it.[19]

The most famous of contemporary female authors was Mary Wollstonecraft, a fierce critic of the slave trade. Her views are illustrated here in a side swipe at Edmund Burke of 1790.

The slave trade ought never be abolished if Burke's ideas hold sway; and, because our ignorant forefathers, not understanding the native dignity of man, sanctioned a traffic that outrages every suggestion of reason and religion, we are to submit to the inhuman custom, and term an atrocious insult to humanity the love of our country, and a proper submission to the laws by which our property is secured. – Security of property! Behold, in a few words, the definition of English liberty. And to this selfish principle every nobler one is sacrificed.[20]

Abolition embraced an extraordinary range of contemporary interests and talents. It had a particular resonance for a variety of writers and poets. One of these was William Cowper, who attacked slavery in his poem 'The Negro's Complaint' of 1793.

> Forced from home and all its pleasures,
>   Afric's coast I left forlorn,
> To increase the stranger's treasures,
>   O'er the raging billows borne.
> Men from England bought and sold me,
>   Paid my price in paltry gold;
> But, though slave they have enroll'd me,
>   Minds are never to be sold.
>
> Still in thought as free as ever,
>   What are England's rights, I ask,

Me from my delights to sever,
  Me to torture, me to task?
Fleecy locks and black complexion
  Cannot forfeit Nature's claim;
Skins may differ, but affection
  Dwells in white and black the same.

Why did all creating Nature
  Make the plant for which we toil?
Sighs must fan it, tears must water,
  Sweat of ours must dress the soil.[21]

Better remembered perhaps is William Blake's 'The Little Black Boy' (1789). Today, it may seem to offer a confusing image, but it was in essence a radical, democratic assertion of equality.

My mother bore me in the southern wild,
And I am black, but O! my soul is white.
White as an angel is the English child:
But I am black as if bereav'd of light.

My mother taught me underneath a tree
And sitting down before the heat of day,
She took me on her lap and kissed me,
And pointing to the east began to say.

Look on the rising sun: there God does live
And gives his light and gives his heat away.
And flowers and trees and beasts and men recieve
Comfort in morning joy in the noon day.

And we are put on earth a little space,
That we may learn to bear the beams of love,
And these black bodies and this sun-burnt face
Is but a cloud and like a shady grove.

For when our souls have learn'd the heat to bear
The cloud will vanish we shall hear his voice.
Saying: come out from the grove my love & care
And round my golden tent like lambs rejoice.

Thus did my mother say and kissed me.
And thus I say to little English boy.
When I from black and he from white cloud free,
And round the tent of God like lambs we joy:

Ill shade him from the heat till he can bear,
To learn in joy upon our fathers knee.
And then I'll stand and stroke his silver hair,
And be like him and he will then love me.[22]

The abolitionist campaign paralleled its political and literary assaults on the slave trade with a practical campaign against the slave lobby. The boycott of slave-grown sugar (led, again, by women), which proved highly effective and received a great deal of publicity, is described here by Maria Edgeworth in two extracts from the 1790s.

Have you seen any of the things that have been lately published about the negroes? We have just read a very small pamphlet about ten pages, merely an account of the facts stated to the House of Commons. Twenty-five thousand people in England have absolutely left off eating West India sugar, from the hope that when there is no longer any demand for sugar the slaves will not be so cruelly treated. Children in several schools have given up sweet things, which is surely very benevolent; though whether it will at all conduce to the end proposed is perhaps wholly uncertain, and in the mean time we go on eating apple pies sweetened with sugar instead of honey. At Mr Keier's, however, my father avers that he ate excellent custards sweetened with honey. Will it not be rather hard upon the poor bees in the end?[23]

★

We met at Clifton Mr and Mrs Barbauld. He was an amiable
and benevolent man, so eager against the slave-trade that when
he drank tea with us he always brought some East India sugar,
that he might not share our wickedness in eating that made by
the negro slave.[24]

*Not surprisingly, those most closely involved in the slave trade –
merchants, shippers and planters – all made their own appeals to the
public and to Parliament. Traders to Africa petitioned in 1788, asserting the enormous value of the slave trade to Britain.*

But the effects of this [African] trade to Great Britain are
beneficial to an infinite extent. In its immediate effect it employs
about 150 sail of shipping, which carry annually from this country upwards of a million of property, the greatest part our own
manufactures; and in its more remote effects, there is hardly any
branch of commerce in which this nation is concerned that
does not derive some advantage from it. But the beneficial
effects of this trade have been nowhere so eminently striking
as in the sugar colonies in the West Indies, where it has been
proved by experience, that Europeans cannot bear the labour
of the field; so that those valuable possessions would most probably have remained to this moment uncultivated and useless to
a great degree had they not been assisted by the African labourers; it is therefore fair to include every advantage which this
country enjoys by means of its West India colonies, among the
benefits of the African trade, more particularly that for slaves;
and if their Lordships will take the trouble to look back to the
condition of the British nation at the time of commencing this
trade, and observe its progress in navigation, in commerce, in
manufactures, opulence, and power, they will find its acquire-
ments of those great national objects in pretty exact proportion
to its pursuits in the African trade, and the consequent improvement of the British colonies and settlements in America.

In conclusion, this Committee make no scruple to assert,

that the African trade is so blended with our commerce, and so interwoven with our general interests, that if at any time, through neglect, mismanagement, or misfortune, this nation should be deprived of its benefits, it will then suffer a very great and irreparable loss, a maim in its commerce, dignity, and power, of which it is impossible it can ever recover.[25]

Similarly, West Indian groups were anxious to protect their interests against abolitionist attacks. On 5 November 1790 the Assembly of Jamaica petitioned the King to argue their case.

To The King's Most Excellent Majesty.
The humble address and petition of the Assembly of Jamaica,
Most gracious Sovereign,
We, Your Majesty's dutiful and loyal subjects, the Assembly of Jamaica, justly considering Your Majesty as the equal and impartial protector of all Your subjects, however remote, beg leave to approach the throne, with the utmost humility, to represent to Your Majesty,

That it appearing from the minutes of the British House of Commons, in the years 1788 and 1789, that various petitions had been presented to that honourable House from different corporations and bodies of Your Majesty's subjects in Great Britain, praying the interposition of Parliament in abolishing the African slave trade, grounded chiefly on supposed and imaginary sufferings, from improper treatment of the negro labourers in this and the rest of the sugar islands, we held it incumbent on us, in vindication of our insulted honour, in defence of our chartered rights, and in support of our property lawfully acquired, to enter into an extensive investigation, as well concerning the many false charges and injurious aspersions which were contained in some of the said petitions, as in regard to the fatal consequences which might be apprehended, in case the proposed measure of prohibiting the further importation of African labourers should be enforced by the authority of a British Act of Parliament . . .

have adventured their property on West India securities, either on mortgage, bond, annuity, or otherwise, and of the sugar refiners in the said city of Bristol, was also presented to the House, and read; Setting forth, That the petitioners learn with serious alarm that, on the proposed investigation in the Committee of the House of Commons of the petitions against the slave trade, a motion will be made for its entire abolition, on which trade, the petitioners conceive, the welfare and prosperity, if not the actual existence, of the West India Islands depend: That it has been found by recent enquiries, conducted with the greatest exactness, that the African and West India trade constitute at least three-fifths of the commerce of the port of Bristol, and that, if upon such motion a Bill should pass into a Law, the decline of the trade of the city of Bristol must inevitably follow, as the African trade and the great West India commerce, connected therewith and dependent thereon, form so considerable a part of it, and this to the very great loss of the petitioners, and to the ruin of thousands of individuals who are maintained thereby, but who are not sensible of the impending danger; and that the petitioners, many of them from their own experience, and all of them from the reports of judicious people conversant with the West Indies, on whose representations they can rely, are fully convinced that the cultivation of the West India colonies cannot be carried on to any degree of advantage, should that trade be abolished by which they have hitherto been supplied with negro labourers from Africa by the subjects of this country; and that, as the West India Islands are the great market for the British herrings, that fishery, which has ever been considered as the nursery of our seamen, and the source of wealth and employment to numbers of the subjects of this kingdom, must be materially affected by any diminution of the consumption in those islands; and the petitioners beg leave to represent the hardships to which the intended measure will expose the British planter, in putting him on a worse footing than the subjects of our great rivals in trade and colonization, the French, Spaniards, Dutch and Danes, especially the two former, who have unbounded tracts of rich land, which yield tropical productions with little labour and skill . . .[27]

The Parliament forum was increasingly dominated by William Wilberforce. Here, in the debate of May 1789, he attacks both the slave trade and its dire consequences for Africa.

A report has been made by H.M.'s Privy Council, which, I trust, every gentleman has read, and which ascertains the slave trade to be just such in practice as we know, from theory, it must be. What should we suppose must naturally be the consequence of our carrying on a slave trade with Africa? With a country vast in its extent, not utterly barbarous, but civilized in a very small degree? Does any one suppose a slave trade would help their civilization? Is it not plain, that she must suffer from it? That civilization must be checked; that her barbarous manners must be made more barbarous; and that the happiness of her millions of inhabitants must be prejudiced with her inter-course with Britain? Does not every one see that a slave trade, carried on around her coasts, must carry violence and desol-ation to her very centre? That in a Continent just emerging from barbarism, if a trade in men is established, if her men are all converted into goods, and become commodities that can be bartered, it follows, they must be subject to ravage just as goods are; and this, too, at a period of civilization, when there is no protecting Legislature to defend this their only sort of prop-erty, in the same manner as the rights of property are maintained by the Legislature of every civilized country. We see then, in the nature of things, how easily the practices of Africa are to be accounted for. Her Kings are never compelled to war, that we can hear of, by public principles, by national glory, still less by the love of their people. In Europe it is the extension of commerce, the maintenance of national honour, or some great public object, that is ever the motive to war with every Monarch;

but, in Africa, it is the personal avarice and sensuality, of their Kings; these two vices . . . we stimulate in all these African Princes, and we depend upon these vices for the very maintenance of the slave trade. Does the King of Barbessin want brandy? He has only to send his troops, in the night time, to burn and desolate a village; the captives will serve as commodities, that may be bartered with the British trader.[28]

The fight for abolition was, as we have seen, a protracted affair on all fronts. But the British slave trade was brought to an end, from May 1807, by the Act for the Abolition of the Slave Trade.

Whereas the two Houses of Parliament did, by their Resolutions of the 10th and 24th days of June 1806 severally resolve, upon certain grounds therein mentioned, that they would, with all practicable expedition, take effectual measures for the abolition of the *African* slave trade, in such manner and at such period as might be deemed advisable: and whereas it is fit . . . that the same should be forthwith abolished and prohibited . . . be it therefore enacted . . . that from and after the 1st day of May 1807, the *African* slave trade, and all manner of dealing and trading in the purchase, sale, barter or transfer of slaves, or of persons intended to be sold, transferred, used or dealt with as slaves, practised or carried on in, at, to or from any part of the coast or countries of *Africa*, shall be . . . utterly abolished, prohibited and declared to be unlawful; and also that all . . . manner of dealing, either by way of purchase, sale, barter or transfer, or by means of any other contract or agreement whatever, relating to any slaves, or to any persons intended to be used . . . as slaves, for the purpose of such slaves or persons being removed or transported either immediately or by transshipment at sea or otherwise, directly or indirectly from *Africa*, or from any island, country, territory or place whatever, in the *West Indies*, or in any part of *America,* not being in the dominion, possession or occupation of H.M., to any other island . . . or place whatever, is hereby . . . utterly abolished . . . and declared to be unlawful; and if any of H.M.'s subjects, or any person or persons resident within this United Kingdom, or any of the islands, colonies, dominions or territories thereto belonging, or in H.M.'s occupation or possession, shall from . . . the day aforesaid, deal or trade in, purchase, sell, barter or transfer, or contract or agree for the dealing or trading in . . . any slave . . . he or they so offending shall forfeit . . . for every such offence . . . £100 . . . for each . . . slave so purchased . . . the one moiety thereof to the use of H.M. . . . and the other moiety to the use of any person who shall inform, sue and prosecute for the same.

II. Vessels fitted out in this Kingdom, colonies &c. for carrying on the slave trade shall be forfeited.

III. Persons prohibited from carrying as slaves inhabitants of Africa, the West Indies or America, from one place or another, or being concerned in receiving them, &c. Vessels employed in such removal, &c. to be forfeited, as also the property in the slaves. Owners to forfeit £100 for each slave.

IV. Subjects of Africa, &c. unlawfully carried away and imported into any British colony &c. as slaves, shall be forfeited to H.M.

V. Insurances on transactions concerning the slave trade unlawful: penalty, £100 and treble the amount of the premium.

VI. Act not to affect the trading in slaves exported from Africa in vessels cleared out from Great Britain on or before 1 May 1807, and landed in the West Indies by 1 March 1808.

VII. Slaves on foreign ships taken as prizes of war or seized as forfeitures, shall be condemned as prize, or forfeited to the King and freed from slavery, and may be enlisted in the armed forces or bound apprentices for 14 years.

VIII. Bounties to be paid to the captors of such slaves.[29]

11. Freeing the Slaves

Ending the slave trade was a major triumph. But what next? Abolitionists had stressed for years that their aim was not the immediate freeing of slaves. Wilberforce reminded his readers,

Can it be necessary to declare that the Abolitionists are full as much as any other man convinced, that insanity alone would dictate such a project.[1]

The aim had been simple. Planters, now no longer able to buy new Africans, would henceforth have to treat their slaves better, and thus encourage the slave population to increase via natural growth. This, in some unspecified way, would lead to the natural decay of slavery itself. Again, Wilberforce made the point: 'The abolition would give the deathblow to this system.' But how could anyone actually know what precise effects abolition would have on the slave islands? And how could those effects be measured? It was clearly important to devise a system to monitor abolition.

The immediate mood after abolition in 1807 was one of 'wait and see'. No one really knew what the end of the slave trade would bring, or what would happen in the West Indies. As the war with France finally drew to a close in 1814–15, Europe tried to put itself back together after a generation of warfare. Before the war, the Atlantic slave trade had been a relatively unquestioned feature of European maritime trade and prosperity. But the British, the senior partner among the victors, had renounced their own slave trade and were not about to allow the defeated French to revive its own trade. At the Congress System, the diplomatic effort to refashion post-war

Europe after 1815, shuttled between various European cities trying to create a peaceful Europe along agreed borders, Thomas Clarkson, energetic as ever, travelled in its wake to press for an international abolition of the slave trade. Clarkson's work was greatly helped by the Duke of Wellington, who allowed him to use the diplomatic bags for his anti-slave-trade correspondence. It was an indication of Clarkson's standing (and of the importance attached to his campaign) that he had open access to ministers, officials and royalty wherever he travelled. But Clarkson also needed to be alert: it seemed that diplomacy might allow the French to restore their own Atlantic slave trade. Faced with this threat, the British abolitionist movement was revived in 1814–15 to marshal another massive expression of anti-slave-trade sentiment, in the hope of forcing the hand of British negotiators at the Vienna Congress meetings. Something like one and a half million people (from a population of twelve million) signed British abolitionist petitions. 'The country never has, and I fear never will, express a feeling so general as they have done about the slave trade,'[2] wrote Samuel Whitbread.

The Times was filled with reports of anti-slave-trade activity and Clarkson, convinced that the power of public feeling left the British government no option but to press for international abolition, wrote to his wife: 'We must however go on and persevere in Petitions, to show the Voice of England, and to strengthen Ministers thereby.'[3]

Talleyrand, the chief French negotiator, thought that British abolition had become 'a passion carried to fanaticism, and one which the Ministry is no longer at liberty to check'. The public outcry was but the latest expression of an astonishing turn-around. Until the late eighteenth century, the British had been the most dominant and successful of Atlantic slave traders. But now, as peace settled on Europe in 1815, they were determined to prevent others doing what they had perfected. They (and the abolitionist Americans) were not, however, completely successful, for over the next half century, until the 1860s, when the Atlantic slave trade was effectively brought to an end, three million Africans were shipped to the Americas, largely to Cuba and Brazil. Abolitionists had, then, good reason to be vigilant. But what was really astonishing was the way the British people en masse could be rallied against the slave trade (and later against slavery itself).

Abolitionists needed to be aware because news from the West Indies was worrying. In the islands, pioneering Nonconformist missionaries were attracting and converting more and more slaves by the year, despite the planters' efforts to obstruct them, and as ever more slaves beame Christian, they seemed to offer more strenuous resistance to their bondage. Between the end of the war and 1831, the repression of a trio of slave uprisings, each one more violent than the last, with plantocractic and colonial force that appalled British onlookers, seemed to confirm that West Indian slavery was a system that could be kept in place only by violence on a medieval scale. Throughout, of course, the West India lobby, its power on the wane in London, objected to and obstructed the abolitionists' campaign.

Equally troublesome for abolitionists perhaps was the slow realization that cutting off the supply of Africans would not, in itself, bring slavery in the Americas to an end. This was particularly clear in the case of the US. Although North America had been in the vanguard of abolition in the revolutionary years, and had ended its own slave trade in the 1808, by the 1820s the US had a thriving internal slave system in the cotton fields of the south, with enormous beneficial consequences for the wellbeing of the US in general.

The rising British revulsion against the slave trade in the 1780s and 1790s had been driven forward by the revelations of the brutal details of life (and death) on board the slave ships. The British public, not unused to bloodshed and violence in the daily conduct of life (especially in popular culture and in the legal system), was clearly appalled by simple accounts of life on board those ships. Perhaps, abolitionists now thought, similar revelations about life on the West Indian plantations might have a comparable impact.

There were, of course, many people in Britain who knew the islands very well indeed. In addition, a number of prominent churches and sects had dispatched missionaries to work in the islands to win over the slaves to Christianity. Information about slave life was thus readily available, but it required collecting, editing and disseminating. The government began its own information gathering about Caribbean slave society. Keeping a census of the slave population was the only accurate means of assessing the real demographic impact of the abolition of the slave trade. In the bitter parliamentary struggle about extending the registration of slaves to all West Indian slaves (from a prototype scheme in Trinidad begun in 1812), planters and their backers inevitably resisted the idea of any form of government interference between them and their slaves. But eventually in 1819 an Act was passed authorizing the registration of all slaves from 1820 onwards. The data was slow to accumulate, but after 1820 indisputable demographic evidence began to emerge. The precise story of slave life in the West Indian islands and the impact of the abolition of the slave trade could now be told.

Abolitionists now had access to raw population data which they could use to promote slave emancipation. As well as feeling confident that British public opinion would be greatly influenced by it, they believed that British opinion, if directed properly, would force the planters' hands. A marked change came over the campaign for slave emancipation. Like Clarkson's earlier evidence about the slave trade, the abolitionists' use of slave registration returns shifted the arguments about slavery from the impressionistic and the hearsay to the specific and the documented. Whatever flaws existed within the registration system and the data it produced were minor when set against the powerful evidence it offered.

Planters were not only bitterly opposed to slave registration but also hated the abolitionist movement and resisted any

attempt to make them accountable for the day-to-day management of their plantations and slaves. Above all, they continued
to worry about slave unrest. The shadow of the Haitian revolution continued to hover over planters throughout the
Americas, especially those living in the Caribbean close to Haiti,
which had become an independent black nation as recently as
1804. Planters accused abolitionists and their friends of elevat-
ing slave expectations and encouraging slave unrest. As if to
prove their point, in 1816 the Bussa rebellion (Bussa being the
rebel leader) erupted in Barbados.

The story of slavery in the Caribbean (and Brazil) could be
written in terms of slave resistance. Violence and resistance were
also part of the broader story of African slavery in the Americas
(though the story was notably less violent in North America).
While there was nothing to match the destruction in Haiti,
slave revolts in the British Caribbean were widespread, common
and unpredictable. Planters and colonial authorities worried
how best to head them off or crush them, and never fully
trusted the slaves, who greatly outnumbered them.

Barbados seemed an unlikely place for a slave revolt. Its slave
population was overwhelmingly local-born, and imported
Africans no longer played the major economic or social role
they once did, both there and on many of the other islands.
For a host of obvious reasons smaller islands like Barbados had
not experienced the litany of slave upheaval and repression that
had been commonplace on larger ones – Jamaica, for example.
Nonetheless, planters on Barbados had made a rod for their
own back. Their vociferous denunciation of registration, and
their loose, indiscreet table talk (predictably relayed back
promptly to the slave quarters), helped ferment discontent
among their slaves, persuading them that the planters were denying them the freedom already granted by London. Though false,
such views had a dramatic impact.

Bussa's rebellion of 1816 was crushed: 120 slaves were killed,
144 executed, 132 deported. But relieved Barbadian planters

were in no doubt that slave unrest continued to simmer, fanned by the debate about emancipation: 'The spirit is not subdued, nor will it ever be subdued whilst these dangerous doctrines which have been spread abroad continue to be propagated among the slaves.'[4] Slave owners now greatly feared the federation of enemies hammering at their door. First, and most worrying, were the slaves, with their simple but persistent demand for freedom; second were the British abolitionists, who demanded positive action and change in the slaves' condition; third were the missionaries, who were industrious in winning over armies of slaves to their church or chapel; last, and not least, planters had to contend with the British government, which seemed ever eager to criticize planters on behalf of the slaves. But above all else, the planters feared the slaves.

As we have seen, slaves everywhere had traditionally resisted their bondage – in Africa, on the slave ships and on the plantations – but their resistance was not always violent or physically threatening. It often took the form of whatever stratagem seemed appropriate at the time: foot dragging, feigning ignorance, acting stupid, misunderstanding orders, running away all formed a *leitmotif* to slavery throughout the Atlantic slave empires. But violence was rarely far away, not least because white violence against slaves was so ubiquitous and pervasive. Although slave resistance was universal, it has, until recent years, rarely been seen as an element in destabilizing and ending slavery itself. This is, however, precisely what began to happen in the last years of slavery in the British Empire.

It was the persuasiveness of the raw accounts of slave life – the pain and the suffering of Africans on the slave ships and on the plantations – that swung British opinion against slavery. The abolitionist campaign's clever use of slave sufferings created a public mood that was resolutely opposed first to the slave trade and later to slavery itself. But in fact the inhuman realities of slavery had begun to dawn on the British reading public even before the abolitionist campaign was launched in

1787. Much of that story was bound up with the experiences of black people living in England. Slave cases in English courts, notably the Somerset case of 1772, the words of a small number of black writers and activists living in London in the 1770s and 1780s, and some powerful visual images had helped broadcast the truth about Atlantic slavery. As we saw in the previous chapter, black writers, for example, had provided the public with first-hand accounts of slave life and of black experiences in Britain. The *Narrative of Gronniosaw* (1772), drafted by Hannah More, the poems of Phyllis Wheatley (1773), Sancho's *Letters* of 1782, Cugoano's *Thoughts and Sentiments* (1787) and most famously Equiano's *Narrative* of 1789 formed a genre which found a receptive readership in the years of heightened abolitionist sentiment after 1787. They were very different writers, of course, but they returned, each in their own distinctive way, to common themes: the inhumanity of slavery, the ungodly acts of Christian Britons, and the attainments of industrious, independent black people (that is, the authors) when allowed to flourish outside slavery. Their work formed a small but influential contribution to public understanding of the principle that blacks were, in essence, no different from whites: that they too could be people of sensibility, religious conviction and material accomplishment when freed from slavery. These were of course the very issues taken up and promoted by the abolitionists, all with an eye to establishing the simple but politically corrosive point that blacks were indeed men and women, brothers and sisters.

In this long, protracted campaign against slavery, the full horror of what was being unearthed and revealed sometimes overwhelmed even the staunchest of abolitionists. Nothing had a more graphic impact than the *Zong* massacre of 1781, yet no one was brought to account for that mass murder. Though unique in its cold-blooded slaughter, the *Zong* case was in keeping with the fate of slave rebels and resistant slaves on other ships and on the plantations.

Long before full emancipation in 1838 there were notable victories for the black cause, beginning with the Somerset case in 1772, but despite the small band of determined friends unfailingly promoting the cause of black equality, the basic problem remained that Britain was inextricably linked to, and greatly benefited from, slavery. Clearly, Britain was not a slave society like Jamaica, Virginia or Barbados, but slavery – however distant – continued to play a critical economic and social role in Britain. Life seemed to revolve around the widespread consumption of slave-grown produce. Whatever freedom blacks in Britain enjoyed, they would always be qualified and circumscribed until slavery within the empire was brought to an end.

Britain's slave colonies were scattered throughout the Caribbean, 5,000 miles away. It was one major achievement of the abolitionists that they shifted slavery much closer to Britain, ensuring that it came to play a more immediate role in British politics than geography might suggest would be possible. They ensured that the course of events in the Caribbean, the grim routines of life on the plantations and the violent realities of sea-borne life on the slave ships provided intimate substance to the literary and political war being waged between the slave lobby and their abolitionist enemies. The details of slave life, then, became basic to the ebb and flow of political argument about slavery between 1787 and 1838.

After the return of peace in 1815, there was a greatly heightened awareness in Britain about slaves and slavery. In this, slaves played their own role, initially and most dramatically through Bussa's rebellion in Barbados is 1816. Though the revolt seemed to confirm everything that planters had been saying for many years (that tampering with slavery was bound to lead to slave unrest), the planters' problem was that slavery was being undermined from a number of different directions. Not only were the slaves' own stratagems of resistance gnawing away at slavery: at a grander, strategic level, debates about the slave trade made headlines wherever European diplomats gathered after the war, giving slavery an unprecedented political status. Moreover, the slaves in the Caribbean were acutely aware of the debate in Britain. With planters and merchants, traders, sailors and visitors to the islands all discussing the ways slavery was being handled in London, and slaves' masters talking about the news from London, it was inevitable that West Indian slaves would hear about what was being discussed in Britain. They knew that they had friends in Britain, and they were very conscious that their Caribbean owners were resistant to whatever beneficial changes were being planned for the slaves.

It was also clear that the work of missionaries was having a profoundly destabilizing effect on slavery. British churches laid down strict rules, ordering missionaries working in the slave colonies to steer well clear of political debate and to do their best not to upset the delicate social balance. It was, however, an impossible task. The missionaries' very presence among the slaves was deeply unsettling. So too was their message, however much it might be couched in theological terms. The established Anglican church had long been notoriously lax in its work in the Caribbean, and failed to minister to the slaves (or to the planters for that matter), but that began to change from the 1780s, when a string of Nonconformist missionaries began to make major inroads into the slave communities. Baptists and Methodists, following where German Moravians had begun in the mid-century, set sail for the islands with strict warnings: 'Remember that the object is not to teach the principles and the laws of an earthly kingdom ... but the principles and laws of the Kingdom of Christ.'[5] Needless to say, it was not quite that easy, and there was an inevitable slippage from the theological to the secular. Much of what the missionaries said seemed to the slaves to speak directly to their worldly condition. More significantly, the Christian message quickly passed from the hands of British missionaries into the hands of local black preachers. Christianity – in the form of local chapels, mastery of the Bible, hymns and home-grown preachers – became a potent weapon in the hands of the slaves; black enslaved congregations, Old Testament fire-and-brimstone and communal singing all added up to a Christian rod for the planters' backs.

Many Anglicans, including prominent Evangelicals, felt uneasy about the work of the missionaries in the slave islands. (Some were no less unhappy with the rise of Methodism among working people in Britain itself.) They disliked Methodism's ability to create 'enthusiasms' among people 'of weak judgment and of little or no knowledge'.[6] Such objections, however, could do little to halt the large-scale conversion of slaves on the islands to Nonconformist Christianity. And in any case, everyone agreed that Christianity was the first step towards 'civilizing' the slaves: an essential move towards weaning slaves away from their African 'paganisms' and directing them towards a more civilized personal and communal life. Here was a basic impulse in the broader Evangelical movement: Christianity was both a means and an end, the way of winning over the benighted peoples of the world to a civilized form of society. Most writers keen to achieve black freedom, sooner or later, regarded the 'irreligion' of the slaves as a serious obstacle. Yet while Christianity went hand-in-hand with black freedom, it also produced unpredictable social consequences among the slaves themselves.

Slave conversion was, then, a vital part of the aspirations of all abolitionists. In his *Sketch of a Negro Code* (1792) Edmund Burke specified that 'A competent minister of some Christian church or congregation shall be provided for the full instruction of the Negroes.' He also envisaged punitive measures for slaves who refused to agree to Christianization. In his plan Christian churches would provide slaves with an armoury of personal and social skills to enable them to survive as free people. If slaves could gradually acquire such skills, the task of emancipation would be so much easier. What no one realized, or predicted, was that this Christian drive into the slave quarters would have such remarkable consequences.

It created, for example, a growing band of British supporters of black freedom. The very sects who were converting the slaves in the Caribbean, especially the Baptists and Methodists, were also growing rapidly in Britain, changing the face of British worship, and British Nonconformists naturally felt a bond of sympathy for their enslaved co-religionists. There were, for example, more than a quarter of a million British Methodists by the 1820s, and perhaps 100,000 British Baptists twenty years later, when there were almost 15,000 Dissenting places of worship across Britain. Nonconformity had clearly become a major social force in Britain, providing the campaign against slavery with a new, national network of support. Moreover it was growing most rapidly in new, industrializing areas of rapid population growth. It was as if the people of this 'new Britain' – the Britain we normally associate with industrial change – were the very people who lent their numbers to, and gave voice to, demands for an end to slavery. With its ability to muster growing numbers of British people, Nonconformity, for all its theological and institutional divides, spoke persuasively and with great eloquence in the British surge towards slave emancipation in the 1820s and 1830s. Equally importantly, this same Nonconformist Christianity transformed slave life itself.

After 1807, when planters were no longer able to replenish their enslaved labour force by purchasing Africans, and had to rethink their management systems, abolitionists, government officials and other outsiders looked at the slave colonies with very great suspicion. It was clear to all concerned, on both sides of the Atlantic, that planters, who had always been hostile to the abolition of the slave trade and continued to be resistant to any outside interference with the slave systems in the islands, would drag their feet in any change demanded of them by London.

The immediate consequence of abolition after 1807 was a short-term decline in the slave population. With fewer slaves at their disposal, planters felt obliged to increase their demands on their labour force. They did this by reorganizing their labour force, switching slaves around, and generally interfering with work systems and labour conventions to which slaves had long been accustomed. Planters also began to shuffle slaves around from one property to another, 'rationalizing' their labour force to suit their broader economic interests. Such changes often caused great inconvenience and distress to the slaves. Women and children found themselves undertaking tasks previously reserved for males. Privileged, skilled or elite slaves found themselves thrust into rougher, more demanding work. Slaves who had long been accustomed to better working conditions found themselves toiling in the fields. While the changes made economic sense to the planters, they angered and confused the slaves.

All this took place when rumours swirled among the slaves that the King and/or Parliament and the British in general were keen to free the slaves, and it was only the planters' resistance that was preventing full emancipation. Freedom was clearly in the offing, and slaves' expectations began to change as slavery shifted around them, but in the meantime, slaves' lives had become more strenuous, more demanding and more uncertain, at least in the sugar economy on the older islands. Notwithstanding its brutalities and cruelties, the slave system that had emerged on the sugar islands had become a sophisticated system of agriculture, with its own form of labour discipline, but after 1807 planters began to chop and change it. There were now, for example, more women working in the sugar fields. Similarly there were more 'coloured' slaves in the fields: fairer-skinned children could no longer expect the preferential treatment often accorded to the offspring of black and white. Nor had abolition made slaves more biddable or docile by forcing planters to treat them better.

Planters assumed that as the old generation of Africans died out by natural ageing, a new population of Creole slaves, born into Caribbean slavery and never having known freedom or Africa (except via slave folklore), would be more manageable and biddable. Yet the very contrary seemed to be happening. Planters also assumed that the slaves' truculence was heightened by outside interference: by a critical and inquisitive British government and its colonial officers, and by the swarm of missionaries luring slaves to chapels and prayer meetings. What happened after abolition in 1807 confirmed their greatest fears. Bussa's rebellion in generally peaceable Barbados seemed to clinch their case. What was to follow was, for them, even worse.

The newly developed slave lands in Demerera (Guyana) attracted a new breed of aggressive investors and planters (including Gladstone's father.) Planters there managed their slaves through a draconian system which flew in the face of abolitionist (and government) expectations. Missionaries dispatched to that unforgiving climate were shocked by what they found. 'A most immoderate quantity of work has, very generally, been expected of them [slaves], not excepting women far advanced in pregnancy,' wrote John Smith, a missionary from the London Missionary Society. He continued, 'Redress they have been so seldom able to obtain, that many of them have long discontinued to seek it, even when they have been notoriously wronged.'[7] The exploitation of slaves was basic to the story of Atlantic slavery but it was often at its worst in the early days of settlement and expansion, in effect when societies were raw frontier communities. Demereran planters' rude management of their slaves may be explained by its early state of development; it was comparable, in the early nineteenth century, to seventeenth-century Barbados and Jamaica. But times and sensibilities had changed. What had gone unnoticed and uncriticized two centuries earlier was unacceptable to the ever-more inquisitive society of the early nineteenth century. To outsiders, it seemed that the planters had not changed, and now, in the 1820s, and unlike the earlier days of settlement, their every move was scrutinized by missionaries on the spot. Reports of plantocratic wrongdoings sped back to British congregations.

Slaves in Demerera had long been noted for their resistance, and for fleeing from slave settlements, which were heavily concentrated in the coastal regions and along the rivers. It was a region where barbaric punishment of slaves was commonplace. When John Smith landed there in 1817, slaves flocked to join his new congregations, despite the planters' hostility. In 1823 local slaves rose up in revolt, to be hastily suppressed by colonial and plantocratic forces. The summary and legal punishments were excessive and gory. In response to the killing of three white people, some 250 slaves were killed. Smith too was tried, in a protracted hearing which lasted a month and was made all the more dramatic by Smith's decline into consumption. He died in jail in February 1824 shortly before receiving a royal pardon.

Smith's death provoked an outcry in Britain. But the true outcry should have been reserved for the deaths of so many slaves, slaughtered for a system that had long been utterly indefensible. Nevertheless, Smith's death succeeded in focusing attention on slavery. How could the government, or the vested interests of the sugar industry, justify a slave system which seemed to be able to maintain itself only by such barbaric punishments? What possible benefits could be gained from such legalized and governmentally sanctioned cruelty? The revolt, and the death of the Revd Smith, instantly revived the flagging British abolitionist cause. Less than twenty years since abolition, it was abundantly clear to more and more people that West Indian slavery stood condemned by the actions of its principal proponents and benefactors.

The 1823 Demerera revolt naturally sent shock waves through other slave colonies. Memories of the 1790s remained vivid, and the Americas were once again haunted by a fear of contamination and spread of servile revolt. But the revolt's most important impact was in Britain itself, where humanitarians seized on Smith's death as a means of goading a hesitant government to move towards slave emancipation. Ever more people in Britain were ready to wash their hands of the entire West

Indian slave system, if only because they saw no possibility that it could ever be expected to bring justice, to say nothing of freedom, to the slaves. The mood of profound disgust, and the feeling that slavery should be brought to an end, was captured in a biblical quotation which Smith smuggled out of his prison cell. 'We are troubled on every side, yet not distressed, we are perplexed, but not in despair. Persecuted but not forsaken: cast down, but not destroyed.'[8] But the practical problem remained: what to do?

Viewed from Britain, the Caribbean was in a depressing state in the 1820s. The slave registration returns showed that the slave population was in decline, and would continue to decline until a new generation of slaves entered their child-bearing years. The labour regime controlling the slaves was tighter than ever. Slaves were exposed as never before to enforced family separations, and the loss of valued privileges. And everywhere the new forces of Christianity, normally in the form of Nonconformist missionaries and chapels, were corroding the old slave system. The resistance (and in many cases the open hostility) of planters towards missionaries and towards Christian slaves merely confirmed the need to bring down slavery. At the precise moment when religious barriers (notably against Roman Catholics) were being removed in Britain, it was ironic to see newly converted slaves in the West Indies being harassed and obstructed in their Christian worship. Casting a shadow over the whole ghastly story was the violence that seemed to be the hallmark both of plantocratic management and even of colonial administration. Slave resistance begat violent repression on a scale that contemporaries in Britain could barely believe.

There was nothing new in the violence meted out to slaves: here, after all, was a system conceived in violence, nurtured by cruelty and maintained by draconian brutality. What had changed, however, was the cultural climate in Britain. In years when the British were slowly curbing their own predilections

for legal and punitive violence (in the law and the armed services, for instance) it was hard to look at the Caribbean and see
anything but an old-fashioned brutal culture which was increasingly out of kilter with the imperial heartland. By the mid-1820s,
the slave islands seemed like survivors from a lost epoch. In 1823
it was time, once again, to rally the abolitionist troops.

The new abolitionist campaign really started in 1822 with
the idea that slavery could be undermined by an attack on the
sugar duties. Slave-grown sugar was a highly subsidized system
that saw more cheaply produced sugars raised to the level of
West Indian prices. Without the sugar duties the British
Caribbean islands could not be competitive. The abolitionist
ploy was simple: expose slave-grown sugar to free competition
and it would simply collapse from its own inefficiencies. Some
of the earliest abolitionist arguments (in the early Quaker tracts
by Benezet, for example) had embraced an economic critique
of slavery, though rarely as a pivotal objection. In any case, the
economics of slavery seemed indisputable: here was a profitable
system that brooked no real dispute. By the 1820s, however,
other, cheaper sugars were readily available on the world market.
By the late 1820s the economic critique of slave-grown sugar
had been widely accepted by commentators of all kinds and it
was believed that open competition for sugar would undermine West Indian slavery. *The Edinburgh Review* opined in 1827,
'There is, in fact, but one way to put down West Indian slavery, and that is by allowing the produce raised by comparatively
cheap labour to come into competition with that raised by the
slaves.'[9] James Cropper, a Quaker with East India interests, was
especially prominent in addressing the economics of slave-grown
sugar. Along with other abolitionists he assumed that public
support would – again – be critical, and was convinced that
for this they needed a reprise of the campaign against the slave
trade.

With this in mind the Society for the Mitigation and Gradual
Abolition of Slavery was founded late in January 1823. Within

a year Clarkson – yet again – had been largely responsible for the creation of 250 societies across Britain. For the next decade these societies (large numbers of their members female) provided the impetus for the campaign to end slavery. A central London committee orchestrated the campaign, with the country divided into districts, and all were encouraged to rally support and organize petitions demanding black freedom. The campaign was, instantly, highly efficient, influential and a clear expression of the national antipathy to slavery. It was also more influenced than ever by the energy and activities of female abolitionists, many of them working through their own associations.

The ideological core of the campaign was, however, quite different from its forebears. Though it was always aligned to the older moral and religious objections, the economics of slavery had now shifted to the centre of the arguments. Thus, for the first time, by the 1820s slavery found itself under attack from a powerful combination of objections. The argument that slavery was both wrong *and* uneconomic appealed to huge numbers of British people. The West India lobby found itself facing an impossible task: of trying to prove both the morality and the economic utility of the slave system. On both counts they were outflanked by events and by abolitionist arguments. What possible moral justification could be offered for the recent treatment of slaves in Demerera, or for the persecution of black Christians on the islands? And why should British consumers pay more for their sugar just to keep the slave system in place?

By the mid-1820s planters were clearly on the defensive, and staring at the massive, well-organized, articulate ranks of British people who were now wedded to demands for black freedom – sooner rather than later. Abolitionism had in effect captured both the moral and economic high ground. The strength – and the ultimate irresistibility – of abolition was, as Thomas Clarkson knew, that it 'spoke the national voice'.

★

Early in 1823 the Commons established a key principle by resolving to press for gradual emancipation. The indefatigable Clarkson found support for the principle from all corners of the country, from all political quarters and – critically – from most churches. Despite opposition in the Lords, black freedom no longer divided the nation, but had, instead, become an issue which united the British people as no other. The aim however, was not merely to free the slaves, but to 'civilize' them: 'to Christianize them, to make them more useful to themselves and families than before, to make them better servants to their masters, and to make them more useful members of the community at large.'[10]

Abolitionists were confident that they could so outrage public opinion that emancipation would be inevitable: Parliament would be unable to resist demands for it. The Society for the Mitigation and Gradual Abolition of Slavery was backed by a host of prominent contemporaries. Some of the most trenchant arguments against slavery were couched in religious language and imagery – not surprisingly, since the British, high and low, had come to assume that slavery was unchristian, and since much opposition came from churches.

After 1823, the old, well-tried abolitionist tactics were again used to promote emancipation, and the campaign was, again, characterized by petitions, publications and lectures – often of incredible length – to packed audiences. Lectures lasting two to three hours were not uncommon; overspill audiences, people being locked out, hundreds defying bad weather to get to a lecture – all and more bore testimony to the staggering popularity of the abolitionist campaign. Through all this, female abolitionists and their own, discrete organizations were vital; they were at the heart of the campaign, as organizers, lecturers and audiences. The female contribution to the abolition campaign was important not just in itself but as part of a much broader and more deep-seated shift towards female political activism. Abolitionist publications fluttered down in profusion on an increasingly literate people. Between 1823 and 1831, the Society for the Mitigation and Gradual Abolition of Slavery (afterwards the Anti-Slavery Society) issued more than three million tracts – about half a million in 1831 alone. This was in addition to publications issued by local abolitionist groups and abolitionist material in local and London newspapers.

Despite such public backing, the abolitionist cause languished in Parliament. Wilberforce was old and weary, handing over the parliamentary leadership to Thomas Fowell Buxton. Despite public feeling, by 1830 little headway had been made in Parliament. Moreover, in that same year emancipation was only one of a number of reforming issues confronting Parliament: dominating everything was the reform of Parliament. A younger generation of abolitionists began to tire of their leaders' apparently endless patience in waiting for black freedom, and in 1832 the Agency Committee, founded by George Stephen and Emmanuel and James Cropper (both Quakers) began to press for immediate emancipation. But in that same year, the whole British political scene was overwhelmed by the national panic caused by the terrible cholera epidemic which killed 32,000 people. Many thought that the disaster was divine punishment for a national sin. What sin could have been greater than slavery? And, as if to confirm the Almighty's wrath, the Jamaican slave revolt of 1831–2 cast its own long shadow over British life.

A massive upheaval involving 60,000 slaves, the Jamaican revolt caused the death of 14 whites and led to the killing of 540 slaves. Led by the inspirational preacher Sam Sharpe, and with Baptist slaves at the forefront, the revolt raced out of control through western Jamaica, with the widespread torching of estates. There was something different about this revolt from those in Barbados in 1816 and Demerera in 1822. Sharpe, though still a slave, personified the power of black Christianity, and the disruptive message inherent in biblical imagery. He 'thought and learnt from the Bible, that the whites had no more right to hold black people in slavery than black people had to make the white people slaves.'[11]

News of the Jamaican revolt, and of its violent repression, caused another outcry in Britain. On the eve of the debate on Parliamentary reform, missionaries returning from Jamaica roused British audiences with all the latest news. This added an emotive element to the debates for both black freedom and for the Reform Bill. When a new election was called in August 1832 – using the new reformed franchise – abolitionists seized their chance to force parliamentary candidates to declare their views on emancipation. Something like 200 MPs declared themselves for black freedom. The reform of Parliament in 1832 thus paved the way for the ending of slavery.

Earl Grey's new government resolved to end slavery, but the Lords (again) remained doggedly supportive of the planters. Now, however, the arguments in Parliament were about when, and under precisely what conditions, slaves would be freed. Finally the Abolition of Slavery Bill of August 1833 initiated black freedom in August 1834. But it was a severely limited form of freedom: all slaves under six were to be freed immediately while the rest became 'apprentices' for up to six years, working most of their time (for free) for their ex-owners. Bermuda and Antigua opted for immediate freedom for all local slaves.

Parliament also voted to allocate £20 million on a per capita basis not to the slaves but to the slave owners. Lord Harewood, for example, already fabulously wealthy from his family's sugar trading and West Indian plantations, received more than £26,000 for the 1,277 slaves still in his possession. Many people asked the obvious question: why not compensate the slaves instead?

The apprenticeship scheme (monitored by a new breed of magistrates sent from Britain) was clearly a sop to the planters' demand for labour, but evidence of its failings was widespread, and was used by abolitionists to continue their demands for full freedom. They kept up the pressure, using the old tactics. They clearly had the voice of 'new' Britain, of urban, industrial and

Dissenting British life. While slavery tended to find support in small-town, rural Britain, and the Lords, there was little the slave lobby could do to save slavery, and on 1 August 1838 apprenticeship was brought to an early end and full freedom established.

Convinced that ex-slaves would remember the long litany of personal and collective grievances, planters and the wider colonial society they had dominated for so long had, throughout, feared that black freedom would be ushered in by a settling of old scores. In the event, ex-slaves celebrated their newly won freedom in the most peaceable of fashions. Across the Caribbean, freed slaves made their way to celebrate in parades, and public meetings. But above all they went to church in droves.

It was a staggering turn of events. Here, after all, was a system that had for almost three centuries defined relations between black and white in the Americas and, throughout, been rooted in violence. Yet although slavery had been ended in Haiti by slave revolt in the 1790s and was to end in the US in the bloodshed of the Civil War, the British system ended quietly.

Just as the two major terminal points in the history of British slavery – the abolition of the slave trade in 1807 and the ending of slavery in 1834–8 – were both ushered in by Acts of Parliament, passed in London, so too had the slave trade and slavery been fashioned and shaped, over the past two centuries, by metropolitan interests. Despite the huge distances which separated Britain from the African slave coasts and the slave plantations of the Americas, the metropole had, throughout, been the pivot on which the whole system hinged. Acts of Parliament, government fiat, royal proclamations, orders-in-council, colonial legislation, common-law decisions – all were issued to encourage and legalize the eager and ubiquitous involvement in slavery by British financial and commercial interests. But, as we have seen, the distances between the centre of British political gravity and the colonial heart of slavery created their own peculiar problems.

It was easy for abolitionists in, say 1834, to think of black

abolition of the Slave Trade and any serious attempt being made
for the extinction of slavery. The former event took place in
the year 1807, and it was not until 1823 that Mr Buxton submit-
ted to the House of Commons the first resolution ever moved
in that Assembly that brought in question, and then only in a
very cautious form, the lawfulness of negro slavery. Various
reasons, however, may be assigned for this comparative in-
action, not the least important of which was the fact, that during
the period referred to the public mind was so engrossed with
that terrible conflict going on between this country and France,
and the disastrous consequences that resulted from it, that it
had little time or energy to spare for anything else. For this is
one among many other miserable fruits of war, that it tends to
make nations selfish, and to withdraw their thoughts from all
measures of domestic improvement or philanthropic reform,
to the one absorbing and passionate care for their own safety
or glory. While the country was bleeding at every pore, or lying
exhausted with the wounds it had received during twenty years'
strife – how was it possible to engage the sympathies of the
people on behalf of a poor and despised race, whose sufferings,
however severe, they might well imagine at that time hardly
surpassed their own? Nor does it appear, indeed, that the excellent men who laboured so long and so successfully to put
the traffic in men under the ban of law and opinion, ever
contemplated speedy emancipation as a thing either practicable
or safe, though, no doubt, they expected that the abolition of
the slave trade would ultimately, and by a necessary though very
gradual process, lead to the overthrow of slavery. Their first
efforts, therefore, after the victory of 1807, were confined to
securing such supplementary legislation as was thought necessary to prevent the provisions of the Abolition Act from being
evaded. And truly there was much yet to do in this direction.
For as the offence of importing slaves into the royal dominions, prohibited under that act, was only punishable by pecuniary
penalties and forfeitures, it was soon found that many British

subjects, willing to run the risk of such penalties for the sake of the enormous profits made, were still engaged in the traffic. To put a stop to this, Mr Brougham, in 1811, introduced a bill, which was carried through both Houses of Parliament, declaring the slave trade to be felony, the offender being liable to fourteen years' transportation, or imprisonment for five years. But even this law, admirable and effective as it proved to be in its general operation, still left open a loophole for evasion, since one of its clauses excluded the intercolonial slave trade from its jurisdiction. To meet and remedy the abuses to which this omission gave rise, the Slave Registration Act was passed in 1819, principally through the indefatigable exertions of Mr Stephen. Nor was it a small gain that, through the influence of the Anti-Slavery party in England – in that instance represented chiefly by Mr Zachary Macaulay – an article was inserted in the treaty of Vienna, pronouncing solemn condemnation upon the slave trade, and binding the great Powers, who were parties to that instrument, to labour together for its extinction.

Engaged thus in consolidating and extending the triumph they had won over the infamous traffic itself, the Anti-Slavery party, for many years, suffered the other part of the question to remain in abeyance. By degrees, however, attention began to be directed more and more to the condition of the slaves in our West India colonies.[12]

The first task facing abolitionists after 1807 was to persuade other European maritime nations of the need to abolish the slave trade internationally. The power of British abolitionist feeling clearly influenced the diplomatic discussions at the various sessions of the Congress System between 1814 and 1822, and is made clear in this letter of 25 October 1814 from Lord Castlereagh to Lord Liverpool.

Mr Lord,   Vienna.

I think it right to acquaint your Lordship, that notwithstanding the Duke of Wellington's repeated agitations of the question at Paris, and my own representations to Prince Talleyrand here, no answer whatever has yet been returned to my official note of the 8th instant on the Slave Trade.

The more I have occasion to observe the temper of foreign powers on the question of the abolition, the more strongly impressed I am with a sense of the prejudice that results not only to the interests of the question itself, but of our foreign relations generally from the display of popular impatience which has been excited and is kept up in England upon this subject.

It is impossible to persuade foreign nations that this sentiment is unmixed with views of colonial policy, and their Cabinets, who can better estimate the real and virtuous motives which guide us on this question, see in the very impatience of the nation a powerful instrument through which they expect to force, at a convenient moment, the British Government upon some favourite object of policy.

I am conscious that we have done an act of indispensable duty, under the circumstances in which we have been placed, in making to the French and Spanish Governments the propositions we have done, but I am still more firmly persuaded, that we should be at this moment in fact nearer our object if the Government had been permitted to pursue this object with its ordinary means of influence and persuasion instead of being placed in the predicament of being expected to purchase concessions on this point almost at any sacrifice.

It will be my duty as it will be my personal pride to employ every possible effort to further this object, but I never can cease to feel, that the manner in which the efforts of the Government in this cause were last year received, and the coldness, if not the tone of disapprobation, in which the most efficient arrangements towards a final abolition which had yet been achieved were met both in Parliament and in the country, has neither augmented our means of discharging our public duties upon this, nor on any other question of foreign policy . . .

Your Lordship is sufficiently apprised of the state in which matters have hitherto stood here, to be aware that I could not possibly have brought this question hitherto into discussion. I shall seize the first favourable moment for doing so, but for the reasons already stated, I had rather not hazard a decision till the principal questions of a political nature are at least further advanced towards a decision . . .[13]

Following abolition in 1807, the work of missionaries among the slaves became more striking and influential, with the widespread, systematic conversion of slaves in the Caribbean. Missionaries faced a daunting task, however, made clear in these instructions given by the Missionary Society to their missionaries in the West Indies in 1812: to convert but not to upset the social equilibrium in the slave colonies.

You are going to preach the Gospel to poor Africans in a state of slavery to man. They have been torn from their native country and reduced to a low and degraded situation. As such they will be the objects of your commiseration. But it is not to relieve them from their servile condition that you visit them. That is out of your power. Nor would it be proper, but extremely *wrong*, to insinuate anything which might render them discontented with a state of servitude or lead them to any measures injurious to their masters: this would be to defeat the object of your mission and excite such opposition as might eventually prevent many other missions. These poor creatures are slaves in a much worse sense; they are the slaves of ignorance, of sin, and of Satan; it is to rescue them from this miserable condition by the Gospel of Christ that you are now going.[14]

The end of the slave trade was soon followed by the registration of slaves — a census of all slaves in the colonies. The aim was to scrutinize the slave populations and to ensure no further illicit importations took place, as outlined here by the abolitionist and founder of the Agency Committee, George Stephen, in his Recollections *of 1859.*

September 16th, 1854.

My dear Madam,

The principle of slave registration was identification of every slave, by age, sex, stature, country, marks, and all personal peculiarities. All these distinctive circumstances were to be recorded in public books, under the eye and on the responsibility of public officers specially appointed for the duty; births and deaths were to be similarly entered of record, and a register thus constructed, was to be indispensable as evidence of title to the (so called) property in man. The falsification of the register was to be rendered difficult, though by no means impossible, by a transmission of it in duplicate, from year to year, to a central office in London.

It is obvious that such a system would greatly check the felonious acquisition of slaves by a contraband trade. It could not wholly extinguish it, because by concealing the deaths on a plantation, a fraud by no means difficult, every vacancy could be filled up by fresh importations so long as new slaves would be found corresponding generally, in sex, age, and appearance with the deceased. Such frauds were carried on to a very great extent, and especially in the Mauritius, to the very last day that slavery continued. Still on the whole, the registration, when ultimately carried, worked well, and contributed far more than any statutory penalties to give full effect to the Slave Trade Abolition Acts.[15]

When the attack on slavery was revived in the 1820s it embraced an increasingly persuasive economic critique of west Indian slavery. The favoured position of slave-grown sugar, the emergent attachment to the ideals of freer trade and the availability of sugar grown by free labour elsewhere all added weight to the argument. Here the case is put by James Cropper, the Quaker abolitionist, in a letter to Wilberforce in 1821.

Liverpool, 5th Month 3, 1821.

William Wilberforce,

Respected Friend,

1. I know that anything which respects the great cause which is the subject of my letter, will be a sufficient apology for my addressing thee.

2. In the first place I should state, that I am engaged in the East India trade, and therefore interested in the measure likely soon to be brought before Parliament, of an increase in the duty on East India sugar, against which the merchants interested in that trade here, have petitioned Parliament; but they did not introduce into their petition any thing respecting its influence on the slave-trade.

3. On the opening of the East India trade, I believed that a great experiment was to be tried, – that of a free competition between the products of the East by *free men*, and those of the West by *slaves*. Of the result of that competition, even shackled as it was in the case of sugar, by a difference of 10s per cwt. in the duty, I entertained no doubt; being persuaded, that cultivation by free men, in the country of their birth, must be much cheaper than by the transportation of slaves from Africa to the West Indies. The high freights, and other impediments which the charter of the East India Company caused, prevented the competition of bulky articles; but we had seen the effects in the case of indigo; the introduction of its cultivation in Bengal is but recent, and yet it has now ceased to be raised in any other place to any considerable extent, owing no doubt to the cheapness of its production there. With these views, I did not hesitate to enter extensively into the East India trade; and though now so much overdone, as not to be profitable, yet in these respects I have not been disappointed. The importations of cotton have greatly reduced the prices of that article, and thereby tended to extend its consumption, so that since the opening of this trade, the cotton-manufactures of Great Britain have increased nearly 50 per cent.

4. Besides this great benefit, there is one which the friends of humanity will consider still more important; and that is, that the price of cotton (if not already) is likely, at no great distance of time, to be so reduced, as not to pay for the further importation of slaves. A friend of mine, who has lately been in America, states, that the planters said that the fall in price was not entirely a loss to them, for they had less inducement to work their negroes hard, and they would increase faster. It hence appears, that a low price may pay under good treatment of the slaves, though it might not pay for that abuse of them which requires a continual fresh supply. The slaves in America are rapidly increasing, and the reduced price of cotton will accelerate that increase; so that with the aid of supplies from India, when they shall again have a good crop, (they have had two bad ones in succession,) it may reasonably be hoped it will very soon, if it has not already, put an end for ever to the importation of slaves for the cultivation of this article.

5. East India sugars have been increasingly coming into consumption in this country; and though the whole extent is yet a mere trifle, yet, seeing what has happened in the cases of indigo and cotton, it is no wonder that West India merchants and planters are alarmed, and call out for increasing protection; for I am persuaded, that if a fair competition were allowed, by some reduction, if not an entire equality in duty, that their present system, so far as it may prevent the natural increase of the slaves, must be altered; nothing but high prices can ever support the slave-trade, – nothing but high prices, which cause the over-working of the slaves, can ever render it necessary. The slaves in America are said now to be increasing at the rate of 4 per cent per annum; but I think there is no increase in our importations from our West India Colonies, to indicate any such increase there; a fall in the prices of sugars might probably have that effect in the West Indies.

6. It may fairly be asked, why do the West India planters ask for an increased duty on East India sugars? They, no doubt, wish

either to increase the price of sugars, or to prevent a fall; and how does it happen, that with all the immense difference of distance which they have to be brought, with a difference of 10s per cwt. in their favour, that they are still afraid of the competition of East India sugars? Is not this a most decided admission that their system of cultivation cannot exist, unless the country is taxed to support it? There is evidently a rate of prices necessary to support slave cultivation, under a treatment which prevents their increase, and may require supply by fresh importations. At a lower rate, slave cultivation may be continued, but not the importation of slaves; cotton seems to be approaching this rate. But in America, where the cultivation of sugar is commenced, it is said (without any difference of opinion) to pay incomparably better than cotton; hence I infer, that sugar is not yet approaching to this point. There is, I believe, a point still lower, where every system of slavery must be given up. Has not that point arrived in all our cultivation and manufacture in this country? Who would here accept of thousands of men, if they were offered for nothing? It has been computed, that a family which could comfortably be supported under their own management at 18s per week, would cost, if supported in our parish workhouse, 28s per week. In such a state of things, how could slavery exist in this country, even if allowed by law? Is it not hence fair to conclude, that so long as man bears *any price at all*, production has not reached its lowest point; and so long as he bears a high price, there is at least great temptation for breaking the laws against importation.

7. I am persuaded, that if it had not been for the charter of the East India Company shutting out our intercourse with that country, the African slave-trade would long since have ceased to exist, if it had ever had a beginning; and if left to a fair competition, it cannot now much longer continue.

8. It is surely a benefit to this country to be supplied with sugar at a low price; and what do the West India planters offer to the people of England, as an inducement to give up this advantage? Is it that a system of working the negroes may

continue, which shall retard their natural increase, and prevent that gradual fall in their price which would remove all temptation to import them? Surely the people of England ought not to be taxed, by keeping up the price of an article which may tend to support this infamous traffic.

9. The slave-trade on the coast of Africa has lately been carried on to a shocking extent; and vain and fruitless it would seem have been all our efforts to abolish this trade, (at least as respects the extent of it, though it may be carried on by others,) if the people of England are to be taxed with a high price of sugar, which can have no other tendency than to support it. We have only to clear the way, instead of opposing fresh obstacles, and we may then hope for a reduction in the prices of sugar, as has already been the case with cotton, and with similar effects.

10. When enlightened views have almost universally condemned systems of restriction or prohibition in commerce, shall we in any case be justified in increasing them? and least of all when such a tax on this country may tend to support a most infamous traffic.

11. The West India planters, no doubt, intend their proposed measure as a prohibition; and if so, they call on the government to sacrifice nearly £50,000 per annum, arising from the difference already existing between the duties paid on East and West India sugar.

12. If these views are correct, and I hope they will at least be thought to deserve investigation, the Legislature should pause, and consider well, before it adopts the plan proposed. Every benevolent mind must rejoice at the prospect before us, and must be more disposed to hasten than to hinder that course of events which seems to be bringing about these changes, on a basis more solid than any laws or prohibitions whatever.

I am, very respectfully,

Thy friend,

J. C.[16]

Try as they might to avoid it, the West India lobby had come to appre-
ciate by the early 1820s that their power was on the wane. The minutes
of the West India Committee – once a powerful voice – reprinted here
from June 1823, recognize the planters' and traders' declining influence
in Britain.

In addition to every other inducement to such a course, it is
manifestly essential to the public tranquillity of the colonies
that the negroes should look up to those who have immediate authority over them, and not to the British Parliament,
British Government or British public – as their protectors –
and as the authors of any indulgence or benefit which can be
extended to them – that as the odium of severity and punishment must fall on the resident gentlemen, the grace and merit
of an act of benevolence should be theirs also.

If such a course should not be adopted by the colonial legislatures the committee can only look forward to constant and
angry discussion in the House of Commons, endangering at
every moment the safety of the colonies – and ultimately to
some decided act of interference by the British Parliament, to
which the government will inevitably be driven by the force
of public opinion.

In the meantime no West Indian question, not even such as
relate to objects purely commercial [and appeals for relief], will
be listened to with favour, or even with common justice, by
the great body of the British public. The proposition of equalling
the duties of East and West Indies sugar, though rejected by a
large majority, has been announced as intended to be renewed
– and any further irritation of the public mind, might produce
a fatal change in the decision of Parliament . . .

It is idle to disguise from ourselves that the various parties
who from different motives are hostile to the West Indian interests, are at least as careful, and act upon a more extensive system,
and with greater means of influence, on the public mind, than
the proprietors and merchants connected with the colonies; all

ministers must be more or less dependent on public opinion and Parliament, and consequently as much disposed to ingratiate themselves with such classes as with us; we cannot, therefore, beat them by influence – we must trust to reason – and the only way of getting that weapon in our hands is by doing of ourselves and by ourselves, all that is right to be done, and doing it speedily and effectually.[17]

The planters' and traders' position was eroded in part by the evidence revealed by the slave registrations. It was clear that the enslaved population of the islands was in decline. Abolitionists assumed that this decline was a direct result of the severity of slave labour in the sugar fields. That argument is outlined here by James Stephen, the abolitionist and member of the Clapham Sect, in his work Slavery Delineated *(1830).*

The best criterion of the good or bad condition of the labouring classes in any country, may be found in the increase or decline of their numbers . . . Such is the superfecundity of the human species, more especially among the tillers of the soil, that a rapid increase of population may consist with very considerable hardships, and privations; as I fear is too much the case, in many parts of England at this period: but that their condition is extremely bad, may with certainty be inferred, when the reproductive powers of nature are so far subdued, though in a climate propitious to their constitutions, that their numbers greatly decline.

    Emigrations, general famines, or destructive wars, may indeed form exceptions to the rule; but from these causes of depopulation, the slaves in our sugar colonies are pre-eminently exempt. They are restrained from voluntary emigration; and are now protected by law, as before the abolition they were by pretty general practice, from compulsory removal; they have no military service to perform, except on a minute scale, and on very rare occasions: nor has any general famine been alleged to have occurred in any colony, during a long series of years. Yet the decline of numbers, among the predial slaves, has always been deplorably great; and still exceeds any measure of the same calamity, that is elsewhere to be found, under ordinary circumstances, in the history of mankind. In the last six years, comprised in the official returns laid before parliament, viz. from 1818, to 1824, the loss amounted to 3 per cent.

But these general returns furnish a very inadequate view of the loss among the common field negroes; because they include the domestics of every description, the slaves employed in various occupations in the towns and ports, and the tradesmen or artificers and head-negroes on the plantations, who are neither driven, nor overworked, and among whom it is notorious, the domestics especially, there is much longevity, and a very considerable native increase. A discrimination in the returns, between these different descriptions of slaves would be highly interesting and important.

That the loss of numbers is pre-eminently great or exclusively found among the field-negroes does not necessarily prove, indeed, that excess of labour, is the depopulating cause. Their condition and treatment may be, in other respects, bad and destructive; but if the same calamity occurs only in the sugar colonies, where forced labour is confessedly the most severe, and is there proportionate to the degrees in which sugar is raised; if there is no decline, but on the contrary an increase in the slave population, under the same, or more unfavourable circumstances, wherever that article is not cultivated, and labour consequently is less severe; and if, where there is no forced labour at all, the same race, in the same climate, multiply with great rapidity, surely we must in sound reasoning ascribe the calamity to the one peculiar cause.[18]

As in the 1790s, female abolitionists became a powerful weapon in the final attack on slavery. Thousands of female petitions, signed by tens of thousands of women, descended on Parliament in the 1820s and

*1830s. Many were motivated by a deep sense of outrage about the viol-
ation of female slaves. This extract is from a female petition from
Birmingham in 1833.*

They can no longer forbear to address your Honourable House
in a cause which so deeply involves the honour and the comfort
of so many of their own sex; and if in this act it should be
thought that the zeal of your Petitioners has led them to over-
step the line within which female influence is usually confined
and unobstrusively employed, they hope it will not be attrib-
uted to any deficient sense of what is due either to themselves
or to your Honourable House, but to that still deeper sense of
what is due to so large a portion of their fellow-subjects.[19]

*Observers were struck by the fact that many female abolitionist groups
– like that described here by the Quaker Jane Smeal to her abolitionist frend Elizabeth Pease in Glasgow in 1836 – were supported not
by prosperous women but by working-class and middle-class women.*

The females in this city who have much leisure for philanthropic objects are I believe very numerous – but unhappily
that is not the class who take an active part in this cause here
– neither the noble, the rich, nor the learned are to be found
advocating or countenancing our object . . . our subscribers and
most efficient members are all in the middling and working
classes but they evince great zeal and labour very harmoniously
together.[20]

*News from the West Indies in the 1820s and 1830s played a critical
role in winning over more and more people to the cause of black freedom. The slave rebellions, and reports from the missionaries active among
the slaves, hardened British hearts against slavery. This plea of 1833,
from William Knibb, missionary to Jamaica, was a typical missionary's
appeal to the British people on behalf of West Indian slaves.*

For nearly eight years I have trodden the sun-burnt and slave-cursed island of Jamaica, during which time your gratitude has been often called forth by the pleasing intelligence that God was blessing the instrumentality employed. In almost every part of Jamaica Christian churches have been established, which may vie with any in the world for a devout attendance on the means of grace, and for the simple yet fervent zeal of their members.

Hill and dale, street and hamlet, have resounded with the praise and prayer of the African who had been taught that Jesus died to save him, and the sweet and simple strains of the many-coloured slave population have often sounded delightfully on our ears. Success has attended your missionaries in a manner which has appeared to promise the commencement of the millennium.

But I need not say, that all is lost, that our harps are hung upon the willows, and that the voice of praise is no more heard in our streets. A combined Satanic effort has been made to root out all religion; the sanctuaries of God have been broken down with axes and hammers, and the infuriated yell, 'Rase it, rase it, even to the foundations thereof,' has resounded through the island. Feeling, therefore, as I do, that the African and the creole slave will never again enjoy the blessings of religious instruction, or hear of the benefits of that gospel which Christ has commanded to be preached among all nations, and which he has so eminently blessed in Jamaica, unless slavery be overthrown, I now stand forward as the unflinching and undaunted advocate of immediate emancipation . . .

Already, in Jamaica, the life-destroying system shakes to its foundation, and the defenders of it are confounded. The passing of the Reform Bill will hasten its destruction; and I trust that Christians will unite with politicians and philanthropists, in giving 'a long pull, a strong pull, and a pull altogether,' so that the earth may be relieved of the curse . . . And now, my fellow Christians, I appear as the feeble and unworthy advocate of 20,000 baptists, in Jamaica, who have no places of worship, no sabbath, no houses of prayer; and I firmly believe, and solemnly avow my belief, that by far the greater part of those 20,000 will be flogged every time they are caught praying. Among this deeply injured race I have spent the happiest part of my life, and my spirit is there now: would that I might, under a tree, or on the mountain top, invite them to Christ! I plead on behalf of my own church, where I had 980 members, and 2,500 candidates for baptism, surrounded by a population of 27,000. Their prayers are put up for you; put up yours for them. By prayer we have, by prayer we must, by prayer we will, prevail. God is the avenger of the oppressed, and the African shall not always be forgotten.[21]

The Reform Act of 1832 effectively sealed the fate of slavery. The new House of Commons accepted these resolutions, proposed by Henry Stanley on 14 May 1833, for immediate emancipation.

1. That it is the opinion of this Committee that immediate and effectual measures be taken for the entire abolition of slavery throughout the colonies under such provisions for regulating the condition of the negroes as may combine their welfare with the interests of the proprietors.

2. That it is expedient that all children born after the passing of any Act or who shall be under the age of six years at the time of passing any Act of Parliament for this purpose, be declared free; subject nevertheless to such temporary restrictions as may be deemed necessary for their support and maintenance.

3. That all persons now slaves be entitled to be registered as apprenticed labourers and to acquire thereby all rights and privileges of freedom; subject to the restriction of labouring, under conditions and for a time to be fixed by Parliament, for their present owners.

4. That, to provide against the risk of loss which proprietors in His Majesty's colonial possessions might sustain by the

abolition of slavery, His Majesty be enabled to advance by way of loan to be raised from time to time a sum not exceeding in the whole £15,000,000, to be repaid in such manner and at such a rate of interest as shall be prescribed by Parliament.

5. That His Majesty be enabled to defray any such expense as he may incur in establishing an efficient stipendiary magistracy in the colonies and in aiding the local legislatures in providing for the religious and moral education of the negro population to be emancipated.[22]

Epilogue
The Survival of Slavery

When people first learn about the London-based Anti-Slavery International, the modern descendant of the Anti-Slavery Society founded in 1839, they often seem bemused. Why campaign against slavery today? Slavery surely disappeared a long time ago. In fact at the time of writing, in 2006, the society has more work than it can handle campaigning against slavery in various corners of the globe. The survival of slavery is one of the most perplexing of all aspects of the history of slavery.

Stories about modern-day slavery periodically surface in the media. The subject recently caught the eye of *National Geographic*, and articles about contemporary slavery in Niger, in Ghana and in various countries in Asia have regularly surfaced in the British press in recent years. Though such stories often cause amazement even among well-informed readers, they come as little surprise to students of slavery, and those, like Anti-Slavery International, campaigning in the field against slavery and other forms of human abuses.

One major difficulty, in the West at least, is that we have become accustomed to thinking about slavery uniquely in terms of what happened in the Atlantic world: as the miserable fate which befell the millions of Africans who were shipped into the Americas. Yet just as there were, as I tried to show at the start of this book, other forms of slavery in other parts of the world long before the rise of the Atlantic slave trade, so slavery lived on long after it ended in Brazil in 1888. In places it survived as a direct result of the Atlantic system. Slavery within Africa was strengthened by the Atlantic trade and it often survived as a result of the continuing and voracious demand for African peoples in other parts of the world, most notably in Islamic societies, where Africans were bought and sold, and transported as slaves, long before, and long after the Atlantic slave trade.

The British involvement with slavery underwent a remarkable transformation in the early nineteenth century. In the century before 1807 the British had been the prime shipper of Africans across the Atlantic. Until 1838 the British West Indian colonies had been home to one of the largest groups of slave communities in the Americas. Yet all that changed, very quickly.

What the British and others discovered in the course of the nineteenth century, especially when they embarked on a new phase of imperial expansion, was that slavery was ubiquitous, as it had been before the launch of the slave empires in the Americas. Now, from the 1830s onwards, the British were fuelled by a different kind of moral imperative: by an abolitionist zeal which burned as brightly in the nineteenth century as their now-discarded enthusiasm for slavery had formerly burned in the eighteenth century. The British not only abolished their slave trade (1807) and their slave systems (1838) but embarked on a remarkable crusade, which lasted throughout the nineteenth and into the twentieth century, to ensure that everyone else toed the British abolitionist line. Nations throughout Europe and the Americas, and later around the world, were pressurized to adopt the principle and practice of anti-slavery. Many of them, notably the French, pointed to what they regarded as the volte-face by the British. What moral authority did the British have for their newly discovered abolitionist zeal? Such criticisms (and there were plenty of them) did not, however, deter the British.

They were not satisfied merely by overturning the slave systems imported into the Americas. Wherever the British encountered indigenous slave systems – in Africa, in India, in Arabia – there too they used the power of British diplomacy and military and naval muscle to secure abolitionist compliance. The British anti-slavery crusade was, in effect, global. Collectively, the British came to resemble a born-again

Evangelical who rejected his sinful, slaving past to adopt a pious abolitionism. To many outsiders, the crusade smacked of hollow hypocrisy. If we take the long view of British history it does indeed seem a peculiar turn of events, the crusade coming as it did from the greatest slaving nation of the eighteenth century.

Anti-slavery seemed to be triumphant. In the course of the nineteenth century slave systems across the Americas either faded away or collapsed. There were only fifty years between the ending of British slavery and the demise of slavery in Brazil, the last slave outpost to fall in the America. By 1888, slavery had been swept away across the Americas.

The same could not be said of Africa, however. Indeed, at the very point when Americans shed their appetite for black slaves, there may have been more slaves in Africa than ever before, more even than had been shipped across the Atlantic in the entire history of Atlantic slavery. The degree to which the African systems had been brought into being and perfected by external demands for African slaves – by Europeans, Americans and Arabs – remains a point of dispute.

What is beyond doubt, however, is that there was a continuing demand for Africans in Arabia. Africans continued to be moved northwards across the Sahara, along traditional trade routes, and eastwards from East Africa and the Horn of Africa, to the slave markets of the Islamic world. From Morocco in the west, to the heartland of Arabia (present-day Saudi Arabia) in the east, British naval officers and consular officials regularly tried to stop the persistent Arab demand for black slaves. Here was a region in which slavery had long predated the Atlantic slave system and continued long after its demise. Indeed it survived for more than a millennium, into the twentieth century, and may have engulfed more Africans than the numbers swallowed by the Atlantic slave ships.

By a bizarre twist of historical fate, slavery was even re-introduced into regions of the Western world which had not seen slaves for centuries. Recently historians have begun to

consider the forms of slavery which lay at the heart of the dicta-
torial regimes of the mid-twentieth century. At first glance, what
happened in Nazi Germany and its conquered lands, or in the
vast stretches of Stalinist Russia and its satellite states, may seem
far removed from the subject of this book. In fact, there were
many close similarities. I was initially dubious when I first encountered the arguments that slavery was a basic and necessary
component of both those tyrannical regimes, especially in the
Second World War. It seemed to me that wartime Nazi Germany
and Stalinist Russia occupied a qualitatively different position
from, for example, the slave empires of the Americas. Today, I am
not so sure, in large part because of the impressive and persuasive scholarship which has revealed the full details (and horror)
of slave labour in both the Nazi and Stalinist empires. Wholesale
upheaval and removal of people, relocation of massive communities and nations, millions of captives turned over to enslaved
labour in brute conditions which often defy description – all this
was common at the height of those tyrannies. Moreover, the
numbers involved – measured in their millions in both cases –
stand comparison with the numbers shipped across the Atlantic.
It is thought, for example, that Nazi Germany used upwards of
twelve million slave labourers during the Second World War,
while the numbers shunted into Stalin's labour camps in the
Gulag remain uncountable but are certainly to be measured in
millions.

The consequences of the events in the mid-twentieth
century, when those two European nations (both using slave
labour) effectively tore each other to pieces, continue to pose
political and legal problems for the modern German and
Russian states. Demands for reparation, contrition and the balm
of apology, and the insistence on historical recognition, continue
to echo through the political corridors of Berlin and Moscow.
Though not yet as strident or as powerful (except perhaps in
the US), similar voices have begun to demand similar consid-
eration for the damage done to millions by the old Atlantic

Notes

Chapter 1

1. Thomas Wiedemann, *Greek and Roman Slavery*, London, 1981, p. 1.
2. Plato, *The Laws*, from ibid., p. 83.
3. Xenophon, *The Householder*, from Thomas Weideman, op. cit., p. 185.
4. Xenophon, *Memorabilia*, from N. R. E. Fisher, *Slavery in Classical Greece*, London, 1993, p. 79.
5. Aristotle, *Politics*, from Thomas Wiedemann, op. cit., p. 133.
6. Euripides, *Ion*, from N. R. E. Fisher, op. cit., p. 90.
7. Ibid., p. 833.
8. Plutarch, *The Life of Cato the Elder*, from D. Cherry, ed., *The Roman World: a Sourcebook*, Oxford, 2001, pp. 11–13.
9. From Keith Bradley, *Slavery and Society at Rome*, Cambridge, 1996, p. 62.
10. Pliny the Elder, from Thomas Wiedemann, op. cit., p. 93.
11. Anon, from Thomas Wiedemann, op. cit., p. 192.
12. Pliny, *Letters*, from Thomas Weideman, op. cit., pp. 188–9.
13. Appian, *Roman Civil Wars*, from Thomas Weideman, op. cit., pp. 220–22.
14. Ibid.

Chapter 2

1. W. D. Phillips Jnr, *Slavery from Roman Times to the Early Atlantic Slave Trade*, Manchester, 1985, pp. 98–105.
2. From Iris Origo, *The Merchant of Prato*, Harmondsworth, 1957, pp. 192–3.
3. Ibid.
4. Ibid., p. 101.

5. Ibid., p. 195.
6. Ibid., p. 198.
7. Ibid., p. 101.
8. From W. D. Phillips Jr, op. cit., p. 101.
9. Ibid.

Chapter 3

1. Suhaym, from Bernard Lewis, *Race and Slavery in the Middle East: an Historical Enquiry*, New York, 1990, pp. 28–9.
2. Ibid.
3. Ibid.
4. Nusayb ibn Rabah, from Bernard Lewis, op. cit.
5. Anon, from Bernard Lewis, op. cit.
6. Ibn Shahin, from Shaun E. Marmon, 'Domestic Slavery in the Mamluk Empire', Shaun E. Marmon, ed., *Slavery in the Islamic Middle East*, Princeton, 1999, p. 9.
7. Ahmad al-Mansur, from John Hunwick, 'Islamic Law and Polemics over Race and Slavery in North and West Africa (16th–19th Century)', in Shaun E. Marmon, ed., op. cit., p. 54.
8. Ahmad, b. Khalid al-Nasiri, from John Hunwick, op. cit., pp. 60–61.

Chapter 4

1. From Elizabeth Donnan, *Documents Illustrative of the History of the Slave Trade to America*, 4 vols., Washington, DC, 1930–36, vol. i, p. 28.
2. From W. D. Phillips Jnr, *Slavery from Roman Times to the Early Transatlantic Trade*, Manchester, 1985, p. 174.
3. From Elizabeth Donnan, op. cit., pp. 15–16.
4. Ibid., pp. 41–2.
5. John Barbot, 'A Description of the Coasts of North and South Guinea . . .', from Elizabeth Donnan, op. cit., p. 293.
6. From W. D. Phillips Jnr, op. cit., pp. 190–91.

Chapter 5

1. From Elizabeth Donnan, *Documents Illustrative of the History of the Slave Trade to America*, 4 vols., Washington, DC, 1930–36, vol. i, pp. 42–3.
2. Ibid., pp. 43–4.
3. Ibid., pp. 44–7.
4. Ibid., pp. 125–6.
5. Ibid., pp. 130–31.
6. Ibid., pp. 156–7.
7. Ibid., pp. 164–5.
8. Ibid., pp. 177–8.

Chapter 6

1. From Elizabeth Donnan, *Documents Illustrative of the History of the Slave Trade to America*, 4 vols., Washington DC, 1930–36, vol. i, pp. 134–5.
2. Ibid., pp. 141–3.
3. Ibid., pp. 462–3.
4. Alexander Falconbridge, *Account of the Slave Trade on the Coast of Africa*, 1788.
5. John Newton, *Thoughts Upon the African Slave Trade*, 1788.
6. Alexander Falconbridge, op. cit.
7. Prince Hoare, *Memoirs of Granville Sharp*, London, 1820.

Chapter 7

1. Thomas Roughley, *The Jamaica Planters' Guide*, London, 1823.
2. Basil Hall, *Travels in North America*, vol. ii, 1829.
3. Hugh Jones, *The Present State of Virginia* (1724), ed. R. L. Morton, Chapel Hill, 1956.
4. From Edmund S. Morgan, *Virginians at Home*, Charlottesville, 1952, pp. 53–4.
5. *Virginia Gazette*, 1 December 1768.

Chapter 8

1. Louis B. Wright and Marion Tinling, eds., *The Secret Diary of William Byrd of Westover, 1709–1721*, Richmond, 1941.
2. *Virginia Gazette*, 25 January 1770.
3. From Michael Mullin, ed., *American Negro Slavery: a Documentary History*, New York, 1976.
4. Ibid.
5. Ibid.
6. Ibid.
7. Ibid.
8. *Daily Advertiser* (Kingston), 7 June 1790.
9. *Daily Advertiser* (Kingston), 12 July 1790.
10. *Daily Advertiser* (Kingston), 29 January 1790.
11. Supplement to the *Royal Gazette* (Kingston), 19 August 1780.
12. Colonial Office Papers, 5/1322, 19ff, Virginia Colonial Records Project, Colonial Williamsburg Research Center microfilm. Reprinted by permission of the Controller of Her Britannic Majesty's Stationery Office.
13. From Michael Craton, *Testing the Chains*, New York, 1982, p. 273.
14. Ibid., p. 313.

Chapter 9

1. Isaac Weld, *Travels Through the States of North America*, ed. Joseph J. Kwiat, New York, 1968.
2. Edward Long, *History of Jamaica*, 1774, vol. iii.
3. Ibid.
4. John F. D. Smyth, *A Tour in the USA* (1784), New York, 1928.
5. *Journal of Nicholas Cresswell, 1774–1777*, New York, 1928, pp. 18–19.
6. Edward Long, op. cit., vol. ii, pp. 423–4.
7. Ibid.
8. Thomas N. Ingersoll, '"Release us out of this Cruell Bondegg": an Appeal from Virginia in 1723', *William and Mary Quarterly*, 3rd ser., 51, 1994, pp. 777–82.
9. *Virginia Gazette*, 30 June 1774.

Chapter 10

1. Prince Hoare, *Memoirs of Granville Sharp*, London, 1820, p. 241.
2. Thomas Clarkson, *The History of the Abolition of the African Slave Trade*, London, 1808, vol. i, p. 418.
3. London Corresponding Society, Minute Book, British Library Add. Ms. 27, 811, ff. 4–9.
4. Judith Jennings, *The Business of Abolishing the British Slave Trade*, London, 1997, p. 35.
5. From Judith Jennings, op. cit., p. 92.
6. Ibid., p. 110.
7. Ibid., p. 110.
8. Granville Sharp, *Representation of the Injustice and Dangerous Tendancy of Admitting the Least Claims of Private Property in the Persons of Men in England*, London, 1769.
9. Anthony Benezet, *Some Historical Account of Guinea . . .* (1771), London, 1788.
10. Adam Smith, *The Wealth of Nations*, 1776.
11. Vincent Carretta, ed., *Letters of the Late Ignatius Sancho, an African, in Two Volumes* (1782), London, 1998.
12. Ottobah Cugoano, *Thoughts and Sentiments on the Evils and Wicked Traffic of the Slavery and Commerce of Human Species* (1787), ed. Vincent Carretta, London, 1999.
13. From Prince Hoare, *Memoirs of Granville Sharp*, London, 1820, pp. 374–5.
14. Thomas Clarkson, *The History of the Rise, Progress and Accomplishment of the Abolition of the Slave Trade by the British Parliament*, 1808, vol. i.
15. Vincent Harlow and Frederic Madden, eds., *British Colonial Developments, 1774–1834, Select Documents*, Oxford, 1953, p. 525.
16. Thomas Clarkson, *An Essay on the Impolicy of the African Slave Trade*, 1788.
17. James Ramsay, *On the Treatment and Conversion of African Slaves*, 1784.
18. Olandah Equiano, *The Interesting Narrative and Other Writings*, ed. Vincent Carretta, Harmondsworth, 1998, pp. 231–2.
19. *York Courant*, 21 February 1792.
20. Mary Wollstonecraft, *Vindications of the Rights of Men*, 1790.
21. From *Gentleman's Magazine*, December 1793.

22. William Blake, *Songs of Innocence*, London, 1794.
23. From Moira Ferguson, *Subject to Others: British Women Writers and Colonial Slavery, 1670–1834*, London, 1992, pp. 179–80.
24. Ibid.
25. Vincent Harlow and Frederic Madden, op. cit., p. 527.
26. Ibid., pp. 534–5.
27. Ibid., pp. 530–31.
28. *Cobbett's Parliamentary History*, London, 1763–1835, vol. xxviii, pp. 41–101.
29. A. Aspinall and E. Anthony Smith, eds., *English Historical Documents*, London, 1959, pp. 803–4.

Chapter 11

1. William Wilberforce, *A Letter on the Abolition of the Slave Trade*, London, 1807.
2. F.D. Cartwright, ed., *The Life and Correspondence of Major Cartwright*, London, 1826, vol. ii, p. 84.
3. Thomas Clarkson, Letter, 30 June 1814, Clarkson Papers, Huntington Library, San Marino, California.
4. From Michael Craton, *Testing the Chains: Resistance to Slavery in the British West Indies*, Ithaca, New York, 1982, p. 266.
5. Mary Turner, *Slaves and Missionaries:The Disintegration of Jamaican Slave Society, 1787–1834*, Urbana, Illinois, 1982, p. 9.
6. Thomas Clarkson, Letter, 20 May 1796, Clarkson Papers, op. cit.
7. From Michael Craton, op. cit., p. 269.
8. James Walvin, *Black Ivory: a History of British Slavery*, London, 1992, p. 278.
9. Quoted in James Walvin, *England, Slaves and Freedom, 1776–1838*, London, 1986, p. 145.
10. Thomas Clarkson, 'Speech Used at Forming of Committees, 1823–1824', Clarkson Papers, op. cit.
11. From Michael Craton, op. cit., p. 321.
12. Joseph Sturge, *Memoirs*, 1864.
13. Vincent Harlow and Frederic Madden, eds, *British Colonial Developments, 1774–1834, Select Documents*, Oxford, 1953, pp. 550–51.

14. Ibid., p. 549.
15. George Stephen, *Anti-Slavery Recollections*, 1859.
16. James Cropper, Letter to William Wilberforce, 5 Month 3 1821, in *Letters Addressed to William Wilberforce*, London 1822.
17. Harlow and Madden, op. cit., pp. 557–9.
18. James Stephen, *Slavery Delineated*, 1830.
19. From Clare Midgley, *Women Against Slavery: The British Campaigns*, London, 1992, p. 97.
20. Ibid., p. 85.
21. *Memoirs of William Knibb*, 1849.
22. Harlow and Madden, op. cit., pp. 587–8.

Further Reading

I have listed the suggestions for further reading under the themes of each chapter. For readers keen to follow the more specialized literature on slavery, the best starting point is the annual biblio-graphy edited by Joseph Miller and colleagues in *Slavery and Abolition* (Routledge, London). For the most recent version, see Thomas Thurston and Joseph C. Miller, 'Slavery: Annual Bibliographical Supplement (2004)' in *Slavery and Abolition*, ed. Gad Heuman, London, vol. 26, No. 3 December, 2005.

Chapter 1: Slavery in the Classical World

W. W. Buckland, *The Roman Law of Slavery*, Cambridge, 1908/1970
M. L. Bush, ed., *Serfdom and Slavery*, London, 1996
M. I. Finley, *Ancient Slavery and Modern Ideology*, London, 1980
M. I. Finley, ed., *Classical Slavery*, London, 1987
N. R. E. Fisher, *Slavery in Classical Greece*, London 1993
Thomas Wiedemann, *Greek and Roman Slavery*, London, 1981

Chapter 2: Slavery and Medieval Europe

Pierre Bonassie, *From Slavery to Feudalism in South-Western Europe*, Cambridge, 1991
Pierre Dockes, *Medieval Slavery and Liberation*, London, 1982
Richard A. Fletcher, *The Conversion of Europe*, London, 1997
Richard Hellie, *Slavery in Russia*, Chicago, 1982
J. N. Hilgarth, *The Spanish Kingdoms, 1250–1516*, Oxford, 1978, 2 vols
Rodney Hilton, *Bondsmen Made Free*, London, 1977
Joseph F. O'Callaghan, *The Learned King: the Reign of Alfonso X of Castille*, Philadelphia, 1993
Iris Origo, *The Merchant of Prato*, Harmondsworth, 1979

David Antony Edgell Pelteret, *Slavery in Medieval England: from the Reign of Alfred until the 12th Century*, Woodbridge, Suffolk, 1995

Chapter 3: Slavery and Islam

P. M. Holt, Ann K. S. Lambton and Bernard Lewis, eds., *The Cambridge History of Islam*, Cambridge, 1970, vol. ii

John Hunwick, ed., *Sharia in Songhay*, Oxford, 1985

Bernard Lewis, *The Muslim Discovery of Europe*, London, 1982

Shaun E. Marmon, ed., *Slavery in the Islamic Middle East*, Princeton, 1999

Ronald Segal, *Islam's Black Slaves: the History of Africa's Other Black Diaspora*, London, 2001

John Ralph Willis, ed., *Slaves and Slavery in Muslim Africa*, London, 1985, 2 vols

Chapter 4: The Origins of Atlantic Slavery

P. D. Curtin, *The Rise and Fall of the Plantation Complex*, Cambridge, 1990

David Eltis, *The Rise of African Slavery in the Americas*, Cambridge, 2000

P. E. Lovejoy, *Transformations in Slavery: a History of Slavery in Africa*, Cambridge, 1983

W. D. Phillips, *Slavery from Roman Times to the Early Atlantic Slave Trade*, Manchester, 1985

Johannes Postma, *The Dutch and the Atlantic Slave Trade*, Cambridge, 1990

Robin Blackburn, *The Making of New World Slavery*, London, 1997

Chapter 5: The Coming of the British

Hilary Beckles, *A History of Barbados*, Cambridge, 1990

Nicholas Canny, ed., *The Oxford History of the British Empire*, vol. i, *The Origins of Empire*, Oxford, 1998

Herbert Klein, *The Atlantic Slave Trade*, Cambridge, 1999

Andrew Porter, ed., *Atlas of British European Expansion*, London, 1991
'Slavery in the Americas', *William and Mary Quarterly*, vol. lix, no. 3, July 2002

Chapter 6: Slave Ships

David Eltis et al., *The Trans-Atlantic Slave Trade: a Database on CD-ROM*, Cambridge, 2000
Herbert Klein, *The Atlantic Slave Trade*, Cambridge, 1999
David Richardson, 'The British Empire and the Atlantic Slave Trade, 1660–1807', *Oxford History of the British Empire*, ed. P. J. Marshall vol. ii, *Eighteenth Century*, Oxford, 1998
'New Perspectives on the Atlantic Slave Trade', *William and Mary Quarterly*, vol. lviii, no. 1, January 2001

Chapter 7: Slaves at Work

James Axtell, *Beyond 1492: Encounters in Colonial North America*, New York, 1992
Trevor Burnard, *Mastery, Tyranny and Desire*, Chapel Hill, 2004
Alfred W. Crosby, *Ecological Imperialism: the Biological Expansion of Europe, 900–1900*, Cambridge, 1991
Douglas Hall, *In Miserable Slavery: Thomas Thistlewood in Jamaica, 1750–1786*, London, 1992
B. W. Higman, *Plantation Jamaica, Capital and Control in a Colonial Economy*, Kingston, Jamaica, 2005
D. W. Meinig, *The Shaping of America: a Geographical Perspective on 500 Years of History*, vol. i, *Atlantic America, 1492–1800*, New Haven, 1986
Stuart Schwartz, *Sugar Plantations in the Formation of Brazilian Society, Bahia 1550–1835*, Cambridge, 1985

Chapter 8: Slave Resistance

Michael Craton, *Testing the Chains: Resistance to Slavery in the British West Indies*, New York, 1982

246246246246##Further Reading

Gad Heuman, ed., *Out of the House of Bondage: Runaways, Resistance and Marronage in Africa and the New World*, London, 1986
Gad Heuman and James Walvin, eds., *The Slavery Reader*, Part 7, 'Slave Resistance', London, 2003
Richard Price, ed., *Maroon Societies*, New York, 1973

Chapter 9: Slave Communities

Sylvia R. Frey and Betty Wood, *Come Shouting to Zion*, Chapel Hill, 1998
Michael Gomez, *Exchanging our Country Marks*, Chapel Hill, 1998
Gad Heuman, *The Caribbean: a Short History*, London, 2006
Gad Heuman and James Walvin, eds., *The Slavery Reader*, Part 4, 'Family Gender and Community', London, 2003
Rhys Isaac, *Landon Carter's Uneasy Kingdom*, New York, 2004
Philip D. Morgan, *Slave Counterpoint: Black Culture in the Eighteenth-century Chesapeake and Lowcountry*, Chapel Hill, 1998

Chapter 10: Abolishing the Slave Trade

David Brion Davis, *The Problem of Slavery in the Age of Revolution, 1770–1823*, New York, 1975
Seymour Drescher, *From Slavery to Freedom: Comparative Studies in the Rise and Fall of Atlantic Slavery*, New York, 1999
David Eltis and James Walvin, eds., *The Abolition of the Atlantic Slave Trade*, Madison, 1981
Adam Hochschild, *Bury the Chains: the British Struggle to Abolish Slavery*, London, 2005
Judith Jennings, *The Business of Abolishing the British Slave Trade, 1783–1807*, London, 1997
John Oldfield, *Popular Politics and British Anti-Slavery*, Manchester, 1995
Steven M. Wise, *Though the Heavens May Fall: The Landmark Trial that Led to the End of Human Slavery*, London, 2006

Chapter 11: Freeing the Slaves

Moira Ferguson, *Subject to Others: British Women Writers and Colonial Slavery, 1670–1834*, London, 1992

William A. Green, *British Slave Emancipation: the Sugar Colonies and the Great Experiment, 1830–1865*, Oxford, 1976

Clare Midgley, *Women Against Slavery: the British Campaigns, 1780–1870*, London, 1992

David Turley, *The Culture of English Anti-slavery, 1780–1860*, London, 1991

Mary Turner, *Slaves and Missionaries: the Disintegration of Jamaican Slave Society, 1787–1834*, Urbana, 1982

James Walvin, *England, Slaves and Freedom, 1776–1838*, London, 1986

Marcus Wood, *Blind Memory: Visual Representations of Slavery in England and America, 1780–1865*, Manchester, 2000

Documents

I have tried throughout to cite documentary material that is accessible in printed form. Readers keen to look further at documentary evidence could begin with the following collections, which have proved invaluable for this book.

Michael Craton, James Walvin and David Wrights, eds., *Slavery, Abolition and Emancipation*, London, 1976

Elizabeth Donnan, *Documents Illustrative of the History of the Slave Trade to America*, Washington, DC, 4 vols., 1930–35

Peter J. Kitson and Debbie Lee, eds., *Slavery, Abolition and Emancipation*, 8 vols., London, 1999

Michael Mullin, ed., *American Negro Slavery*, New York, 1976

Willie Lee Rose, ed., *A Documentary History of Slavery in North America*, New York, 1976

Acknowledgements

I could not have researched and written this book without the help and encouragement of a number of colleagues and friends. Simon Winder of Penguin initially planted the idea in my mind: I hope he thinks the final outcome worthwhile. I undertook much of my reading and research in three welcoming and supportive libraries. Firstly at La Trobe University, where I was privileged to be a Fellow in the Institute for Advanced Studies; the Director, Gilah Lehrer, and an old friend, Alex Tyrrell, went out of their way to make my time there happy and productive. Secondly, James Horn, then Director of the Rockefeller Library at the Colonial Williamsburg Foundation, enabled me to enjoy the facilities of the library. Thirdly, Andrew O'Shaughnessy, Director of the Jefferson's Studies Center at Kenwood, made it possible for me to work at Monticello, Virginia. I was greatly helped by two colleagues in York, Rosemary Morris and Peter Rycraft. Both steered me towards important literature in what were, for me, unfamiliar areas. Charles Walker, my agent, was again supportive throughout. I am very grateful to both Chloe Campbell and Anne Askwith for their exemplary editing of my manuscript: it was much improved by their efforts. But my greatest debt, as always, is to Jenny Walvin.

Index

PENGUIN HISTORY

THE DECLINE AND FALL OF THE BRITISH ARISTOCRACY
DAVID CANNADINE

'How real history should be written: the mixture of dashing judgments and riveting detail' Michael Foot, *Guardian*

In the late nineteenth century, Britain's aristocracy were still the richest and most powerful people in the country. But in the hundred years that followed, their glamour tarnished, their fortunes withered and their power had faded – their self-appointed role as God's elect had come to an end.

Here, David Cannadine tells the very human story behind their decline. He describes the vast estates carved up and sold, the generation of sons lost in the First World War, the rise of a newly rich and untitled elite, and the labour movement that overturned patrician domination of public life. Authoritative and witty, *The Decline and Fall of the British Aristocracy* provides a wonderfully illuminating account of this seismic change.

'Anecdotes, facts, names, quotations and statistics are piled up, swept along by a fluent and often witty prose' Roy Foster, *Independent on Sunday*

'Magnificent ... of critical importance in understanding how Britain has changed ... This is history at its very best' Lawrence Stone, *London Review of Books*

'Remarkable ... A brilliant, multifaceted chronicle of economic and social change' Robert Blake, *The New York Times*

PENGUIN HISTORY

PAGANS AND CHRISTIANS
IN THE MEDITERRANEAN WORLD FROM THE SECOND CENTURY AD
TO THE CONVERSION OF CONSTANTINE
ROBIN LANE FOX

'This brilliant book is a wholly unexpected and central contribution to its subject.
What is more it is readable and rereadable, even gripping' Peter Levi, *Spectator*

How did Christianity compare and compete with the cults of the pagan gods in the
Roman Empire? This scholarly work from award-winning historian, Robin Lane
Fox, places Christians and pagans side by side in the context of civil life and
contrasts their religious experiences, visions, cults and oracles. Leading up to the
time of the first Christian emperor, Constantine, the book aims to enlarge and
confirm the value of contemporary evidence, some of which has only recently
been discovered.

'A massive and humane study. On my shelf it will rest with pride between Edward
Gibbon and Peter Brown' Charles Thomas, *Daily Telegraph*

'Here is richness indeed …on the one hand a magisterial analysis and
reconstruction of an apparently remote and alien society, on the other a detailed
study of the single most significant process in our history and still the most
important determinant of our present attitudes and beliefs'
Donald Earl, *The Times*

'This book is important indeed' Henry Chadwick, *Financial Times*

PENGUIN HISTORY

GULAG: A HISTORY
ANNE APPLEBAUM

**Winner of the Pulitzer Prize for General Non-Fiction 2004 &
the Duff Cooper Prize 2004**

THE INTERNATIONAL BESTSELLER

'Important and moving … a terrifying and unforgettable story' Antony Beevor

'Terrifying, searing … one of the great untold stories of the twentieth century …
a triumph' Richard Overy, *Sunday Telegraph*

'Extraordinary … heartrending, painful … devastating' T. J. Binyon, *Daily Mail*

The Gulag was Russia's forgotten holocaust. The largest network of concentration
camps ever created, it murdered millions and haunted all those who came out
alive. Here, for the first time, is the full, moving story of its countless victims:
how they lived, laboured, suffered – and survived to bear witness to one of
history's most terrible crimes.

'An outstanding book, whose importance is almost impossible to exaggerate'
Michael Burleigh, *The Times Literary Supplement*

'A magisterial study that brings to life the hell of Russia's Gulags … it moves as
much as it shocks' Simon Sebag Montefiore, *Daily Telegraph*

'She has constructed from novels, records and scraps of paper a heaving,
breathing testament of experience … and made the names of Solovetsky, Kolyma,
Norlisk and others resound with the same dull echo of evil as Auschwitz' Hugh
MacDonald, *The Herald*

'This book is a monument to their suffering, and to read it is to honour that
suffering' Adam Zamoyski, *Spectator*

PENGUIN HISTORY

THE MITROKHIN ARCHIVE

CHRISTOPHER ANDREW AND VASILI MITROKHIN

In 1992 the British Secret Intelligence Service exfiltrated from Russia a defector whose presence in the West had remained secret until the publication of this book. Vasili Mitrokhin worked for almost thirty years in the foreign intelligence archives of the KGB, which in 1972 he was made responsible for moving to a new HQ just outside Moscow. Mitrokhin – a secret dissident – spent over a decade noting and copying highly classified files which, at enormous personal risk, he smuggled daily out of the archives and kept beneath his dacha floor. This unprecedented treasure-trove of KGB material, which extends from the Lenin era to the 1980s, has been described by the FBI as 'the most complete and extensive intelligence ever received from any source', and has enabled Christopher Andrew, the leading Western writer on modern intelligence, to cast a new light on the history both of the Soviet Union and of the East–West conflict which spanned three quarters of this century.

'The historical scoop of the decade' *Independent*

'This tale of malevolent spymasters, intricate tradecraft and cold-eyed betrayal reads like a cold war novel' *Time*

'Sensational … so far the most informed and detailed study of Soviet subversive intrigues worldwide' *Spectator*, Books of the Year

'Co-authored in a brilliant partnership by Christopher Andrew and the renegade Soviet archivist himself … This is a truly global exposé of major KGB penetrations throughout the Western world' *The Times*

PENGUIN HISTORY

THE MITROKHIN ARCHIVE II
CHRISTOPHER ANDREW AND VASILI MITROKHIN

'Stunning ... the stuff of legend ... a unique insight into KGB activities on a global scale' *Spectator*

The Baltic, 1992: A shabbily dressed old man enters a British embassy with a sheaf of top-secret documents hidden at the bottom of his battered suitcase. Ex-KGB worker Vasili Mitrokhin was about to reveal the most sensational intelligence archive the world had seen.

'The long-awaited second tranche from the KGB archive ... co-authored by our leading authority on the secret machinations of the Evil Empire' *Sunday Times*

The Mitrokhin Archive II reveals in full the secrets of this astonishing cache, showing for the first time the extent of the KGB's influence around the world, from making friends with Fidel Castro in Cuba to starting the Soviet invasion of Afghanistan. For over twenty years, the KGB believed that the Third World was the arena in which it could win the Cold War against the West.

'Headline news ... as great a credit to the scholarship of its author as to the dedication and courage of its originator' *Sunday Telegraph*

Telling untold stories of conspiracies combined with bizarre black comedy on a global scale, this exposé of the world's most powerful secret organization will transform our understanding of the Cold War.

'Adds an unexpected dimension to our understanding of [East-West relations] ... Now the required addition can be made to the historical record' *The Times Literary Supplement*

PENGUIN HISTORY

GULAG: A HISTORY ANNE APPLEBAUM

'Important and moving … a terrifying and unforgettable story' Antony Beevor

'Terrifying, searing … one of the great untold stories of the twentieth century … a triumph' Richard Overy, *Sunday Telegraph*

'A magisterial study that brings to life the hell of Russia's Gulags … it moves as much as it shocks' Simon Sebag Montefiore, *Daily Telegraph*

THE COMING OF THE THIRD REICH RICHARD J. EVANS

'Monumental … gripping … the definitive account for our time' Andrew Roberts, *Daily Telegraph*

'Impressive … perceptive … humane … the most comprehensive history in any language of the disastrous epoch of the Third Reich' Ian Kershaw, author of *Hitler*

NATASHA'S DANCE: A CULTURAL HISTORY OF RUSSIA
ORLANDO FIGES

'Awe-inspiring … *Natasha's Dance* has all the qualities of an epic tragedy' Frances Welsh, *Mail on Sunday*

Orlando Figes's enthralling, richly evocative history has been heralded as a literary masterpiece on Russia, the lives of those who have shaped its culture, and the enduring spirit of a people.

EMPIRE: HOW BRITAIN MADE THE MODERN WORLD
NIALL FERGUSON

'The most brilliant British historian of his generation … Ferguson examines the roles of "pirates, planters, missionaries, mandarins, bankers and bankrupts" in the creation of history's largest empire … he writes with splendid panache … and a seemingly effortless, debonair wit' Andrew Roberts, *The Times*

'Thrilling … an extraordinary story' *Daily Mail*
